IMPACT OF E-COMMERCE ON CONSUMERS AND SMALL FIRMS

Impact of e-Commerce on Consumers and Small Firms

Edited by

SALVATORE ZAPPALÀ
University of Bologna, Italy

and

COLIN GRAY
Open University, UK

ASHGATE

Published by
Ashgate Publishing Limited
Gower House
Croft Road
Aldershot
Hampshire GU11 3HR
England

Ashgate Publishing Company
Suite 420
101 Cherry Street
Burlington, VT 05401-4405
USA

Ashgate website: http://www.ashgate.com

British Library Cataloguing in Publication Data
Impact of e-commerce on consumers and small firms
   1. Electronic commerce 2. Small business – Technological
   innovations 3. Consumer behaviour 4. Internet marketing
   I. Zappalà, Salvatore II. Gray, Colin
   381.1'42

Library of Congress Cataloging-in-Publication Data
Impact of e-commerce on consumers and small firms / edited by Salvatore Zappalà and Colin Gray.
       p. cm.
   Includes index.
   ISBN 0-7546-4416-2
  1. Electronic commerce. 2. Internet marketing. 3. Small business--Computer networks. 4. Consumer behavior. I. Zappalà, Salvatore. II. Gray, Colin.

HF5548.32.I46 2006
381'.142--dc22
                                 2006009521

ISBN-10: 0-7546-4416-2
ISBN-13: 978-0-7546-4416-3

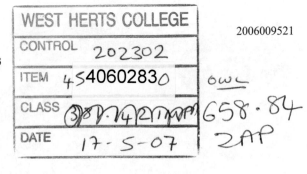
Printed and bound in Great Britain by Antony Rowe Ltd, Chippenham, Wiltshire.

Contents

List of Contributors

Elena Bocci Research Assistant at the Faculty of Psychology, University of Rome 'La Sapienza'; Research Trainee at the European Ph.D on Social Representations and Communication.

Felice Carugati Professor of Educational Psychology, Department of Education, University of Bologna.

Francisco Costa Pereira Professor of Psychology of Advertising and Consumer Behaviour, and Coordinator of the Advertising Observatory at the Polytechnic Institute of Lisbon.

David Deakins Dean of Research, Professor of Entrepreneurship and Director of the Paisley Enterprise Research Centre, University of Paisley.

Laura Galloway Lecturer in Entrepreneurship in the School of Management and Languages, Heriot-Watt University, Edinburgh.

Heather Fulford Lecturer in Information Systems, Business School, Loughborough University.

Colin Gray Professor, Open University Business School; President of the Institute for Small Business and Entrepreneurship; Trustee, Small Enterprise Research Team.

Tatjana Grek Kooperationsstelle Hamburg.

Erich M. Kirchler Professor, vice Dean of the Faculty of Psychology, University of Vienna; former President of the International Association for Research in Economic Psychology.

Lothar Lissner Head of Department of the Ministry for Science and Health, Free Hanseatic City of Hamburg.

Marco G. Mariani Researcher, Faculty of Psychology, University of Bologna.

Elvis Mazzoni Researcher, Department of Education, University of Bologna.

Robert Mochrie Lecturer in Economics in the School of Management and Languages, Heriot-Watt University, Edinburgh.

Elfriede Penz Assistant Professor in International Marketing & Management, at the Vienna University of Economics and Business Administration.

Annamaria Silvana de Rosa Professor of Psychology of Attitudes and Social Representations, Faculty of Psychology, University of Rome 'La Sapienza'; Coordinator of the European Ph.D on Social Representations and Communication and of the SO.RE.COM Thematic Network.

Mikko J. Ruohonen Professor and Chief Executive, School of Economics and Business Administration, University of Tampere.

Guido Sarchielli Professor of Work and Organizational Psychology, Faculty of Psychology, University of Bologna.

Laura Sartori Researcher, Department of Communication, University of Bologna.

Sara Saurini University of Roma 'La Sapienza'.

Daniele Scarpi Researcher, Department of Management, University of Bologna.

Abdel Monin Shaltoni Researcher, Birmingham Business School, University of Birmingham, and Lecturer in e-Marketing, Faculty of Administrative Sciences, University of Petra.

Jane Tebbutt Managing Consultant, Tangerine Consulting, former Head of Research at Business Link for London.

Carlo Tomasetto Researcher, Department of Education, University of Bologna.

Sabine Wendt Project Manager of Air-Craft Project, Kooperationsstelle Hamburg.

Rute Xavier Master in Communication and IT at the 'Instituto Superior de Ciências do Trabalho e da Empresa' (ISCTE) Lisbon.

Salvatore Zappalà Professor of Psychology of Economic Behavior, Faculty of Psychology, University of Bologna.

Introduction

Colin Gray and Salvatore Zappalà

Current State of e-Commerce in Europe

The European Union's (EU) Electronic Commerce Directive in 2000, whilst focussing mainly on providing a framework for cross border online services within Europe, states very clearly that its objective is to foster the potential for e-commerce to offer 'significant employment opportunities in the Community, particularly in small and medium-sized enterprises (SME), and to stimulate economic growth and investment in innovation by European companies'. Most of the Directive then goes on to address a range of contractual, legal and information issues in order to allow consumers 'to take full advantage, without consideration of borders, of the opportunities afforded by electronic commerce'. The EU and individual Member States have provided the policy objectives and regulatory framework. The purpose of this book is to look inside the frame at how some of Europe's 20 million firms and 370 million or more consumers have been trading electronically with each other, what influences their decisions to go online and what encourages and facilitates their electronic trading.

Impact of e-Commerce on Consumers and Small Firms describes factors influencing the process of adoption and use of e-commerce, both in firms (mainly small and medium enterprises) and among consumers. Although the EU's e-commerce Directive and a number of other studies use a narrow definition of e-commerce to include transactions done and services provided entirely online, this book takes a broader definition where important elements of trade and transactions are conducted using information and communications technologies (ICT). Generally, e-commerce is the term widely used to refer to business transactions between firms or directly with consumers that is conducted wholly or substantially online, while the broader concept of 'e-business' includes not only e-commerce but also the various processes where ICT applications – such as customer relationship marketing (CRM), electronic data interchange (EDI), knowledge management (KM) systems, enterprise resource planning (ERP) and so on – are used to improve business efficiency, effectiveness and growth. The focus of this book is the adoption of e-commerce, the simpler transactional phenomenon that entails access, especially broadband, to the Internet and implies the active use of a website.

A 2000 EU survey on firms' e-commerce adoption, conducted at the start of the new millennium, revealed (Table I.1) that access to the Internet was already high and growing, adoption of a website was variable and online sales were generally at low levels (European Commission, 2001). The same year saw the launch of the EU's *e-Europe Action Plan* in Lisbon with ambitious e-commerce and e-business objectives for fundamental changes to business processes and collaboration among significant numbers of SMEs. Five years later, the review of the action plan (European Commission, 2004) revealed that these objectives have been very slow to appear and that:

> the effective take up of new business processes and the adoption of new business models to exploit the potential of ICT remains a challenge, especially for the millions of European SMEs.... European performance is affected by the large proportion of SMEs, which are still lagging behind larger enterprises not only in terms of ICT infrastructure deployment but also in the level of sophistication of ICT use (European Commission, 2004, p. 9).

This lack of sophistication applies not only to the use of technology but also to innovative approaches to the market, particularly in the creating and meeting of new consumer needs. However, as Table 1 shows, the technological base has been in place for some time and it may be that there is a lag as a new generation of entrepreneurs emerge to take advantage of new e-commerce opportunities.

Table I.1   Percentages of SMEs with e-business applications in 2000

	FIN	S	DK	UK	D	NL	E	I	EL
Internet access	91	90	86	62	82	62	66	71	54
Own website	58	67	62	49	65	31	6	9	28
E-commerce purchases	34	31	36	32	35	23	9	10	5
E-commerce sales	13	11	27	16	29	22	6	3	6

Source: European Commission (2001)

In 2000, ICT adoption and use of was clearly not uniform across the EU, with northern Member States, particularly the Scandinavians (Finland, Sweden and Denmark), reporting much higher adoption rates than the southern Member States (Spain, Italy and Greece). Although not summarized in Table 1, this *digital gap* with central and eastern Europe was even wider. The e-commerce use of the Internet to buy and sell products and services reflected similar patterns. In addition, there were significant size differences between firms, with larger firms being much more likely to use ICT applications to transform their business processes and practices (e-business) than medium (50-249 employees) or small (10-49 employees) firms. However, it needs to be noted that this large scale EU survey, excluded *microfirms* of less than 10 employees, even though they account for 93 per cent of all EU firms and employ around one-third of the EU labour force. Other surveys suggest that size effects among microfirms tend to be even more acute and that they tend to be slower to adopt ICT. European SME Observatory studies conducted around the same time (European Commission, 2002) revealed distinct size differences in 2001 with a significantly lower adoption rate among microfirms. Indeed, microfirms were more likely to have a mobile phone (nearly 80 per cent) than a website (36 per cent).

The 2002 *e-Europe Benchmarking Report* on the level of e-commerce adoption in 15 European countries stated that e-commerce 'faces particular difficulties. It is growing, but much slower than expected and seems to be mainly taken-up by well-established companies'. Nevertheless, in 2002 there were also encouraging signs that access to the Internet had taken off among Europe's small businesses with the later SME Observatory studies confirming that some 74 per cent of SMEs had access to the Internet. Although clear size patterns remained, with 73 per cent of microfirms, 88 per cent of small firms and 97 per cent of medium firms connected to the Internet, it is now clear that majority of SMEs in Europe have passed the beginner's stage of using basic computer-based applications. Indeed the 2004 EU report confirmed this trend and reported significant increases in Internet access by consumers and firms across Europe, with 87 per cent of EU microfirms online and 41 per cent of all firms connected by broadband but little shift in the overall pattern of online purchases and sales (Ottens, 2004).

This was further confirmed by the latest findings from the EU's 'e-Business W@tch' project that has been tracking the adoption and diffusion of e-business related ICT adoption and activities among some 10,000 company decision-makers since 2001 (e-Business W@tch, 2004). Although there are signs that the digital north-south and east-west divides between regions and some industry differences are diminishing as late adopters catch up, there are still significant size differences. There are also signs that public policy has played an important role in bringing SMEs to the threshold where e-commerce and e-business are possible. The *e-Europe Action Plan,* the main EU policy to develop SMEs as e-businesses, has the specific aim of a 'widely available broadband infrastructure' as the platform for achieving its goals. National policies have targeted similar objectives. As Table I.2 shows, there is at least a partial link between expenditure on ICT and adoption of broadband (OECD, 2002).

Patterns of public and private ICT expenditure in Table I.2 are consistent with the levels of ICT adoption in Table I.1. Over the past ten years, the northern EU Member States increased their share of GDP spent on ICT from already high proportions in 1993 (especially Sweden). The southern EU partners (Italy, Portugal and Spain) have also increased but from a much lower base and by more modest increases. However, the relationship is not always consistent. Although Sweden has consistently invested more and has the highest broadband adoption rate, Britain has spent proportionately more than Denmark (and the US) with a lower average adoption rate, as has Italy with respect to Portugal and Spain. This will be partially due to financial and physical infrastructural factors but also to the cultural, economic and personal factors that influence the adoption rates by consumers and by the largest number of businesses in all countries – the SMEs.

By the time of the first review of the e-Commerce Directive in November 2003, however, the EU was more optimistic about the prospects for wider adoption of

Table I.2 ICT expenditure as a percentage of GDP 1993–2001

	1993	1994	1995	1996	1997	1998	1999	2000	2001	2002 OECD broad- band*
UK	4.83	4.64	4.83	4.9	4.89	4.82	5.15	5.56	5.62	1.3
DK	4.05	3.85	3.98	4.1	4.26	4.77	5.04	5.38	4.99	6.7
Italy	1.92	1.85	1.88	1.78	1.87	2.01	2.21	2.41	2.48	1.2
Portugal	1.34	1.33	1.48	1.48	1.49	1.73	1.86	1.96	1.93	1.5
Spain	1.66	1.56	1.54	1.56	1.66	1.78	1.85	1.96	1.94	2.1
Sweden	5.17	4.97	4.82	4.73	5.25	6.24	6.48	6.92	6.77	6.8
Germany	3.02	2.97	2.84	2.96	3.28	3.62	3.95	4.25	4.22	3.2
EU15	3.23	3.13	3.13	3.17	3.43	3.57	3.9	4.17	4.17	2.3
USA	4.54	4.55	4.7	4.93	5.03	5.21	5.31	5.47	5.3	5.8

* OECD: broadband subscribers/100 inhabitants
Source: Eurostat, Structural Indicators, December 2002.

e-commerce among firms and consumers. However, even though it is widely acknowledged ICT applications increase significantly the speed and content of communications, the links between ICT adoption and innovation in SMEs are assumed rather than understood. These remain to be demonstrated even though there is some evidence of productivity improvements and increased market efficiencies (Clayton, Criscuolo and Goodridge, 2004). It is clear that what is needed is a clearer comprehension of the factors that facilitate the adoption and the use of e-commerce technologies, at the level of both the firm and the consumer.

Structure and Themes

Impact of e-Commerce on Consumers and Small Firms addresses the problems we have described by exploring, from the perspective of the small firm not that of the established large firm, three key aspects:

1. factors that influence the adoption of innovations and ICT applications,
2. how ICT is used to improve the effectiveness of commercial transactions,
3. theoretical and practical factors that enable more effective use of the Internet.

From a theoretical perspective, the book follows an economic-psychological approach recognizing that neighbouring disciplines have something important to contribute. A fundamental assumption of this book is that e-commerce implies a commercial and a 'relational' transaction. Firms adopting and using e-commerce have to take into account not only the technological and organizational aspects of the implementation, but also the potential users of the web sites, with their own attitudes, skills, enthusiasm and fear of technology. On the other side, a greater number of consumers have to keep the pace with, and use effectively the, services offered through the Internet by enterprises. Thus, to complete successfully a transaction firms and consumers have to exchange not only money and products but also information and trust. The fact that conducting commercial transactions on the net affects directly the two actors of the transaction, poses important research questions. Entrepreneurs attitudes to technology and innovation, firms' strategic decision making and organizational changes, customers' perception of risks, search behaviour or actual use of the net are some of the issues and questions involved in the not so easy neither so fast e-business revolution. These issues may, and are, investigated by different perspectives. The study of e-commerce is, in fact, a new field which is developing its theoretical and empirical foundations and which is based on several disciplines (Turban et al., 2002).

This book had as its starting point an international workshop held in Rimini, in September 2003, organized by Salvatore Zappalà and supported by the Faculty of Psychology of the University of Bologna and the International Association for Research in Economic Psychology (IAREP). We acknowledge the contribution of Guido Sarchielli for providing support at critical moments and of IAREP Presidents, Erich Kirchler and Stephen Lea, for being there at the planning and at the closure of the workshop.

Experts in business management, organizational behaviour, marketing and consumer behavior attended the workshop and presented theoretical and empirical papers on the adoption and use of e-business and e-commerce, taking into account the two sides of the transaction, the firms or the consumers. All the papers addressed theoretical issues tested through empirical work and were available in advance, in order to facilitate discussion at the workshop itself. They have since been reviewed by the author/s, in the light of peer comments and discussions at the workshop, to improve the theoretical and empirical perspectives on each topic.

The chapters have been grouped in three broad areas: firstly, issues concerning the adoption of ICT and e-commerce by small firms; secondly, firms' use of ICT applications to support their marketing and sales transactions; thirdly factors that influence consumers' online purchases decisions.

Looking at the chapters in more detail, Colin Gray opens with a critique of different stage models of ICT adoption, using data on EU and UK small firms' ICT adoption to contrast different orientations towards innovation and growth of early and late ICT adopters. This is followed by Tomasetto and Carugati who address the social influence processes arising when a high status versus peer status source asks employees to learn and to use new technologies. Zappalà and Sarchielli describe the influence that two psycho-social variables, namely organizational climate for innovation and attitudes to Internet, have on ICT adoption. Ruohonen examines new business models for exploiting the potential of the web, such as alliances and clusters among firms and their need to be supported by new, improved and more professional leadership styles. The three following chapters in this first area then look in detail at ICT and e-commerce adoption in three different areas: firstly, the large metropolitan context of London which has some of the highest concentration of ICT adoption in Europe together with areas of very low adoption. This chapter, by Jane Tebutt, contrasts with the ICT adoption in rural Scotland. Mochrie, Galloway and Deakins describe the Internet forums that promote the adoption and use of web based technologies among Scottish small rural businesses, comparing the different roles of growth-orientation and export-orientation in driving this process. The third of these chapters is set in a specific industry in Germany. Wendt, Grek and Lissner report the preliminary results of a three years project, supported by the German Federal Ministry of Education and Research, introducing e-procurement in SMEs in the aviation industry. This chapter deals with many technical aspects of the introduction of e-procurement. Questions concerning work processes and conditions for an effective usage of e-procurement are also examined.

The second group of chapters explores internet marketing and the prerequisite of website usability and contents. This group starts with Xavier and Costa Pereira's account of Internet-based marketing (e-marketing) characteristics and the description of the main e-marketing strategies adopted among Portuguese firms. The next chapter, by Shaltoni, analyses current literature on e-marketing and proposes three different levels of e-marketing adoption strategies, related to different orientations to business displayed by different types of firm. Fulford describes characteristics of websites of small firms that want to attract consumers from overseas and suggests a three stages approach to tailor websites towards the needs of targeted site visitors. Mazzoni then uses an ergonomic perspective on website usability and describes how ease of use may improve the efficiency of small firm websites and internet related business operations. This chapter provides a link to the final group of chapters that focus on consumer purchase decisions.

The third group of chapters starts with Sartori who contrasts different consumption levels and styles between consumers from Italy and the USA and describes cultural, cognitive and social processes involved in consumers' decision to go online. This is followed by Penz and Kirchler's experiment which simulates an online shopping experience and which examines how relevant aspects of real websites, but also knowledge of the company and the type of product influence consumers' decision making process, the intention to purchase online and satisfaction with the shopping experience. Then, Mariani and Zappalà explore the perceptions of risk and trust in e-commerce adoption describing how perception of probability and perception of consequences of negative events in online shopping influence consumers' online behaviour. Scarpi then focuses on the effects of utilitarian and hedonic features of products on e-consumer choice. The purchase of tour packages on the Internet or in the traditional channels is influenced also by what customers think about the internet besides the specific risks and advantages of the two channels. This is what de Rosa, Bocci and Saurini observed in a study on the purchase of tour packages on the Internet.

The book concludes with a chapter from Zappalà and Gray that integrates the common themes that have emerged. These concern some of the social processes influencing a firm's decision to adopt ICT, the learning processes supporting the stage adoption and use of e-business, and risk perception, a factor that makes consumers and small firms reluctant to adopt ICT. The chapter, and the book, concludes with a brief review of current ICT developments and trends.

This book is on the frontier of behavioural research on the crucial area where consumers and firms interact and where older technologies are making way for the new. If it helps those who are beginning to engage in e-commerce understand the processes involved and why other e-commerce actors (firms, consumers, business associations, hardware and software providers, consultants and so on) behave as they do, perhaps the adoption process will go more smoothly and new e-businesses emerge more quickly.

References

Clayton, T., Criscuolo, C. and Goodridge, P. (2004), *e-Commerce and Firm Performance: An Assessment Using Multiple Survey Sources and Linked Data*, Report to the European Commission, DG Eurostat and DG Enterprise, Luxembourg.

e-Business W@tch (2004), *The European e-Business Report, 3rd Synthesis Report*, European Commission: Enterprise Directorate, Brussels.

European Commission (2001), *e-Commerce and ICT Usage by European Enterprises*, Eurostat, Brussels.

European Commission (2002), *Observatory of European SMEs 2002 / No. 1, Highlights from the 2001 Survey*, EC Enterprise Directorate, Brussels.

European Commission (2004), *Challenges for the European Information Society beyond 2005*, COM(2004) 757 final, Brussels.

Organization for Economic Cooperation and Development (OECD) (2002), *Broadband Access for Business*, OECD, Paris.

Ottens, M. (2004), *Internet Usage by Individuals and Enterprises: 8,* Eurostat, Luxembourg.

Turban, E., King, D., Lee, J., Warketin, M. and Chung, M. (2002), *Electronic Commerce 2002, A managerial perspective*, Prentice Hall, New Jersey.

PART I
Impact of e-Commerce on Small Firms

Chapter 1

Stage Models of ICT Adoption in Small Firms

Colin Gray

Introduction

Global competition and the potential of ICT to increase massively the speed of communication and access to information offer enormous business opportunities though added complexities mean that individual firms are finding harder to manage on their own. Small and medium enterprises (SMEs), with their more limited resources and significantly weaker market power, find the competitive pressures are even more intense. This has increased the pressure on SMEs to cooperate more in networks, to share information, development costs and risks. Networking – sometimes referring to the tight or loose social ties that bond groups of business owners and managers, sometimes to the information and communication technologies (ICT) that enable faster connections between businesses with mutual interests – has come into the limelight as policy makers across Europe have become alert to the pressures of globalisation. The networks that policy makers have in mind are generally supply and value chains that link SMEs to larger 'focal firms' but sometimes their attention is on the agglomerations of SMEs (clusters) that can produce innovations that are successful in world markets. The key to future development, growth and networking is seen as lying in the effective adoption of ICT.

Despite a slow start, there is now widespread use of ICT by SMEs across Europe. Use of personal computers is almost universal, the vast majority of firms and consumers access the Internet, and now many SMEs are networking their computers through internal intranets or through dedicated extranets with external partners. Even so, the 2002 European SME Observatory revealed strong size effects and that some 30 per cent of microfirms (SMEs with less than 10 employees) were not connected to the Internet (EC, 2002). Some 43 per cent of microfirms without access at that time felt it did not apply to their type of business or product. This was followed by concern that their investment would not pay off (18 per cent) and a similar number felt that they lacked of appropriate ICT skills (17 per cent). Although these concerns still exist, more recent EU surveys reveal that access to the Internet has taken off dramatically and, by 2003, half of the EU's 370 million inhabitants had access and 87 per cent of firms were connected (Ottens, 2004). However, this means that around 13 per cent of microfirms are still resisting the adoption of the Internet or finding no use for it. Also, the adoption of e-commerce still seems stuck at the bottom of the adoption curve with 19 per cent of individuals, but only 12 per cent of firms, reporting that they had purchased something online – and just 5 per cent and 7 per cent respectively reporting that they had made sales online. It is clearly important to have a better understanding of the adoption process. In the following sections, a number of different models of ICT adoption are described and considered in the light of empirical research conducted among SMEs in Britain.

Models of ICT Adoption

When ICT applications, such as personal computers, modems and e-mail, were first introduced, small businesses, especially the smaller microfirms, were initially slow to adopt the new technologies. Although this is no longer true, the adoption and use of ICT is not uniform across Europe and needs to be better understood. Attempts to explain and analyse ICT adoption among SMEs appear to fall into three broad approaches:

1. supply-side, *technology-determinist*, rational process where the supply of more advanced ICT applications creates its own demand through the benefits of superior business performance;
2. demand-side, rational and *business strategy* response by small firm owners to ICT-induced competitive, market and socio-economic changes whereby, through use, they move to another stage of business development as they master earlier stages and become aware of the business benefits of more advanced ICT applications;
3. *social network* approach where adoption is not necessarily a linear process and will not happen until the owner is ready, a state that depends on the everyday influences such as individual expectations, peer pressure and the business milieu that shape opinions, attitudes and behaviour of small firm owners.

It needs to be stated that it is unlikely that none of these models alone adequately explains or predicts the adoption of ICT by small firms. However, in line with many other aspects of small firm behaviour and performance, usually effects associated with firm size and industry need to be taken into account. For instance, very small firms and the self-employed are often motivated to sustain a lifestyle that preserves their independence rather than to achieve business or financial success (Gray, 1998). Some small firm lifestyles may be resistant to the adoption of new technologies whereas other small firm owners may view ICT as the means for defending their autonomy. Medium firms in the ICT sector, business services, distribution and manufacturing are likely to be more aware of new applications and to have in-house ICT skills and so be more open to a technology-push approach. Growth-oriented small firms, whose size-related resource limitations make them more alert to value-for-money, productivity and efficiency issues, are more likely to take a more strategic approach, often driven by the cost-reduction or time-saving potential of ICT. Most small firms, however, do not have a formal or explicit strategy and most, especially the microfirms, suffer from information, knowledge and skills gaps. For many of these small firms and microfirms, networks, which can range from informal local clusters to more formal inter-firm relationships governed by contracts, offer real economic and business advantages (Perry, 1999). The microfirm sector is where the social network diffusion model might be most useful in understanding and promoting adoption.

Referring to Tables I.1 and I.2 in the Introduction, it is clear that supply side issues in investment, in the development of ICT applications and in the provision of infrastructure do influence adoption patterns, at least at the macro level. However, this is always more difficult to detect at the micro level, which is the main concern of this chapter. The 'adoption ladder' (see Figure 1.1) developed by Cisco for the UK government's information age partnership study (DTI, 2001) is one of the most widely used technology-push models. Indeed, it is used in the EU to support the next stage of development which envisages specialised small firms linked through ICT connections in real and virtual clusters as 'digital business ecosystems' (Nachira, 2002).

Although the adoption ladder provides a sense of technological progression, it is too linear to describe processes that are often non-linear and very complex. Indeed, there is no evidence that the rungs in the DTI ladder actually do represent evolutionary steps by which SMEs transform themselves into e-businesses (Sparrow, 2001). Nor does this ladder help in understanding how ICT alters what SMEs can do or the resource implications of successful adoption. Even though the model has

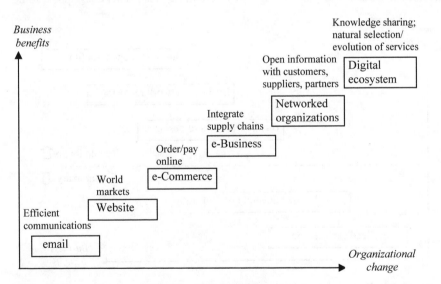

Figure 1.1 e-Business adoption ladder
Source: Adapted from DTI (2001), and Nachira (2002)

organizational changes as one of its axes, there is no indication of the dynamic processes that drive SMEs from one stage to the next.

The business-strategy approach, with its concerns for demand-side issues, is well represented by an earlier ICT adoption model, which focused on small firm demand and customary modes of working. This accepted that the business opportunities and organizational change of ICT adoption can indeed be described in stages, or different phases, but that SMEs will enter at any point according to their immediate business needs and according to the current capabilities in the firm (Venkatraman, 1994). The Venkatraman model of integration of ICT into the business in Figure 1.2 distinguishes between small *evolutionary* changes, where ICT applications are used to improve the effectiveness and efficacy of existing business practices and processes, and changes where ICT results in *revolutionary* changes to processes, business conduct and, indeed, what the core business is.

The dotted line separates the bottom stages where incremental change can take place from stages where a fundamental change in the nature and processes of the business needs to occur. The bottom incremental stages could include the adoption of simple ICT applications that do not require a major change to existing business routines and systems, such the introduction of word processing, databases, e-mail, networked computers and so on. The more advanced stages above the dotted line require a strategic decision for their adoption, including budgeting and planning, and imply fundamental changes to the firm. However, this is not a path followed by many small firms which tend to respond to immediate need and do not necessarily follow a staged, rational process. A non-linear approach is more likely to describe their behaviour in the evolutionary stages but not in the revolutionary stages where the knowledge demands and strategy needs are more acute. This does appear to be

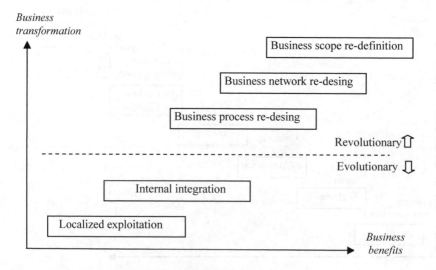

Figure 1.2.   Business integration ICT adoption model
Source: Adapted from Venkatraman (1994) (reprinted with permission)

a useful model for describing the routes taken by some SMEs that have transformed themselves through the considered use of ICT applications into proper and successful e-businesses. These firms remain a very small minority. This model does not take into account the 'trial and error' approach adopted by many SME owners, many of whom may view the dotted line between incremental, evolutionary changes and fundamental, radical, revolutionary changes as a point of no return beyond which a return on investment cannot be guaranteed with any degree of certainty. The majority of SMEs, especially the very small microfirms, do not adopt a rationale strategic approach to business and this generally includes the decision of how and when to invest in ICT.

A more considered approach to understanding patterns of ICT adoption by SMEs must start from examining how they acquire information and use it in their decision-making. A useful 4-step 'staircase of Internet engagement' stage approach (see Figure 1.3), based on information needs of small firms, not on technology push, was adopted by the British Library (Allcock *et al.*, 1999), following a study on SME use of the Internet as an information and learning resource.

The British Library staircase takes the perspective of the SME owner-managers, linking technological evolution to their capability to learn, manage new ICT knowledge and introduce business changes. Importantly, the British Library's dynamic model shows that business problems, unfulfilled expectations and information weaknesses may send SMEs back down the 'staircase' as well as up. Ironically, although it is an information-needs based model, it does not address where small firm owners find their information on ICT or what impels them to do so. The older social network approach is enjoying a resurgence of interest and provides a much richer theoretic framework, focusing strongly on the social and economic drivers of competition, cooperation and the exchange of information and knowledge.

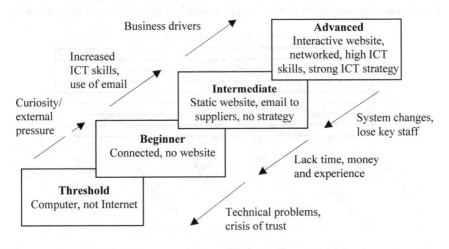

Figure 1.3   British Library staircase of Internet engagement
Source: Adapted from Allcock et al. (1999) (reprinted with permission)

Everett Rogers (1983), who is discussed in more detail in the next chapter by Tomasetto and Carugati, highlighted the role of social networks as crucial determinants of innovation adoption. He identified how the pressures of uncertainty over the outcome, unknown risks and lack of information raised the importance of social and occupational networks as sources of information. As more network peers adopt a given innovation, communication concerning the risks and outcomes increases within the networks until a critical mass of network members is reached when the dissemination and demonstration effects gather their own momentum and the adoption of the innovation is a success. Even prior to that, a threshold is reached when a sufficient number of network peers have adopted the innovation to convince a larger number of other members to adopt. The stronger the ties between network members, the faster and more trusted the communications between them so the diffusion effects are likely to be faster (Granovetter, 1978). This describes the adoption patterns of a very wide ranges of different products and services, including seeds, medicines and consumer goods as well as ICT innovations such as computers, e-mail, websites, mobile phones and broadband (Rogers, 1983; Foxall and Goldsmith, 1994; Smoreda and Thomas, 2001).

Innovation adoption patterns follow similar normal distribution curves (see Figure 1.4). According to social network theory, innovative adopters (roughly 2.5 per cent of the market) are usually already involved with the innovation area and have a very strong curiosity to try the latest fads and gadgets. With respect to ICT adoption they may be 'geeks' or just people fascinated by new technology. They tend to have higher income and educational levels than their peers. As their enthusiasms lead them to communicate their experiences, they are a vital first step in the diffusion process. However, the next group, the early adopters, are a much larger and more significant group (around 13.5 per cent). Similar to innovative adopters with respect to their curiosity regarding ICT, they tend to be more business-minded and prepared to take risks (Foxall and Goldsmith, 1994). They are less obviously

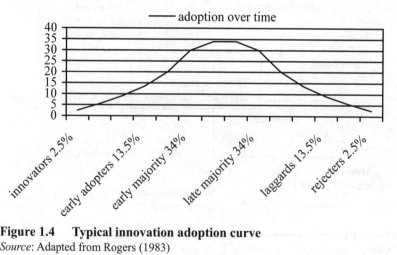

Figure 1.4   Typical innovation adoption curve
Source: Adapted from Rogers (1983)

'faddists' or obsessives, though clearly attracted by the new product (broadband, e-commerce and ICT applications in general). Being closer in characteristics to the mass markets, their adoption is extremely important to the ultimate successful diffusion of the innovation, which comes when the innovation is taken up by the early majority adopters (34 per cent). Successful innovations will then be taken up by large numbers (34 per cent) of late majority adopters, eventually tailing off when the laggards (13.5 per cent) enter the market.

This adoption curve, which is similar to a product life cycle curve, is a useful way to examine the adoption patterns of ICT applications of all types. Following the laggards in the SME sector, some studies (Gray and Juhler, 2000; Gray, 2002) suggest that there is an additional category of 'rejectionists' (say 2.5 per cent or more) who seem determined not to adopt. Generally, early adopters are rational, relying on empirical evidence that the product works in ways that they want, tend to be more evaluative and deliberate in their decisions but are driven by a personal involvement and interest in the product domain (in-house ICT skills, planned growth strategy, etc.). ICT usage amongst small firms in Britain has been tracked by a number of studies including those conducted by the Small Enterprise Research Team (SERT), an independent non-profit research body based at the Open University Business School (OUBS). Four recent surveys (1996, 1999, 2001 and 2003) shared a sufficient number of respondents (394) to trace adoption patterns over time. Table 1.1 compares, at the three time points, the adoption rates of e-mail, websites and e-commerce of innovative and early adopters of e-mail in 1996 with SMEs that did not adopt e-mail in that year.

In line with social network theory, the innovative and early adopters of e-mail were only 17 per cent of SMEs in 1996. Thereafter, they consistently accounted for much higher new adoptions of Internet e-mail, websites, broadband and e-commerce in succeeding years. Also in line with social network theory, the rate of adoption of Internet e-mail, websites and broadband began to tail off by 2003 as majority adopter small firms followed the early adopters. Thus, the early 1996 adopters of e-mail were twice as likely three years later in 1999 to have adopted a website and, by 2001, almost six times as likely to have adopted broadband (both necessary to conduct e-commerce). By 2003, there is a noticeable convergence in adoption rates between the two groups (though it was clear from the responses to questions on usage that many late adopter SMEs do not update their websites or upgrade their systems as frequently as early adopters). It seems likely that these early adopter effects will be reflected in the adoption of mobile/wireless technologies as early adopters switch to newer technologies.

The different patterns of adoption in Table 1.1 provide convincing evidence of early adopter effects. The learning and familiarity effects associated with introducing e-mail appear to have positively influenced the adoption of the more advanced website applications, such as broadband. Social network diffusion models, in emphasising the social influences on SME decisions and different personal consumer profiles at different phases in the adoption process, are more subtle and explanatory than simple technology-push or business-pull stage models. In particular, they help in

Table 1.1   ICT adoption patterns in early-adopter UK SMEs, 1996-2003
(percentages)

	1996 e-mail innovative/early adopters (17% of the 394 sample, n = 67)			1996 e-mail later/non adopters (83% of the 394 sample, n = 327)		
	e-mail	Own website	Broadband; e-commerce	e-mail	Own website	Broadband; e-commerce
1996 Adoption						
e-mail	100			0		
1999 Adoption						
Internet e-mail	91			39		
Website		44			22	
2001 Adoption						
Internet e-mail	98			69		
Website		58			44	
Broadband			63			11
e-commerce			13			7
2003 Adoption						
Internet e-mail	91			77		
Website		59			50	
Broadband			61			54
e-commerce			11			6

Source: SBRT 1996, 1999, 2002; SERTeam 2003

understanding how the very small microfirms can enjoy some of the benefits that ICT offers in developing their businesses without sacrificing their autonomy (which is precious to most microfirms).

In all three approaches discussed above, it needs to be stressed that the decision-maker, the small firm owner-manager, needs to be personally ready before moving on to the next stage and that the ICT adoption process inevitably involves learning and new knowledge. Readiness refers not only to the consolidation of learning and operational knowledge from previous adoptions of technology or change but also to the positive attitudes and expectations that precede change (Gray and Juhler, 2000; Parasuraman, 2000). Readiness is the psychological and practical point at which an individual is prepared to proceed to the next stage – a state determined by a particular mix of experience, capabilities, resources, education, age, peer pressure, business imperatives, motivation and circumstance. The social network effects discussed above are very important, especially with SME owners who lack confidence, experience or ICT capabilities. Thus, more generally, ICT adoption models for SMEs need to take into account:

- *individual* personal readiness (including abilities, skills and motivation to handle ICT equipment and applications as well as the capacity to sense future possibilities);
- *organizational* readiness (including the financial, human resource, technological, marketing and strategy dimensions);
- *external* social, technical and business readiness (including economic climate, stakeholder analysis, supply-chain relations and political or regulatory dimensions).

Personal readiness is linked to business objectives, experience and increased familiarity in dealing with ICT. Organizational readiness relates to functional capabilities. The external business environment influences readiness not only in terms of business opportunities but also the state of e-business development, including telecoms infrastructure, security of credit-card transactions literacy of the population. Trust, public policy and consumer attitudes are also important (WITSA, 2001). External readiness is also influenced by peer pressure (often through their networks), relations with large firms and disproportionate costs of regulations compliance. Indeed, as Figure 1.3 showed, external barriers to ICT adoption plus the effects of introducing even newer technologies, can also push firms back to an earlier stage. Small firms are cautious about wasting precious resources on unproven technologies, preferring to wait until innovative ICT applications have become mature products. In order to guide future research, OUBS have synthesised, in Table 1.2, the strengths of the three main ICT adoption approaches while also taking into account the three levels of readiness required for more advanced ICT adoption.

One key assumption of the model is that it will be the entrepreneurial SMEs which have explicit growth strategies, and more consequent openness to external events and opportunities, that will progress more surely from one stage to the next. Implicitly embedded in this model are the processes of consolidation (operational learning, knowledge of new routines and capabilities, new working relations and skills, etc.) that need to be completed at each stage for readiness to grow at personal and organizational levels. Even though many SMEs agree that these technologies will bring about improved communications with customers and suppliers and improved business efficiency, this belief does not impel them from one stage to the next. They need a new mindset developed from personal confidence and concrete evidence from prior experience, plus strongly convincing evidence of the potential, for example, of an ICT application to increase turnover or broaden their customer base. The motivation to adopt new ICTs is often to achieve goals other than or in addition to the theoretical benefits of e-business (which are generally held to include improved communication between partners, customer and knowledge management, transformation of internal business processes, security from confidentiality and fraud, and so on). In the earliest stages, adoption may be an emotional rather than rational process. Indeed, only a minority of SMEs use business plans and very few of these plans include a consideration of the business implications of ICT and e-commerce for the firm (Wilson and Deans, 2000; Quayle, 2001).

Table 1.2 OUBS stages of SME adoption and use of ICT model

READINESS ISSUES		
Individual/personal	Organizational	Business envirnomental

Pre-stage. Uninvolved: naïve, indifferent, hostile

Cultural/lifestyle concerns	Lack of resources; unemployed; sole-trader	Low ICT contact; no market demand

Stage 1. Threshold: Keen to try ICT; unsure how

Low technical knowledge; ICT business potential curiosity	Communication important; customer, staff demand	Customers/peers online; supplier, government pressure; local ISP, ADSL

Stage 2. Beginner: Recently online but unsure of where to go next

Confident with e-mail, Internet; ready for website	Internal e-mail; sales-customer activities; skills-productivity issues	Market/ network push ICT use; sources of advice not obvious

Stage 3. Intermediate: Internet e-mail, website, no ICT strategy

Owner grows ICT knowledge; sees benefits of Web, ready to use ICT in admin. and ops.	ICT skills and efficiency issues; network benefits	Use of advice and support networks; stronger competition push on costs, access/delivery issues

Stage 4. Advanced: ICT an integral part of business strategy

ICT capabilities developed; ready for new approaches to business	Knowledge issues; outsourcing; ASP; ICT integrated in systems	Strong competitor and customer ICT skills; clear regulatory and legal frameworks

Stage5. Innovative: Capability to exploit ICT strategically in process/product innovations

Entrepreneurial; high ICT literacy; managers/ workers in effective autonomous working	Shared corporate culture and vision; knowledge management/sharing; networked	Strong value-chain; strategic partnership + support networks; global competition

Empirical Findings on SMEs Adoption

The following sections report findings from empirical studies conducted by OUBS which cast more light on the factors that influence patterns of ICT adoption among SMEs and provide some support for the OUBS model of ICT adoption (Table 1.2). In particular, these findings show that early adopters of one ICT application:

1. tend to be early adopters in others,
2. tend to be more entrepreneurial in their growth strategies and
3. tend to be *core* or 'opinion-former' members of their networks.

To a large extent the first proposition has already received some support from the SERTeam analysis presented in Table 1.1. However, further ICT adoption and use by early-adopters still needs to be considered in relation to their businesses.

These issues were addressed by OUBS in the NEWTIME project, an EU-funded study on the effects of recent introduction of broadband in small firm networks in six EU countries for two years over 2000-2003. The networks, selected locally by each partner, were a mix of business associations, supply chains and local less formal clusters. Two were in urban areas and the rest in peripheral EU regions. The NEWTIME project focused on microfirms in the intermediate stage of ICT adoption of the OUBS model. The study developed a framework that took into account not only the impact that broadband has on networks but also the complex patterns of behaviour, performance and strategies among the individual microfirms. NEWTIME research is both qualitative and quantitative – consisting of an initial baseline survey of 55 participating microfirms (Gray et al., 2002) and an exit survey, at the end of the 12-month research period, of the 45 microfirms in the 8 networks, plus recorded observations from the mentors who interacted with the networks during the one year research period (March 2002–March 2003). In particular, the mentors observed and probed attitudes and practice towards the adoption of broadband and other ICT applications, as well as individual and collective growth strategies of firms in their networks.

Early adopter effects

By selection, all NEWTIME participants were either innovative or early broadband adopters. Based on mentor observations and participant responses to a number of questions on their use of ICT and broadband, the sample split evenly. Half of the sample were innovative adopters, having adapted, modified or developed software or hardware for their own specific business use. In line with the differences between innovative and early adopters as expected by social network theory, the introduction of broadband further increased the *readiness* of the innovative adopters to adopt and try even more advanced ICT applications, which in many cases included systems for collaborative working and e-commerce. Indeed, the innovative adopters were also more likely to report an increased use of the Internet and Internet based services, in line with their stronger interest in technology. As Table 1.3 shows, they were also deeply inserted in their networks.

The innovative adopters are be drawn to or supported by strong ties with other network members and are seen by themselves and other network members as core members. This is supportive of the social network theory of innovation diffusion. Indeed, mentor observations also support the proposition that innovative and early adopters in one ICT application tend to be early adopters of others, including the adoption of e-commerce. However, the early adopters were not so strongly linked to their networks and, thus, were even less likely to be core members. This suggests that they may be more driven by their own business needs and that they perhaps make use of their networks in a more instrumental way than innovative adopters. Although the importance to strongly tied networks of innovative adopters as opinion-formers seems clear with respect to ICT adoption, however, they may not have the same role in the business use of ICT for e-commerce. The entrepreneurial effects are examined in this next section followed by a more detailed assessment of the network effects.

Table 1.3 Innovative vs. early adopter network features, 2003 (percentages)

Network features	Innovative adopter	Early adopter	All
Strong ties	74	32	53
Core members	73	18	46
Total (n)	22	22	44

Source: NEWTIME project (IST 2000 29568; see also www.newtime.org.uk)

Entrepreneurship effects

It might be expected that the second proposition would also hold – that innovative adopters would also be entrepreneurial. However, in the NEWTIME study, the exit survey revealed no significant differences in business performance between the innovative and early adopters or of the impact of broadband upon their businesses. Around 60 per cent of both reported that they had performed better than their sector and 40 per cent of both reported a positive impact of broadband on their businesses.

Table 1.4 Innovative vs. early adopter future strategies, 2003 (percentages)

Business strategies	Innovative adopter	Early adopter	All
Growth/new markets	23	48	35
More ICT development	36	24	30
Organizational improvements	23	24	23
No plan/other	18	5	12
Total (n)	22	21	43

Source: NEWTIME project (IST 2000 29568; see also www.newtime.org.uk)

Far from the innovative adopters being more entrepreneurial as a group, they are actually less growth-oriented and less likely to seek to develop new products for new markets than the early adopters. In fact, fascination with technology seems more important to innovative adopters than their business objectives. Interestingly, one quarter of both groups intend to apply ICT solutions to internal organizational matters which indicates that early adopters of broadband are also likely to be early adopters of e-business. In line with the characteristics of the early adopter in Roger's innovation diffusion model, it is the NEWTIME early adopters who are also significantly more entrepreneurial minded compared to the more technologically oriented innovative adopters. It appears that a technology-push stage model of ICT adoption may reflect the behaviour of technology-oriented SMEs but fails to capture the business-drivers or reflect actual usage and potential needs with respect to ICT in entrepreneurial small firms. However, the business-pull model does seem to apply to the many of entrepreneurial early adopters, most of whom made significant changes to their businesses as a result of introducing broadband (especially in extending their sales further afield into new markets).

Just over one third (35 per cent) of the firms could be described as entrepreneurial in the sense of having business growth objectives. A very high 80 per cent of these entrepreneurial firms reported that, in the year they adopted broadband, their firms performed better than average against their sector and against their region. They were critical of support from ICT vendors and telecoms but this was not a case of small firm individualism. They were very positive regarding support they receive from their network and had increased significantly contact with other network members and their own business performance as a result of adopting broadband. Overall, they were active network participants and it is to be assumed that the 40 per cent of these entrepreneurial firms who were also core members (a select 14 per cent segment of the whole sample) are likely to be effective *network entrepreneurs*.

Network effects

With respect to the third proposition, the findings above suggest that innovative adopters are effective opinion formers on matters of technology and ICT while early adopters, or an active minority of them, do seem to be opinion-formers on business matters. Both are important in the adoption of e-commerce. However, the power of their influence on the adoption of e-commerce is likely to also depend on the external environment including the nature and purpose of the network. In the second quarter of 2002, the SERT examined network effects among small firms in Britain. Table 1.5 outlines the business use of the three main types of network: association (business, professional and trade bodies), supply/value chains and informal cluster networks.

A high 85 per cent of respondents engage in some form of networking. The balance between social contact and the business functions, such as the sharing of business and technology advice, and seeking new customers are clear. Both social and business activities are both significantly more important in cluster networks, which are mainly composed of microfirms. However, associations are also used a lot by members for business and technology advice (a finding that should reassure chambers of commerce and trade associations). Thus there are strong network effects among small and microfirms. The high demand for technology advice also suggests that many small firms (one third of those that are members of a local cluster) do adopt a rational and informed business-pull approach towards ICT adoption even though the social and business attractions of their networks dominate. Results from the initial baseline survey of the NEWTIME project also revealed a curiosity and very positive attitudes towards ICT as those firms moved from that beginner stage to an intermediate stage with the introduction of broadband. Table 1.6 summarises attitudes towards ICT in NEWTIME microfirms at the start of the project.

The vast majority (78 per cent) of NEWTIME microfirms felt that the next step in ICT adoption was either necessary or very important to their business. Once again, it was the microfirms in the less formal local clusters that were more likely (88 per cent) to hold these strong attitudes. However, in looking at their actual use of ICT at the start of project (Table 1.7), the cluster firms seem to be more collaborative in their networking with 60 per cent already using a local area network (LAN) and

Table 1.5 SMEs network use, 2002 (percentages, multiple mentions)

Network use	Association	Supply chain	Cluster	All networks	All SMEs
Social contact	38	35	62	41	46
Business advice	52	42	59	50	42
Technology advice	30	29	33	29	25
New customers	20	23	31	23	20
New suppliers	14	17	23	15	14
Joint marketing	13	12	17	11	10
Joint purchasing	9	8	11	8	7
Recruiting staff	3	3	3	3	3
Sample (n)	810	343	507	992	1168
Percent	69	29	43	85	100

Source: NatWest/SBRT Quarterly Survey of Small Business in Britain, 2002

Table 1.6 ICT attitudes in NEWTIME firms, 2002 (percentages)

ICT value to firm	Association	Supply chain	Clusters	All
Necessary	21	69	28	35
Very important	59	7	60	43
Important	21	14	8	17
Not necessary	7	7	4	7
Sample (n)	14	15	25	54

Source: NEWTIME project (IST 2000 29568; see also www.newtime.org.uk)

Table 1.7 Modes of connection in NEWTIME firms, 2002 (percentages)

ICT connections	Association	Supply chain	Clusters	All
Website	86	73	80	80
Local area network	67	43	60	61
Internal Internet	36	31	20	28
Partner extranet	14	0	48	26
e-commerce	63	25	0	19
Sample (n)	14	15	25	54

Source: NEWTIME project (IST 2000 29568; see also www.newtime.org.uk)

nearly half (48 per cent) linked to their partners through an extranet (compared with only 14 per cent of business association members and no members of supply chain networks).

Business association networks also seem to be more advanced ICT users (including the use of ICT applications that facilitate collaboration), and supply chain less so. However, the use of ICT by firms in supply chains (presumably to support internal operations and direct e-mail links with focal customers) is seen as essential. The NEWTIME exit survey cast more light on the ICT influence on communications in microfirm networks finding that e-mail had become the preferred mode of communication following the introduction of broadband (pushing ahead of face-to-face communications, and older technologies such as fax). There were clear differences between those in networks that have strong ties (53 per cent) between members and those with weak ties (47 per cent). In general, microfirms in networks with weak ties tended to remain at *status quo* and reported far fewer changes resulting from broadband or from their network involvement. Of those in networks with strong ties, half increased their network involvement and their frequency of contacts compared with just 10 per cent and 29 per cent respectively of those with weak ties.

Discussion

The findings from both the SERT analysis and the NEWTIME study, in revealing strong early adopter effects, provide support for the social network theory of innovation adoption and diffusion. The differences between innovative adopters, with their focus on technology, and the early adopters, who have more of an entrepreneurial business focus, was very strongly in line with social network theory but it also serves to highlight the complexity of relationships and roles in functioning networks It is clear that effective networks have to address at least three different aspects of concern to microfirms – the social dimension, the technology dimension and the business dimension. These reflect the different dimensions that individual microfirm owner-managers have to manage (Gray, 1998). This is clear from Table

1.5 where those in clusters – which is the most common form of networking among microfirms – are linked by social ties as much as business ties and appear to be more willing to conduct collaborative activities. The clusters are also a significant source of ICT advice to the individual firms. As Table 1.6 shows, ICT development is very important to the NEWTIME firms though the firms in cluster networks seem more interested in the increased communications with other members than in developing e-commerce. Thus the social aspects of the network are important in tying the network together, and sharing knowledge on ICT applications, but may also inhibit a more competitive and entrepreneurial approach to their development as businesses.

The OUBS model of ICT adoption takes these tensions into account, with business and marketing pressures gradually assuming greater power as drivers of ICT adoption over the more personal and social aspects. Thus, the innovative adopters are very important at the early stages – possibly even providing the main *raison d'etre* of the network for many members – but the influences of the more business-minded early adopters begin to become more to the fore. In fact, the local clusters in Denmark and Portugal did spend the earlier stage on evaluating and implementing broadband-based internal communications systems before moving to the next stage of focussing on external communications with potential or actual major customers. At the same time, they identified additional ICT needs to support their increasing customer focus. The NEWTIME firms that actually began to move into more revolutionary business integration of ICT by adopting e-commerce in their marketing and sales tended to be individual early adopters, not innovative adopters, with a more considered approach to their ICT investments in support of their marketing outside their regions.

Finally, it is important to examine the policy implications of the studies and findings reported in this chapter. One implication of the OUBS model is the need to recognize that each stage of ICT development represents a different set of dynamics between entrepreneurs, their firms and the markets they operate in. Policy initiatives risk being ineffective if they are 'directed' at firms at different stages of ICT readiness and development. The ICT support needs to be integrated with initiatives that support business management and strategy development. In many regional and local development policies this takes the form of encouraging the establishment of local clusters to promote entrepreneurship and innovation. The clear evidence presented here is that ICT applications that support e-commerce are adopted by SMEs for a variety of motives, to meet a variety of expectations and at a variety of speeds. It is equally clear that for most SMEs the strongest influences on their adoptions decisions are peers and like-minded other firms in their networks of contacts and friends. In part, cluster initiatives are an attempt by policy makers to foster those network effects in order to support innovation which is interesting. However, there is a danger that, in focussing too tightly on entrepreneurial firms, other types of firms that play a crucial role in the functioning of effective networks, such as non-entrepreneurial innovative adopters or the more considered late majority adopters, may be marginalized. For e-commerce to take off and for new e-businesses to emerge the challenge remains to attract and enthuse the majority adopters, which may be a job for the early adopters rather than policy makers.

References

Allcock, S., Webber, S and Yeates, R. (1999), *Business Information and the Internet: Use of the Internet as an Information Resource for SMEs*, British Library Research and Innovation Report (136), London.

Department of Trade and Industry (DTI) (2001), *Business in the Information Age: International Benchmarking Report*, Department of Trade and Industry, London.

European Commission (EC) (2002), *Observatory of European SMEs 2002 / No.1, Highlights from the 2001 Survey*, EC Enterprise Directorate, Brussels.

Foxall, G. and Goldsmith, R. (1994), *Consumer Psychology for Marketing*, Routledge, London.

Granovetter, M. (1978), 'Threshold Models of Collective Behavior', *American Journal of Sociology*, Vol. 53, pp. 1360 -1380.

Gray, C. (1998), *Enterprise and Culture*, Routledge, London.

Gray, C. (2002), 'Entrepreneurship, Resistance to Change and Growth in the Small Firm', *Journal of Small Business and Enterprise Development*, Vol. 9, pp. 61-72.

Gray, C. (2003), 'Managing the Impact of Broadband on Microfirms and their Networks', *The European Journal of Teleworking*, Vol. 9, No. 1, Autumn, pp. 4–16.

Gray, C. and Juhler, K. (2000), 'Impact of Information and Communication Technologies in EU Rural Areas', SBRT, Milton Keynes.

Gray, C., Langkjaer, K. and Oliveira, A. (2002), 'SME Networks: Broadening their Reach and Success', Paper presented at the 3rd eBusiness and eWork Conference, Prague.

Nachira, F. (2002), 'Towards a Network of Digital Business Ecosystems: Fostering the Local Development', DG INFSO Discussion Paper, September, European Commission, Brussels.

Ottens, M. (2004), *Internet Usage by Individuals and Enterprises: 8*, Eurostat, Luxembourg.

Parasuraman, A. (2000), 'Technology Readiness Index (TRI): A Multiple-Item Scale to Measure Readiness to Embrace New Technologies', *Journal of Service Research*, Vol. 2, pp. 307-320.

Perry, M. (1999), *Small Firms and Network Economies*, Routledge, London.

Quayle, M. (2001), 'E-Commerce: the Challenge for Welsh Small and Medium Size Enterprise', Paper presented at the Business week in Wales, Cardiff.

Rogers, E. (1983), *The Diffusion of Innovations*, Free Press, New York.

Small Business Research Trust (SBRT) (2002), *NatWest/SBERT Quarterly Survey of Small Business in Britain*, Vol. 18, No. 2.

Small Enterprise Research Team (SERTeam) (2003), *NatWest/SERTeam Quarterly Survey of Small Business in Britain*, Vol. 19, No. 4.

Smoreda, Z. and Thomas, F. (2001), 'Social Networks and Residential ICT Adoption and Use', Paper presented at the EURESCOM summit meeting, Heidelberg.

Sparrow, J. (2001), 'A Knowledge-Based View of Support for Small Business Management of E-Business Activities'. Paper presented at the 24th National Small Firms Policy and Research Conference, Leicester.

Venkatraman, N. (1994), 'IT Enabled Business Transformation: From Automation to Business Scope Redefinition', *Sloan Management Review*, Vol. 35, pp. 73-97.

Wilson, M. and Deans, K. (2000), *E-Business and SMEs in the Otago Region of New Zealand,* Southern Cross University, Otago.

WITSA, (2001), *International Survey of Electronic Commerce, 2000 Edition,* World Information Technology and Services Alliance.

Chapter 2

Social Influence and Diffusion of Innovations in Education

Carlo Tomasetto and Felice Carugati

Introduction

When a new idea, a new product or a new technology appears in our social system, each of us should carefully consider its merits and defects, and after a brief period decide to adopt those innovations that will bring us an advantage, and reject those that are useless or harmful. Nevertheless, it is clear that in daily life we usually behave quite differently.

First of all, we can almost never know exactly which innovations will actually turn out to be more useful than the technologies and behavioral patterns that we are used to: some of them could turn out to be more disadvantageous, after all. Moreover, even if the innovation's promoters have produced scientific data which could help to evaluate their proposals, not all of us are adequately qualified to evaluate such information (Lissoni, 2000).

What we can more realistically do is start to look around us, observing what happens to the first adopters in our circle of neighbours, friends, and work colleagues; it is likely that we will try to exchange information with them about the innovation, paying attention to their opinions and impressions. Our final decision will probably follow this intense work of constructing shared knowledge trough social interaction, rather than being based on pure logical rationality.

In this chapter we highlight some contact points between research on innovation diffusion and processes of social influence, and we propose that a theoretical model of influence can help to understand the impact of social interactions on innovative behaviors. Then we will report an empirical study carried out in Italian compulsory schools, in which we examined whether teachers, potential adopters of a new didactical tool, are affected by the interaction with a source promoting the innovation. More specifically, the status of the source could be equal (it was a group of teachers as well) or higher (i.e., a group of principals) than the status of the potential adopters. The social influence model predicts that under certain condition this status imbalance should produce a remarkable effect upon the adopters' response.

Social Interaction and Innovation Diffusion

Gabriel Tarde (1890), with his classical theory of imitation, asserted that the dialectics between the masses and the élites who lead them gives rise to societal changes. It is by the example and actions of the élites that the rest of the social community comes to adopt new behavioral models and ideas, which were previously unknown or opposed by the majority.

Later, Ryan and Gross's classical study (1943) on the diffusion of hybrid seeds in Iowa pointed out the importance of interaction and reciprocal influences between adopters. One of the key evidences of this research, which was the first to use the term 'diffusion', was that non-economic factors (such as relationships with neighbours) decisively influenced farmers' decisions to adopt new seeds. Through these exchanges of information farmers came to give meaning to the innovation, assessing the benefits and the convenience of adopting it for their own farms.

The intuition of Tarde, and above all that of Ryan and Gross, was more systematically developed by Everett Rogers in his well known 'Diffusion Theory of Innovation' (1962) (this theory is introduced by Gray in the first chapter of this book in relation to the influence of early adopters on entrepreneurial networks). Rogers defines the whole process of diffusion as 'a special type of communication in that the messages are concerned with new ideas' (Rogers, 2003, p. 5). Despite the importance accorded to them in Rogers' definition, issues concerning communication and reciprocal influences still remained in the background of innovation literature, until the last few years. Rogers himself, in the last edition of his book, has recently paid much more attention to the role of communication networks and their impact on the decisions of potential adopters.

Integrating experimentally based models of social influence into the framework of innovation diffusion studies might help an understanding of the ways in which communication processes actually shape innovative behaviors and attitudes. A promising example of such integration is recently provided by Kincaid (2004), who uses a model of *bounded normative influence* to explain an apparent paradox: the fact that a counter-normative and minority idea, which is by definition an innovation at the first stages of its diffusion, comes to be accepted by a gradually increasing number of people, until it eventually becomes the model of reference for the social system. Kincaid's hypothesis is that an innovation does not diffuse throughout an entire system, but in relatively isolated local sub-systems, composed of people who are in close contact with each other and hence are more susceptible to reciprocal influences. In these bounded sub-systems the innovators' voices are not as minority as they are in the rest of the system, and the likelihood of influencing new adopters is greater (Latané, 1981). In turn, each new adopter will come into contact with members of other surrounding sub-systems (families, neighbours, colleagues...) and, according to the same principle, will be able to exert his influence on these additional groups of individuals, in a widening circle of bounded influences.

Many contributions have also stressed the importance of local opinion leaders as promoters of innovation. Opinion leaders are individuals whose prestige is acknowledged within their community, and whose advices on various issues are particularly sought after by other members of the system. When few selected opinion leaders adopt the innovation, many other members of the system rapidly follow their example, due to simple modeling or because they have been persuaded by communication coming from these acknowledged authorities. In particular, opinion leaders attain an essential importance as sources of social influence when the innovation is perceived by potential adopters as risky, with uncertain outcomes, or difficult to manage (Dearing, 2004).

Literature claims for many criteria to define a member of a social system as an opinion leader: personality traits (for example, a generic tendency to seek out novelties), above-average socio-economic status, wide-ranging nets of interpersonal links with other members of the same group, with persons outside the reference group and also with change agents (Rogers, 2003). Thus characterized, opinion leaders are definitely not conceivable as peers to other members of their social systems (Dearing, 2004), just like Tarde's imagined élite innovators. A uni-directional conception of social influence emerges, in which privileged, high status members with elevated socio-cultural capital, exert their influence towards lay-members of the social system, depicted as simple targets of modeling or persuasion processes.

The models discussed so far seem to describe social influence as a normative influence ('I think or I do what the reference members of my group expect from me') and an informative influence ('I believe that what the reference members of my group say or do is right because I trust them') (Mucchi Faina, 1998). But are these the only possible form of social influence in the field of innovation?

Models of Social Influence

All models of social influence seek to explain how people acquire or change attitudes, knowledge and behaviors when interacting with other individuals and groups (Butera and Mugny, 2001). The above-mentioned attempts to articulate diffusion research with social influence follow the classical North American studies on influence which focus on the persuasive effectiveness of acknowledged authorities (Milgram, 1974), powerful sources (French and Raven, 1959), and majority groups (Asch, 1955; Cialdini and Goldstein, 2004; Deutsch and Gerard, 1955; Latané, 1981).

The European research partly took a different orientation. Up until the 1960s, Moscovici showed that even subjects lacking in psycho-social resources – low status groups and minorities, in particular – could influence other people's behavior (Moscovici, 1976). Moscovici's experiments demonstrated that sources equipped with power, authority and numerical support obtain support for their ideas, but this support is often superficial and purely formal; vice versa, ideas proposed by minority, and in general by non-dominant, groups though publicly rejected can give rise to deep and long-lasting changes in the targets' attitudes and behaviors. Later research showed that precisely these 'neglected' sources could encourage divergent thinking (Nemeth, 1986), creativity (Mucchi Faina, Maass and Volpato, 1991) and, in a word, innovation. Many studies on group performance have also shown that the latest joiners of an organization, often considered a priori as weak and conformist victims of the influence exerted by the older group members, are actually capable of introducing significant innovations in work methods (Choi and Levine, 2004; De Dreu and De Vries, 2001; De Dreu and West, 2001).

In an attempt to give a unitary explanation of the different possible processes of influence (minority or majority, public or private, superficial or deep, etc.), Pérez and Mugny (1993) elaborated a theoretical model that they called 'Conflict Elaboration Theory' (CET). The basic assumption of the CET states that influence result from the way in which a target elaborates the conflict between its position (opinion, belief or behavior), and the one held by the source. To simplify, two main ways of elaborating the conflict are possible: the first one is oriented to the comprehension of the content of the message (i.e., the ideas of the source), whereas the other one is centered upon the defense of the target positive self-image.

For example, if we have to solve a mathematical problem, or learn to use a new computer, we will probably try to find out what a mathematician or a computer expert would do in our place, because the authority of their status guarantees us more reliable information: thus, we should be positively influenced by his advice and keep it into a great account. And yet, our response could be different. For example, if we also consider ourselves sufficiently competent computer users, we could resist to the expert's opinion, and the more the expert insists on his suggestions, the more irritated we will become. This phenomenon of reactance is rather general (Brehm, 1966) and means that in many situations in which an individual feels his/her independence is at risk, s/he arrives at an irrational decision just so as not to conform to others' influence, and to restore a positive image of him/herself (Wicklund, 1997).

Sometimes, however, the expertise of the source is clearly superior to ours, or his hierarchical level in the organization to which we belong is such that it impedes our resistance to his influence. In this case we would have a situation of *informational constraint* (Quiamzade and Mugny, 2001), in which the source gets others to adhere to his proposals, but in a very superficial way, without any particular reflection on the part of the target of influence: we listen or imitate what the source says not because we are convinced, but because we have no choice, or because in that moment it is convenient for us, or otherwise – more simply – just because 'the expert said it' (Maggi, Butera and Falomir, 2001). Given the superficiality of the implied cognitive process, it is unlikely that we will spontaneously utilize knowledge thus acquired in other contexts or to resolve other problems (Butera, Mugny, Legrenzi and Pérez, 1996). If the comparison occurs in a markedly competitive context, a high status source can constitute such a threat as to induce us to refuse (or accept purely out of formal courtesy) the information that we gain from it: in the terms of Mugny and coll., these are influence exchanges in which the information content is not deeply elaborated, since all our attention is kept by the relational concern of defending our positive self-image.

Fortunately there are many other situations – which CET defines as 'informational dependence' – in which the goal is not to excel, but to cooperate with others to attain the best possible result. These are the cases in which relational concerns are not at stake, and our cognitive resources can be devoted to the elaboration of the information that we can gain from the source of influence. It could be the case of two scientists who decide to work together on the same research, providing each other with their respective competencies: in practice, they influence each other reciprocally, providing each other with knowledge that they did not have before, without calling into question their positive image as competent scientists (Mugny, Tafani, Butera and Pigière, 1998). If it is clear that the goal is not to defend our image, but to improve our knowledge or adopt more efficient behaviors, comparing ourselves with a high status source can provide us with valuable information that we can then elaborate and generalize to different situations (Quiamzade and Mugny, 2001).

Mugny *et al.* also insist on the fact that even low status sources, such as people with competencies equal to if not inferior to ours, can profoundly influence our behavior. It is true that even if these sources provide us with new information, or a different way of looking at things than we are used to, nothing guarantees us that this information is in itself correct; yet the great advantage is that these latter sources do not threaten our identity, especially when we also consider ourselves novices with regard to the problem we face. In this case a so-called *conflict of incompetencies* is established: these sources do not provide knowledge to imitate, but they show us that alternative points of view do exist. If we realize that a newcomer, or a not very brilliant person, proposes an unexpected viewpoint on a problem, we might think that it is worth the effort of searching for other possible solutions, thus gaining an unexpected stimulus to our creative potential (Nemeth, 1986; Butera, Mugny, Legrenzi and Pérez, 1996).

In effect, it seems that these 'neglected' sources have a significant indirect influence, since they are able to modify our knowledge and our behavior with regard to issues that are related but not identical to the object of interaction (Crano and Chen, 1998; Wood et al, 1994). Moreover, this effect seems to appear even if the target of the influence has explicitly rejected the proposals formulated by the source (Mugny, 1982). In terms of innovation diffusion, the role of minority or low status sources would not be that of encouraging the adoption of a pre-packaged, top-down innovation, since they do not have neither the power nor the prestige to attain this goal; rather, these sources could have the role of stimulating the innovative skills that all individuals, groups and organizations are able of expressing autonomously.

Implications for Educational Innovation

Keeping in mind the CET framework, let's return to the issue of innovation diffusion. What happens when an innovation is introduced in the school system? Modern school systems have passed through unceasing attempts to innovate their established routines. Generations of general school reforms, thousands of projects aimed at solving specific problems (e.g., inclusion of ethnic minorities or the struggle against dropping out), experimentations of new techniques or innovative learning tools (e.g., computers in the classrooms), are all examples of attempts at transforming the old 'school as it is' (boring, ineffective, out of time...) into a new 'school as it should be' (stimulating, effective, closer to the real world...) (Tyack and Cuban, 1995; Cuban, 2001). Despite the evidence that many of these school innovations are introduced in school systems through compulsive intervention, many studies point out that the introduction of any innovation in schools is mediated by interpersonal relationships between promoters and adopters (Hargreaves, Lieberman Fullan and Hopkins, 1998). In fact, these studies often describes individuals playing roles that are easily recognizable as the change agents or the opinion leaders described by diffusion theory.

Scholars' attention is often focused on the role of the principal, considered as the gate-keeper who can open or shut the doors of the school to any innovation attempt (Fullan, 2001). The principal is expected to support innovation, both on a material level of finding resources, as well as on a social level of leading the process of change. With a duty is to secure the conditions for supporting teachers in their paths of innovation, the principal has to be a professional and didactical point of reference to whom teachers can easily rely on.

Contrary to principals, teachers are rarely recognized as promoters of innovation, despite the fact that in any school can be easily found teachers who, formally or informally, function as reference leaders for their peers: they adopt or elaborate original ideas and they often try to involve their colleagues in the experimentation of the novelties. The case of learning technologies is somewhat exemplary: the diffusion of new technologies in schools has always coincided with the presence of impassioned teachers, who take it upon themselves to explain how things work to their less expert colleagues, as well as helping them with maintenance and technical management of the new tools (Cuban, 1986).

According to the CET, it can be reasonably conceived that the same innovation can be accepted more or less favorably by teachers, depending on the status of the source that introduces and promotes it in a given school. If it is the principal who promotes an innovation, influence is exercised by a source of status (and power) superior to potential adopters: information on the innovation could be trustworthy on the one hand, but on the other it could imply a potentially very strong identity threat due to the hierarchical imbalance between two partners (who is proposing the innovation and who is supposed to adopt it). The result could be a decisive rejection of the proposal (at that point the identity threat would be untenable), or a very superficial acceptance. On the other hand, when the information on the innovation is delivered by a colleague (source of equal status), no sort of identity threat due to asymmetrical social comparison would be activated. No longer worrying about their relationship of subordination to the source of influence, potential adopters could concentrate their attention on the content of the innovation, sharing the usefulness of changes in their way of teaching and, thus, turning out to be more open towards educational innovation in general.

To empirically test the hypotheses derived from CET, regarding the adoption of educational innovation by teachers, we conducted a quasi-experimental research involving 347 elementary school and middle school teachers in Italy (Tomasetto, 2003; Tomasetto and Carugati, 2003).

Social Influence and Teachers' Evaluation of a Computer-Based Learning Activity

The research was conducted in 2001–2002, after a four years period in which Italian schools had been involved in a project aiming at the diffusion new media in the classrooms. Considerable resources (about $ 600,000) were invested in computer equipment and in-service teachers training to make multimedia equipment an everyday teaching tool (Ministero dell'Istruzione, 2000). Our study involved 242 teachers working in elementary schools (69.7%), and 105 teachers working in junior high schools (30.7%). Males were 9.5% of the total; the average age of the participants was 43. We presented these teachers with a description of a teaching activity similar to those promoted at that time by the Ministry project, based on the use of text editing software by students; teachers were then asked to evaluate the didactic quality of the activity described (this was naturally a fictitious proposal, as it was explained to the participants in the de-briefing). In other words, we asked potential adopters to evaluate a learning innovation.

The description of the learning activity was identical for all participants, but in the different experimental conditions some crucial aspects of its presentation were manipulated. In fact, teachers were presented with a text in which a source of superior status (described as 'a group of principals'), or a source of equal status ('a group of teachers') supported the didactic effectiveness of the described activity. Furthermore, we also manipulated the risk of failure to implement the activity: in conditions of high risk, teachers were warned that if, in case they themselves had wanted to experiment with the activity in their classrooms, they would have had to work very hard to avoid the risk of not being able to carry it out. Vice versa, in conditions of low risk the warning emphasized that in similar experiences there had never been any recorded cases of the teachers failing. Finally we divided the participants into 'competent' vs. 'not very competent' in information technology, on the basis of their own self-evaluation of using text editing software, the Internet and e-mail. We thus implemented a 2 (source proposing the activity: superior vs. equal status) x 2 (risk of failure in the activity: high vs. low) x 2 (teacher's competence in information technology: high vs. low) experimental design.

After reading the description of the activity, the participants had to evaluate its didactic quality. We calculated an overall index of direct influence by summing up three items (the proposal is 'interesting', 'effective for teaching', 'worth implementing in class').

We also asked teachers to express their general attitudes towards computers and new media by means of a special index composed of 6 items. This second measurement was meant to examine whether the context of social influence (that is, comparison with the source proposing an innovation) could have an impact not only on how the proposed learning activity was evaluated, but also on teachers' attitudes towards more general aspects of technological innovation. This second index measured the generalization of influence.

We carried out two separate analyses of variance (ANOVA) with post-hoc single planned contrasts. The results show that the conditions of social influence do affect the responses of potential adopters to an innovation. Figure 1 illustrates the didactic evaluation of the learning activity provided by the teachers in different experimental conditions.

A main effect of the teachers' information technology competence was observed: those who consider themselves more competent in using the computer feel that the activity would be more effective for learning ($F_{(1,326)} = 8.790$; $p < .01$). More interestingly for us, the three-way interaction (Computer competence x Risk of failure x Source of influence) is also significant ($F_{(1,326)} = 5.543$; $p < .02$).

In detail, planned contrasts show that the teachers' evaluations change depending on the source of the innovation, in particular when a high risk of failure is evoked. When a high risk of failure is anticipated, expert teachers evaluate the activity very positively if this is proposed by a high status source. Nevertheless, the expert teachers evaluate the activity as marginally less effective when the claim for innovation comes from the same high status source, but the risk of failure is erased, ($p<.06$). On the other hand, when teachers consider themselves as low competent computer users, the effect of social influence appears to be significant only when the risk of failure is high. In this case, the same activity is considered

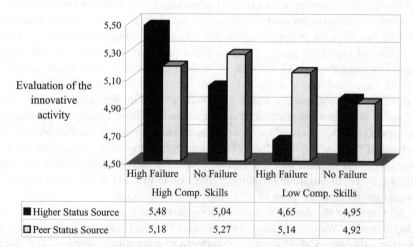

	High Comp. Skills		Low Comp. Skills	
Evaluation of the innovative activity	High Failure	No Failure	High Failure	No Failure
■ Higher Status Source	5,48	5,04	4,65	4,95
☐ Peer Status Source	5,18	5,27	5,14	4,92

Figure 2.1   Evaluations of the innovative activity in the four experimental conditions, Direct influence (1 = very negative; 7 = very positive)

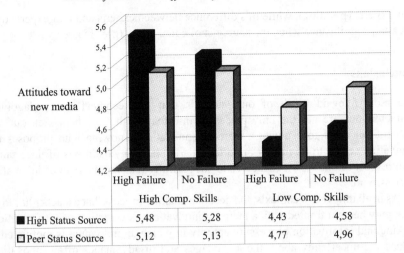

	High Failure	No Failure	High Failure	No Failure
	High Comp. Skills		Low Comp. Skills	
■ High Status Source	5,48	5,28	4,43	4,58
▢ Peer Status Source	5,12	5,13	4,77	4,96

Figure 2.2   Attitudes toward new media in the four experimental conditions, Generalization of influence (1 = very negative; 7 = very positive

more effective when it is supported by a source of equal status, rather than a source of superior status (p<.001).

It is important to note that when the risk of failure is made to rise, the high status source induces the overall most positive evaluation of the activity (by expert teachers), just as it induces the overall most negative evaluation (by teachers who are less expert; p < .05). On the contrary, when the innovation entails a low risk of failure, the source of influence loses importance, and there is no significant difference in teachers' answers.

The dynamics of influence also effect teachers' general attitudes towards new technology (generalization of influence, see Figure 2.2); the univariate ANOVA shows a significant effect of the interaction between status of the source of influence and teachers' competence in information technology ($F_{(1,328)}$ = 6.2; p < .02), in addition to the simple effect of the latter ($F_{(1,328)}$ = 20.7; p < .001).

In detail we can observe that the teachers who judge themselves as less competent in information technology prefer to obtain information about innovation from their colleagues. In fact, their attitudes are significantly more favorable to technological innovation when the influence source has equal (m = 4.86) rather than superior status (m = 4.50; p < .05). On the contrary, when teachers consider themselves as competent in computer skills, the effect of the high status source (m = 5.37) is not significantly different from the equal status source (m = 5.12; p = .138). In any case, these expert teachers seem not to be afraid of an identity comparison with the high status source, as we might have expected from the CET. Rather, they seem to consider the principals' opinions particularly credible and trustworthy. In fact, when it is the principals who exert influence, the attitudes of the expert teachers are much more favorable towards innovation than those of the non-experts (p < .001), while this difference between experts and non-experts does not attain significance when the source is of equal status (p = .15).

Conclusions

The most relevant result of our study is that the technical and pedagogical characteristics are not the only pieces of information that teachers seek out and elaborate in order to evaluate a learning innovation: knowing who proposes the innovation seems to be just as important, particularly in conditions of uncertainty with respect to one's own capacities to successfully manage the path of innovation in classroom.

As in all innovative contexts, the decision-making process that a teacher has to go through when confronted with a learning innovation 'is essentially an information-seeking and information-processing activity in which an individual is motivated to reduce the uncertainty about the advantages and disadvantages of an innovation' (Rogers, 2003, p. 14). In fact, whatever teachers can find out by observing, listening and questioning colleagues and/or principals turns out to be essential. It is not surprising that innovators invest a substantial portion of their resources in searching for the best persuasion strategies towards potential adopters, confiding from time to time in the hierarchical authority or informal construction of shared learning about innovation (ibid.).

The results of our study show that, with imaginable disappointment for innovation promoters, there is no one source more capable than others of influencing adopters' opinions. Indeed, there is a source of influence that is normally very highly valued in innovation processes (i.e. that of superior hierarchies of potential adopters) which induces both the most favorable attitudes towards innovation (in adopters who consider themselves very competent), as well as the most negative ones (in adopters who consider themselves less competent). How should this difference be interpreted? Based on the CET we should have expected the opposite effect, because those who consider themselves competent on a topic normally attribute more value to their own decision-making autonomy, and, if possible, they avoid conforming to pressures from higher status sources (Falomir et al., 2002). It is probably necessary to refer to the specific culture of the school system, in which teachers still claim their own didactic autonomy (Leiter, 1996), and there is no hierarchical authority with real coercive power over their way of teaching. Perhaps teachers who consider themselves as competent in the subject matter (using computer equipment) can easily manage the asymmetrical relationship with the source of superior status, because they know that useful information can come from it, but not such pressures as to infringe upon their decision-making autonomy. Vice versa, teachers who already perceive their lack of computer competence as a threat, perhaps because they feel they do not have complete control over a new learning tool, can not add a relational type threat to this as well; for this reason it could be easier for them to accept proposals for change coming from a source of equal status. All this confirms the need, already pointed out by others (Filkestein and Personnaz, 2002), not to overlook the cultural and relational specificities of single organizations in which social influences processes take place.

Our results refer to a process of technological-pedagogical innovation in the educational field, and we hope that efforts to integrate multiple theoretical frames in the study of innovation will be extended to other social and organizational contexts. The issues of consumers and companies facing the risks and the open prospects of the computerization of commercial trade, widely discussed in other chapters of this book, seem to be suitable for a similar attempt. In fact, people who come in contact with e-commerce have to face up to an innovation in a situation of uncertainty with regard to its implications, and interaction with other people (e.g., experts, other consumers, and so on) could provide them information that can reduce uncertainty. We therefore believe that the systematic use of experimentally-based models of influence, albeit complex, can contribute advancing the comprehension of a wide range of innovation diffusion processes, both from the theoretical and the applied standpoint.

References

Asch, S.E. (1955), 'Opinions and Social Pressure', *Scientific American*, Vol.193, pp. 31–35.

Brehm, J.W. (1966), *A Theory of Psychological Reactance*, Academic Press, New York.

Butera, F. and Mugny, G. (2001), *Social Influence in Social Reality*, Hogrefe & Huber Publishers, Ashland, Ohio.

Butera, F., Mugny, G., Legrenzi, P. and Pérez, J.A., (1996), 'Majority and Minority Influence, Task Representation, and Inductive Reasoning', *British Journal of Social Psychology*, Vol. 35, pp. 123–136.

Choi, H.S. and Levine, J.M. (2004), 'Minority Influence in Work Teams: The Impact of Newcomers', *Journal of Experimental Social Psychology*, Vol. 40, pp. 273 –280.

Cialdini, R.B. and Goldstein, N.J. (2004), 'Social Influence: Compliance and Conformity', *Annual Review of Psychology*, Vol. 55, pp. 591–621.

Crano, W.D. and Chen, X. (1998), 'The Leniency Contract and Persistence of Majority and Minority Influence', *Journal of Personality and Social Psychology*, Vol. 74, No. 6, pp. 1437–1450.

Cuban, L. (1986), *Teachers and Machines*, Teachers College Press, New York.

Cuban, L. (2001), *Oversold and Underused: Computers in the Classroom*, Harvard University Press, Cambridge, London.

De Dreu, C.K.W. and De Vries, N.K. (2001), *Group Consensus and Minority Influence*, Blackwell, Oxford.

De Dreu, C.K.W. and West, M.A . (2001), 'Minority Dissent and Team Innovation: The Importance of Participation in Decision Making', *Journal of Applied Psychology*, Vol. 86, pp. 1191 –1201.

Dearing, J.W. (2004), 'Improving The State of Health Programming by Using Diffusion Theory', *Journal of Health Communication*, Vol. 9, pp. 21–36.

Deutsch, M. and Gerard, H.B. (1955), 'A Study of Normative and Informational Influence upon Individual Judgement', *Journal of Abnormal and Social Psychology*, Vol. 51, pp. 629–636.

Falomir, J.M., Invernizzi, F., Mugny, G., Muñoz-Rojas, D. and Quiamzade, A. (2002), 'Social Influence on Intention to Quit Smoking: The Effect of the Rhetoric of an Identity Relevant Message', *Revue Internationale de Psychologie Sociale*, Vol. 15, No. 1, pp. 81–96.

Filkestein, R. and Personnaz, B. (2002), 'Influence Sociale entre Groupes de Statut Asymetrique: Une Approche Expérimentale dans une Contexte Judiciaire', *Revue Internationale de Psychologie Sociale*, Vol. 15, No. 1, pp. 5–29.

French, J.R.P. and Raven, B.H. (1959), 'The Bases of Social Power', in Cartwright, D. (Ed.), *Studies in Social Power*, Institute for Social Research, Ann Arbor, pp. 150–167.

Fullan, M. (2001), *The New Meaning of Educational Change (3rd Ed.)*, Teachers College press, New York.

Hargreaves, A., Lieberman, A., Fullan, M. and Hopkins, D. (Eds.) (1988), *International Handbook of Educational Change*, Vol. 2, Kluever Academic Publishers, Dordrecht.

Kincaid, D.L. (2004), 'From Innovation to Social Norm: Bounded Normative Influence', *Journal of Health Communication*, Vol. 9, pp. 37–57.

Latane, B. (1981), 'The Psychology of Social Impact', *American Psychology*, Vol. 36, pp. 343–365.

Leiter, J. (1986), 'The Organizational Context of Teachers' perceived control over decision making', *Sociological Focus*, Vol. 19, No. 3, pp. 263–288.

Lissoni, F. (2000), 'La Diffusione delle Innovazioni', in Malerba, F. (a cura di), *Economia dell'Innovazione*, Carocci, Roma, pp. 283–314.

Milgram, S. (1974), *Obedience to Authority*, Harper & Row, New York.

Moscovici, S. (1976), *Social Influence and Social Change*, Academic Press, London.

Ministero dell'Istruzione (2000), *Programma Sviluppo Tecnologie Didattiche. Rapporto di monitoraggio 2000*, www.istruzione.it/innovazione_scuola (02/2005).

Mucchi Faina, A. (1998), *L'Influenza Sociale*, Il Mulino, Bologna.

Mucchi Faina, A., Maass, C. and Volpato, C. (1991), 'Social Influence: the Role of Originality', *European Journal of Social Psychology*, Vol. 21, pp. 183–198.

Mugny, G. (1982), *The Power of Minorities*, Academic Press, London.

Mugny, G., Butera, F. and Falomir, J.M. (2001), 'Social Influence and Threat in Social Comparison Between Self and Source's Competence: Relational Factors Affecting the Transmission of Knowledge', in Butera, F. and Mugny, G. (Eds.), *Social influence in social reality*, Hogrefe & Huber Publishers, Ashland, Ohio, pp. 225–245.

Mugny, G., Tafani, E., Butera, F. and Pigière, D. (1998), 'Contrainte et Dépendance Informationnelles: Influence Sociale sur la Représentation d'un Groupe d'Amis Idéal', *Connexions*, Vol. 75, pp. 55–72.

Nemeth, C.J. (1986), 'Differential Contributions of Majority and Minority Influence', *Psychological Review*, Vol. 93, pp. 23–32.

Pérez, J.A. and Mugny, G. (1993), *Influences Sociales. La Théorie de l'Elaboration du Conflit*, Delachaux et Niestlé, Neuchâtel.

Quiamzade, A. and Mugny, G. (2001), 'Social Influence Dynamics in Aptitude Tasks', *Social Psychology of Education*, Vol. 4, pp. 311–334.

Rogers, E.M. (1962), *Diffusion of Innovations*, Free Press, New York.

Rogers, E.M. (2003), *Diffusion of Innovations* (5th Ed.), Free Press, New York.

Ryan, B. and Gross, N. (1943), 'The Diffusion of Hybrid Sees Corn in Two Iowa Communities', *Rural Sociology*, Vol. 8, pp. 15–24.

Tarde, G. (1890), *Les Lois de l'Imitation*. Etude Sociologique, Alcan, Paris.

Tomasetto, C. (2003), 'Dealing with Educational Innovation: Adoption and Resistance to School Change in a Psycho-Social Perspective', *Studies in Communication Sciences – Special Issue: New Media in Education*, Vol. 3, pp. 271–275.

Tomasetto, C. and Carugati, F. (2003), *Innovare i Contesti dell'Apprendimento: Influenza Sociale e Costruzione delle Innovazioni nella Scuola*, XVII Convegno Nazionale A.I.P – Sezione di Psicologia dello Sviluppo, 22–25 settembre 2003, Bari.

Tyack, D. and Cuban, L. (1995), *Tinkering Toward Utopia*, Harvard University Press, Cambridge, MA, London.

Wicklund, R.A. (1997), 'The Theory of Psychological Reactance: A Reliably Revolutionary Perspective', *Contemporary Psychology*, Vol. 42, No. 8, pp. 679–681.

Wood, W., Lundgren, S., Ouellette, J.A., Busceme, S. and Blackstone, T. (1994), 'Minority Influence: A Meta-Analytic Review of Social Influence Processes', *Psychological Bulletin*, Vol. 115, pp. 323–345.

Chapter 3

Climate for Innovation, Attitudes to Internet and ICT Adoption in Small Firms

Salvatore Zappalà and Guido Sarchielli

Internet and e-Commerce Diffusion in Italy

The adoption of information and communications technology (ICT) among small firms in Italy, including broadband access and Internet connectivity, is increasing; also online purchasing is growing and playing a significant role in companies, but online selling is stagnating (Anee, 2003; Mate, 2001, 2003). Surveys monitoring the adoption, development and impact of e-business in the European economy (European Commission, 2004) and within single European countries (see chapters 1 and 5 in this book, respectively by Gray and Tebbutt) show the same trend. The e-Business Watch (2004) reports that the percentage of companies allowing customers to order and pay online is, in 2003, similar to those of previous years, and in the five more monitored European countries (France, Germany, Spain, United Kingdom and Italy), amounts on average about 9 per cent. In Italy, Mate (2003) reported a percentage of 5.5 of small firms selling online.

Thus, even though the use of Internet spreads among companies, a more developed, technical, use of the net is still lacking. Nearly two-thirds (63 per cent) of Italian small firms interviewed by Mate (2001) had a website, which was used by most of them (80 per cent) to present products and services. For these earlier adopters, most of these activities had a low degree of risk because the financial investment in the website was often low (Loparco, 2000). Over time, however, support from local and national institutions, which are encouraging the adoption of ICT infrastructure among small firms, has led to an increase in financial investment (Campodall'orto, 2003). Even so, some small firms sometimes buy information systems that underutilize, while some others do not invest in any information systems at all.

Considering this and the widespread diffusion of information systems supporting the use of word editors, spreadsheets, databases and browsers to surf the net, one may wonder why the adoption of sophisticated systems is still limited. Which psychological and social variables facilitate or slow down the adoption of ICT and, particularly, e-commerce within small firms? What do entrepreneurs think about the internet? Does employees' collective acceptance support or discourage the use of a new technology?

Research has examined psychological and social factors predicting the adoption of ICT in the workplace, especially among large companies. Unlike large firms, however, small firms cannot rely on specialized technical staff or a data management department. A better understanding of the determinants of ICT adoption within small firms would help to support entrepreneurs to develop more realistic aims and avoid risk that can arise when adopting ICT.

This chapter reviews research on two psycho-social variables, attitudes towards ICT and organizational climate towards innovation. Their influence on ICT adoption, and more generally on organizational behavior and decision making, has been largely observed in many studies. These two variables were measured in a survey investigating organizational and psycho-social determinants of web site and e-commerce adoption in a sample of small firm entrepreneurs. Method and main findings of this survey are reported in the later sections of the chapter.

Individual Adoption of New Technology

In recent years, many local and government institutions have financially supported small firms to buy information technologies to improve their competitiveness and productivity. Unfortunately, acquiring appropriate ICT is a necessary but not a sufficient condition for using them effectively. Employees are in fact the final user of ICT and they may show different behaviors. They may resist and avoid the use of such technology. They may use only the simpler and most basic procedures of the technology; or they may explore and discover advanced procedures to best exploit the possibilities offered by such technology. The actual use of ICT by organizational members is thus crucial both for those responsible for implementing the technology and for those that have to demonstrate the financial and business advantages that ICT (should) allow to reach.

Individual acceptance of ICT has been investigated by different theoretical perspectives. Technology Acceptance Model (Davis, 1989; Davis, Bagozzi, Warshaw, 1989) and Diffusion of Innovation (DOI) theory (Rogers, 1995), have been widely used and received consistent empirical support. Other important theoretical contributions about the intention to adopt ICT are Task Technology Fit (TTF) theory (Goodhue and Thompson, 1995) and Socio-Cognitive Theory (Bandura, 1997).

Technology Acceptance Model (TAM) is based on the theory of reasoned action developed by Fishbein and Ajzen (1975). This theory posits that intentions to perform a behavior are a function of two basic determinants, a psychological one (attitude towards the behavior) and the other reflecting social influence (subjective norms). Attitude refers to a general affective response towards the behavior, and is influenced by beliefs about the consequences of performing the behavior. Subjective norms are defined as the person's beliefs that specific individuals or groups approve or disapprove the behavior. The actions with respect to an object (the behavior) follow directly from behavioral intentions towards that object.

In TAM, as in the theory of reasoned action, attitudes predict intention, and intention predicts behavior. Unlike theory of reasoned action, at least in its initial formulation, TAM does not include subjective norms, and posits that only two beliefs, perceived usefulness and perceived ease of use, influence an individual's attitude toward using an ICT. Perceived usefulness is defined by Davis as 'the degree to which a person believes that using a particular system would enhance his or her job performance', while perceived ease of use is defined as 'the degree to which a person believes that using a particular system would be free of effort' (Davis, 1989, p. 320).

Research has demonstrated the validity of TAM in predicting intention and actual usage, in work and non-work settings and across varieties of software applications as text editors and spreadsheets, but also electronic mail, the internet or a specific web site (Adams, Nelson and Todd, 1992; Chuan-Chuan Lin and Lu, 2000; Lederer, Maupin, Sena and Zhuang, 2000; Moon & Kim, 2001; Straub, Keil and Brenner, 1997).

Rogers' theory, proposed for the first time in 1983, suggests that innovations are adopted through a process of uncertainty reduction (Rogers, 1995). Individuals collect and synthesize relevant information on an innovation, such as a new ICT application, from the social system to which they belong, thus developing specific beliefs about potential advantages and disadvantages of that innovation. Beliefs causing individuals to accept or reject the innovation are related to five attributes of it: relative advantage, complexity, compatibility, trialability and observability. Moore and Benbasat (1991) expanded this set and developed an instrument to measure the perceived characteristics of an innovation.

TAM and Rogers' theory share, as a common theme, the relevance given to beliefs and attitudes, which are considered as crucial antecedents of the adoption of an innovation (Agarwal, 2000). In her review, Agarwal (2000) summarizes research on other relevant antecedents of innovation. These include the social influence exerted by the acceptance (or rejection) of the technology from co-workers, supervisors or friends; individual differences among employees, such as gender, age, cognitive style or personality; and managerial interventions supporting employees' motivation to engage in use behaviors.

More recent theoretical and empirical research is extending the concept of acceptance. Cooper and Zmud (1990) proposed a six stage model of ICT implementation, suggesting that if technology is to provide its advantages, the adoption has to be followed by a routine and more advanced stage of usage. The actual usage of an innovation, and not only the intention to use, is increasingly used as a dependent variable (e.g., Culpan, 1995; Davis, 1993; Moon and Kim, 2001), while longitudinal field studies have shown that cognitive and social determinants of acceptance have different patterns of influence before and after the implementation of a new system. For instance, Karahanna, Straub and Chervany (1999) examined, in a large financial institution, the actual use of new software in half of the employees that were already using the system, and the intention to use the same software in the other half that had not yet started to use it. The findings suggested that whereas social pressures from organizational environments (especially top management and one's supervisor) were most effective in overcoming the initial inertia of new adopters, attitudes and usefulness beliefs were most effective in predicting the intention to continue to use the new software. Another important finding of this research is that new potential adopters had a richer set of beliefs than individuals already using the system. The authors argued that to cope with the uncertainty surrounding the adoption decision, individuals try to grasp a wider set of characteristics of the technology, as trialability, usefulness or visibility, compared to experienced users who focus on fewer and more task centered attributes. Similar findings were obtained by Venkatesh and Davis (2000) that testing an extended version of TAM, observed that social norms influenced the intention to use a new system in mandatory, but not voluntary, usage contexts.

In summary, despite the impressive increase in hardware and software systems in workplaces, so that in many cases their use is no more 'mandatory' but just 'ordinarily expected', the issue of acceptance of information technology and its appropriate and effective use is well alive. Additionally, information systems are updated or change so quickly that even experienced users are frequently faced with the choice of adopting a new release (or a new software) or to continue using the old one. Significant progress has been made in explaining user acceptance of information technology at work, and a couple of beliefs, perceived usefulness and perceived ease of use, have received consistent and systematic empirical support. Other cognitive beliefs, especially related to the characteristics of the innovation, have been shown to predict the intention to use a new system. Some social factors, such as expectancies held by co-workers and supervisors, are especially important in the initial stages, when technology is mandated.

Organizational Climate

Organizational climate is a widely used concept related to individual and collective organizational behaviors. Schneider (1990) defined organizational climate as 'employees' perceptions of the events, practices, and procedures and the kinds of behaviors that are rewarded, supported, and expected in a setting' (p. 384). The distinctive features of Schneider's definition are that climate concerns 'perceptions', which are 'shared' among individuals and that are based on work unit practices, procedures and rewards promoting behaviors consistent with a specific outcome of interest (Klein and Sorra, 1996). Moreover, climate is portrayed as an intervening variable resulting from differences in human resource management or organizational design, that has a mediating effect on output measures such as performance, productivity and satisfaction (Sparrow and Gaston, 1996).

By briefly reviewing the history of climate research, Schneider, Bowen, Ehrhart and Holcombe (2000) refer the first conceptualization of the social climate concept to Kurt Lewin, who used this concept to describe psychological conditions created by leaders of boys' groups. In a famous study, Lewin trained different leaders to behave in a democratic, authoritarian or laissez-faire leadership style, and then observed boys' and groups' reactions. The groups in the democratic condition were, for instance, more cooperative and participative during class work; members of these groups liked being part of the group and showed less dominating behaviors compared to boys in the authoritarian condition. Lewin concluded that the different 'atmospheres' that emerged in the groups were strongly influenced by leaders' different behaviors, and that climate was an abstraction resulting from behaviors and attitudes held in a specific setting. Later Rensis Likert focused on how to measure organizational climate in order to modify it or make it more suitable to organizational development. Measurement techniques developed by Likert came to represent climate as the aggregation of individual data from attitude scales. Thus, behaviors and social processes went slowly on the background, and organizational climate took on a more cognitive perspective, focusing on sense-making processes. Such processes describe how managers or employees perceive and develop a representation of what is going on around them, within the organization, and then react to their own representation (Weick, 1995).

Two important theoretical and methodological questions concerning climate refer to the unit, or level, of analysis to measure 'organizational' climate and the minimum sufficient level to say that perceptions are 'shared'. Research has consistently used two units of analysis, the organizational and the team level. Sparrow and Gaston (1996), for instance, measured organizational climate in 93 organizations issuing about 50 questionnaires in each company. Questionnaires, measuring 17 climate dimensions, were submitted across three broad managerial levels (managerial, supervisory, manual/clerical) and data were aggregated at the organizational level. Different combinations of the 17 climate dimensions were represented in eight clusters, or climate maps, ranging from negative to positive climates. It was observed that most organizations of the same industry were members of only two or three of the eight clusters. This seems to suggest that organizational climate varies more across industries than within industries, probably linked to specific dimensions of technology and growth, but also suggests that narrow variations of the climate may exist within the same industry.

Measuring climate at the team level was instead proposed by Anderson and West (1998). They argue that the appropriate level of analysis at which to examine shared perception of climate is the proximal work group, defined as the 'permanent or semi-permanent team to which individuals are assigned, whom they identify with, and whom they interact with regularly in order to perform work-related tasks' (p. 236). Within the group it is more likely that individuals have the opportunity to interact and to co-construct perceptions. The two authors observed that group processes, facilitating the expression of creativity, influenced the number and quality of innovations introduced in 27 British hospitals by their respective management teams; hospital size and availability of financial resources had no influence on group and hospital innovation (West and Anderson, 1996). In another study, conducted in a large European bank, headquartered in Belgium, De Jong et al. (2003) observed that participation in an interteam network had a positive impact on team members' adoption of standard and customized ICT. The authors argue that consensus among teams on how to solve problems and how to work together within the network promotes a mutual involvement with regard to ICT adoption.

In these studies organizational climate was measured by collecting data at an individual level and then averaging and aggregating the data at a group or organizational level.

During the 1980s, an alternative concept, organizational culture, emerged and has taken an increasing important role in explaining adaptation, change and competitive success in organizations. This concept derives from cultural anthropology; thus organizational culture research, as the anthropological one, is mainly conducted by using qualitative research methods, such as interviews, case studies and observations (Ashkanasy, Wilderom and Peterson, 2000). Organizational culture is viewed as a layered phenomenon and, following Schein (1985), composed of three levels ranging from the relatively observable to the mostly invisible: 1) surface signals, such as language, symbols or myths, relatively easy to observe; 2) underpinning patterns of behavior, such as titles, rituals, norms or values; 3) deeper core values and assumptions, difficult to observe but relevant as they are felt as the more stable and causative elements of culture.

The complex relationships between the organizational climate and culture has been recently extensively discussed (Ashnasy Wilderom and Peterson, 2000) and accepted conclusions are that climate taps into a conscious subset of individual responses, quantitatively representing explicit and self-reported facets of culture (Sparrow and Gaston, 1996), and that climate describes people's everyday experiences of the ways they are managed and their relations with each other (Michela and Burke, 2000).

Schneider et al. (2000) have also suggested that the concept of organizational climate is generic and all inclusive, and that climate has to have a focus, a target. In other words, climate has to be investigated as a climate *for* something. This would also increase the relationship between climate measures and the available criteria of interest. The *something* of interest has concerned, for instance, climate for safety (Zohar, 1980, 2000), climate for service (Schneider, Bowen, Ehrhart, Holcombe, 2000), climate for innovation (West and Anderson, 1996) or climate for implementation (Klein and Sorra, 1996; Klein, Conn and Sorra, 2001). Interest for facet aspects of climate has stimulated the analysis of how a particular type of climate (e.g. safety or innovation) leads to particular work outcomes (accident avoidance or innovativeness). For instance, Klein and Sorra (1996) suggest that a strong implementation climate fosters innovation use by:

a. ensuring employees skills in innovation use,
b. providing incentives for innovation use and disincentives for innovation avoidance;
c. removing obstacles to innovation use.

Similarly, innovativeness was measured as administrative and technical innovations introduced in 27 British hospitals and was expected to be influenced by team processes facilitating a shared climate for innovation. These team processes were operationalized as (West and Anderson, 1996):

1. team objectives: the appreciation and pursuing among team members of goals and outcomes;
2. participation: the active involvement in decision making as occurring in an interpersonally non-threatening environment;
3. task orientation: the shared concern among team members with excellence of performance;
4. support for innovation: the expectation, approval and support of attempts to introduce new and improved ways of doing things at work.

In 1998 Anderson and West presented a psychometric validation of the Team Climate Inventory (TCI), a questionnaire measuring four factors of team climate for innovation: vision (defined as team objectives), participative safety, task orientation and support for innovation. We used TCI to test, in the study we are going to present, relations between climate for innovation and ICT adoption in small firms.

In summary, organizational climate is a psychological and social variable as it is both in organizational members' minds and an attribute of the setting (Schneider et al., 2000). Climate is a picture of a work setting, developed by individuals working in it, and based on leaders' behaviors and organizational rules, procedures and expectations of that setting. The study of climate has evolved from a more general perspective to a more focused one linking climate perceptions to a specific aspect of the work environment, such as safety, innovation or implementation.

ICT Adoption within Small Firms: Empirical Research

During 2002 a cross national study on the diffusion and adoption of ICT in small firms (E-CoSME – e-Commerce in the small and medium enterprises) was conducted in six European regions: Brittany (France), Devon, Cornwall and south Wales (U.K.), Galicia (Spain) and Emilia Romagna (Italy). Questionnaires were used to examine organizational determinants of e-commerce and included questions on firm's size, turnover, full time employees, as well as on computers availability, internet connectivity, web-site and e-commerce adoption. In Emilia Romagna (Italy) besides the organizational determinants, the survey included measures on the psychosocial constructs presented in the introduction. In particular, we used ten items proposed by Moon & Kim (2001) to measure perceived ease of use and perceived usefulness of the internet, and a short version of the Team Climate Inventory. Here we report findings of the survey conducted in Emilia Romagna.

The aims of the survey were: 1) to describe the organizational aspects of small firms adopting vs. non adopting e-commerce, 2) to test whether attitudes towards the internet and climate for innovation have different means in adopting vs. not adopting small firms.

Table 3.1   Type of business

	Frequency	Percent
Manufacture – finished goods	23	28
Manufacture – semi-finished goods	18	22
Business service	22	27
Personal service	5	6
Building, construction	2	2
Distribution (retail, warehouse, transport, ...)	10	12
Hotel, accomodation, catering, ...	4	5
Others	13	15

Table 3.2   Number of full time employees and sales turnover (raw data)

	Full Time Employees						
	1	2–4	5–9	10–15	16–25	> 25	Row Tot.
Less than 80.000 euro	1	0	0	0	0	0	1
80 – 160.000 euro	0	2	1	2	1	0	7
160 – 770.000 euro	0	6	4	3	2	0	15
770 – 1.500.000 euro	0	0	6	7	8	0	21
1.500 – 7.500.000 euros	0	0	2	3	9	12	26
More than 7.500.000 euro		1	1	0	1	6	9
Column Totals	2	9	14	15	21	18	79

Answered to the questionnaire 82 owners, or a close collaborator, of small firms. To maintain uniformity in the E-CoSME research design, a single respondent per firm was used. Firms were randomly selected from two small firms' associations lists, and we managed to include firms of different sectors. About 70 per cent of the contacted owners agreed to answer the questionnaire.

The industry distribution of the sample is reported in Table 3.1. Manufacturing firms, including those producing semi-finished and finished goods, are 50 per cent of the sample, followed by business services (27 per cent) and distribution (12 per cent). The total is greater than 82 because some firms rated their own businesses in more than one category. Firm size was measured by number of full time employees and sales turnover; the two variables are strongly correlated (R Spearman = .70, p<.001), and their distribution is reported in Table 3.2.

Results

Internet and e-commerce adoption

Confirming results of previous Italian research, 80 small firms (almost 98 per cent of the sample) report to have computers connected to the net; one firm reports a stand-alone computer, and the last one declares no computer at all. The most frequent connection is through ISDN (50 per cent), followed by ADSL (23 per cent) and fixed line (23 per cent).

The situation is still positive when considering firm's web site: 71 per cent of the interviewed small firms has its own web site, 10 per cent has the intention to start one in one year and the remaining 19 per cent does not have a web site. But only 12 per cent of firms that have a web site (thus, the 8 per cent of all small firms participating at the survey) has the possibility to order and to pay online; 14 per cent is planning to have such possibility in one year, and 74 per cent of small firms with a web site do not have any e-commerce activity.

Answers about business plans reveal a low level of planning activities. Only 12 per cent of small firms had a written business plan, while 29 per cent had an unwritten plan (in other words, the plan is 'in the mind' of the owner/s). However, findings reported below suggest that there is no difference between firms with 'unwritten' and firms with 'written' business plans. Almost 75 per cent of these written and unwritten business plan included ICT.

Finally, 15 per cent of firms rated e-commerce as very important for their own business, 32 per cent as important in the future and 35 per cent as not important at all. The most common solution for improving ICT skills is to have the staff learn on the job as it goes along (54 per cent), followed by formal training for the staff (41 per cent).

Organizational influences on ICT and e-commerce adoption

Previous research has shown that size (conceptualized as sales turnover or as number of full time employees) is an important determinant of internet and e-commerce adoption. In this survey only the number of full time employees is related to web site adoption (Chi square = 20.4, df = 10, p<.05; see Table 3.3).

More significantly, firms with planned growth targets tend to have their own web site (Chi square= 16.7, df = 6, p <.05; see Table 3.4) as well as a business plan

Table 3.3   Adoption of website and number of full time employees (column percentage)

	No website	Website in one year	Have website
Sole-trader	13	0	0
2–4	19	25	7
5–9	13	25	18
10–15	31	0	18
16–25	25	13	28
More than 25	0	38	30
Total	16	8	57

Table 3.4   Adoption of website and firms' growth targets
            (column percentage)

	No website	Website in one year	Have website
No specific target	19	38	5
Sell/merge	6	0	2
Grow indefinitely	44	0	22
Grow to a planned size	31	63	71
Total	16	8	58

(Chi square = 21,6; df = 6; p <.01), but having a business plan does not mean either having one's own web site or an e-commerce activity.

Finally, confirming the theory of reasoned action, and also common sense, firms with a positive attitude to e-commerce are more probable to make e-commerce compared to those with a negative attitude (Chi square = 16.9; df = 8; p<.05).

Psychological influences on ICT and e-commerce adoption

The Team climate inventory and Attitudes to internet scales, respectively measured on a 5 and a 7 point Likert scale (where 1 = strongly disagree, and 5 or 7 = strongly agree), were submitted to exploratory factor analysis and new scores were computed by summing up items with loadings higher than .40. Eigenvalue greater than 1 was used as criterion in choosing the number of underlying dimensions.

For the Firm Climate Inventory, the following three factors were observed: Support for innovation, Task orientation and Vision (64 per cent of explained variance; Cronbach's alpha respectively .70, .84, .85) (the fourth factor of the original version, Participative safety, was dropped as unsatisfactorily loaded).

Three factors were also found in the Attitudes to internet scale: 1) perceived ease of using internet (e.g. 'It is easy to remember how to use Internet'); the factor 'perceived usefulness of internet' resulted in two different factors: 2) usefulness of internet to improve quality of work (e.g. 'Using internet improves task quality') and 3) usefulness of internet to obtain information in a short time (e.g. 'Using internet enables one to access a lot of information') (78 per cent of explained variance; Cronbach's alpha respectively .70, .87, .88).

Table 3.5 shows that small firms with a web site, compared to those without a web site, perceive internet as a useful tool to obtain more information ($F(2,78) = 3,43$; p<.05); moreover the few firms with on-line activity perceive internet as a not so easy technology, showing a more realistic attitude compared to small firms planning to start e-business within one year ($F(2,58) = 3,37$; p <.05).

Firms with written and unwritten business plans report greater support towards innovation and greater belief that internet may be useful in improving the quality of work (see Table 3.6). Moreover, firms that consider ICT compared to those that do

Table 3.5 **Perceived usefulness and ease of Internet in small firms with web site and on line payments** (averages)

Website	Usefulness of Internet to obtain information	Order and pay on-line	Perceived ease of Internet
No	5.2	No	5.6
In one year	5.9	In one year	6.1
Yes	6.1	Yes	4.6

not consider ICT in the business plan report higher scores on all the three dimensions measuring climate for innovation (see Table 3.7).

Small firms with well defined growth targets and with positive beliefs about e-commerce consider Internet also as a useful tool for improving the quality of work (see Table 3.8 and 3.9).

Finally, considering internet a useful tool in improving the quality of work seems related to an economic impact of ICT: the greater such a belief, the higher the sales turnover (regressing perceived ease and usefulness of internet on sales turnover, the only significant beta observed concerns 'usefulness of internet for quality of work', beta =.32, p<.01, R square = .14).

Table 3.6 **Support for innovation and usefulness of internet in firms with or without business plan** (averages)

Business Plan	Support for innovation	Internet useful for quality of work
No	3.6	4.4
Yes, non written	4.1	5.5
Yes	4.0	4.9
	$F_{(2,75)} = 5.1; p<.01$	$F_{(2,76)} = 3.4; p<.05$

Table 3.7 **Climate for innovation and ICT inclusion in the business plan** (averages)

Plan includes ICT use	Support for innovation	Task orientation	Vision
No, not yet	3.7	3.3	3.4
Yes	4.3	3.9	3.9
	$F_{(1,30} = 5.9; p<.05$	$F_{(1,30)} = 5.5; p<.05$	$F_{(1,30)} = p<.05$

Table 3.8   Perceived usefulness of internet and firms' growth targets (averages)

e-Commerce Importance	Internet useful for quality of work
No specific target	3.6
Grow indefinitely	4.7
Grow to planned size	5.1
	$F(2,76) = 3.4; p<0.5$

Table 3.9   Perceived usefulness of internet and e-commerce importance (averages)

e-Commerce Importance	Internet useful for quality of work
Not important for us	3.9
In the future, now now	5.2
Very necessary for us	6.2
	$F(2,63) = 10; p<.001$

Discussion

Findings from the E-CoSME study provide evidence of the associations between organizational and psycho-social variables and adoption and use of ICT within small firms. The almost complete diffusion of computers and internet connection in a large part of Italian small firms, the wide adoption of web sites as a way to promote firms' products and services, and the still low diffusion of e-commerce is confirmed. The same trend and almost the same percentages were observed in the larger and more recent European e-Business Watch (2004) survey.

The influence of structural components of firms (size, number of full time employees and of customers, sales turnover, planned growth targets) in the adoption of a web site is confirmed and was observed in the Italian and British (Gray and Lawless, 2002) surveys of the E-CoSME project. Such findings suggest that even within the small firms sector a 'size effect' does exist: the larger the firm, with more employees, the more probable it is that it has its own website.

Less clear are, instead, the organizational determinants of order and pay online activity. Again, it has to be noted that the proportion of Emilia Romagna firms adopting e-commerce (8 per cent) is the same as observed in the English (Gray and Lawless, 2002) and Welsh (Brooksbank et al., 2002) E-CoSME surveys. This low percentage may suggest that the adoption of an e-commerce strategy is a complex and slow process for small firms, that barriers to its adoption are still not effectively addressed or that an adequate strategy to support small firms has yet to be found. The adoption of this technology still seems to rely on a small group of 'early adopters', that have not developed clear guidelines on how to manage the process of ICT adoption and management.

On psycho-social variables, our study shows a relationship between climate for innovation and availability of a business plan. This plan may take into account different pathways to innovation (e.g., cost reduction or new products), and ICT adoption may be one of these pathways. But ICT seems to be a very innovative strategy. In fact, firms whose plan includes ICT use show higher scores in all the dimensions of climate for innovation (shared organizational goals, task orientation and an effort to introduce new and improved ways of doing things in the workplace). Besides, the adoption of business plan, defined growth targets and a positive evaluation of e-commerce are related to beliefs on the usefulness of internet for improving the quality of work. Thus, it seems that the climate for innovation and usefulness of internet for quality of work are related to a cognitive anticipation and preparation for the future, as shown by the available and clearer business and growth plans.

Firms that are already using a website and firms potential adopters of a website evaluate internet as a useful tool to obtain information. Firms that are already using e-commerce differ from the potential adopters of this system in evaluating the ease of using internet; the first ones consider internet as less easy compared to the second ones. Actual experiences may have shown that managing an online business is not as easy as, for instance, surfing the net, and that support from technology suppliers, a staff with updated skills or a functioning network with external organizations are necessary conditions to continue using the system. This result supports Karahanna, Straub and Chervany's (1999) findings that users, compared to prospective users, have a more concrete knowledge of the new system that is mainly focused on task centered attributes.

This study has some limitations to be considered when interpreting the results and the implications. There may have been some selection-bias by the two small firms' associations in selecting the study samples to give a positive impression of their members. We asked them for a mixed sample, with firms of advanced ICT users but also with firms not interested in ICT. Our results, confirming previous literature as well as other E-CoSME surveys, suggest that such selection bias was probably well controlled.

In addition, the E-CoSME project mainly investigated objective organizational determinants for which a single respondent was perfectly adequate. More problematic is instead the measurement of the climate for innovation on the basis of a single respondent, the owner or someone of his/her staff. We measured the perception of the climate held by a special member, but future efforts should attempt to obtain multiple respondents for each organization.

Further, social norms, an important social determinant of adoption, were not included in the survey. Entrepreneurs are very busy people and to have a high rate of respondents we kept the questionnaire brief, but future research should provide a more rigorous test of the extended technology acceptance model.

This study has shown that e-business, and particularly e-commerce, is not an easy task for small firms that need to be supported along the many stages of ICT planning, adoption and implementation. To achieve the information society targets and to improve European small firms' competitiveness, governments and associations have to invite small firm owners to focus both on financial resources and investment in the equipment side of innovation as well as on beliefs and collective attitudes towards innovation shared within firms. To overcome the initial inertia and to stimulate firms to properly plan a stage adoption of ICT, change agents, consultants or business support organizations, may emphasize the need for innovation and usefulness of ICT to increase turn-over. Quite early, it becomes more useful to use different arguments, based on the perceived usefulness of ICT and how to deal with potential problems in the technological and organizational side of e-business implementation. Continuing to use an ICT application may depend on the economic advantages of the technology and the motivated and supported employees that judge the new system as useful and easy.

References

Adams, D.A., Nelson, R.R. and Todd, P.A. (1992), 'Perceived Usefulness, Ease of Use, and Usage of Information Technology: A Replication', *MIS Quarterly*, Vol. 16, pp. 227–247.

Agarwal, R. (2000), 'Individual Acceptance of Information Technology', in R. Zmud (Ed.), *Framing the Domains of IT Management: Projecting the Future through the Past*, Pinnaflex Publishing, Cincinnati, Ohio.

Anderson, N.R. and West, M. (1998) 'Measuring Climate for Work Group Innovation: Development and Validation of the Team Climate Inventory', *Journal of Organizational Behavior*, Vol. 19, pp. 235-258.

Anee (2003), *Osservatorio sul Commercio Elettronico in Italia: Edizione 2003*, ANEE, Milano. ('Observatory on electronic commerce in Italy: 2003 Survey')

Ashkanasy, N.M., Wilderom, C.P. and Peterson, M.F. (2000), *Handbook of Organizational Culture and Climate*, Sage, Thousand Oaks, CA.

Bandura, A. (1997), *Self-efficacy: The Exercise of Control,* Freeman, New York.

Brooksbank, D., Brychan, T., Packham, G. and Morse, L. (2002), 'E-Commerce and Small and Medium-Sized Enterprises in South-East Wales: A Clear Case for Intervention?', Paper Presented at the 25th ISBA National Small Firms Policy and Research Conference, 13-15 November, Brighton.

Campodall'Orto, S. (2003), *Crescere con l'e-Business*, Franco Angeli, Milano.

Chuan-Chuan Lin, J. and Lu, H. (2000), 'Towards an Understanding of the Behavioural Intention to Use a Web Site', *International Journal of Information Management*, Vol. 20, pp. 197–208.

Cooper, R. and Zmud, R.W. (1990), 'Information Technology Implementation Research: A Technological Diffusion Approach', *Management Science*, Vol. 36, pp. 123–139.

Culpan, O. (1995), 'Attitudes of End-Users Towards Information Technology in Manufacturing and Services Industries', *Information and Management*, Vol. 28, pp. 167–176.

Davis, F.D. (1989), 'Perceived Usefulness, Perceived Ease of Use, and User Acceptance of Information Technology', *MIS Quarterly*, Vol. 13, pp. 319-340.

Davis, F. (1993), 'User Acceptance of Information Technology: System Characteristics, Users Perceptions and Behavioral Impact', *International Journal Man–Machine Studies*, Vol. 38, pp. 475–487.

Davis, F.D, Bagozzi, R. and Warshaw, P. (1989), 'User Acceptance of Computer Technology: A Comparison of Two Theoretical Models', *Management Science*, Vol. 35, pp. 982–1003.

De Jong, A., De Ruiter, K. and Lemmick, J. (2003), 'The Adoption of Information Technology by Self-Managing Service Teams', *Journal of Service Research*, Vol. 6, pp. 162–179.

European Commission (2004), *The European e-Business Report, 3rd Synthesis Report of the e-Business W@tch*, EC Enterprise Directorate, Brussels.

Fishbein, M. and Ajzen, I. (1975), *Belief, Attitude, Intention and Behavior*, Addison-Wesley, Reading, MA.

Goodhue, D.L. and Thompson, R.L. (1995), 'Task-technology Fit and Individual Performance', *MIS Quarterly*, Vol. 19, pp. 213-236.

Gray, C. and Lawless, N. (2002), Determinants of E-Commerce Adoption in Small Firms, Paper Presented at the 25th ISBA National Small Firms Policy and Research Conference, 13-15 November, Brighton.

Karahanna, E., Straub, D. and Chervany, N. (1999), 'Information Technology Adoption Across Time: a Cross-Sectional Comparison of Pre-Adoption and Post-Adoption Beliefs', *MIS Quarterly*, Vol. 23, pp. 183–213.

Klein, K. and Sorra, J.S. (1996), 'The Challenge of Innovation Implementation', *Academy of Management Review*, Vol. 21, pp. 1055–1080.

Klein, K., Conn, A. and Sorra, J.S. (2001), 'Implementing Computerized Technology: an Organizational Analysis', *Journal of Applied Psychology*, Vol. 86, pp. 811–824.

Lederer, A., Maupin, D., Sena, M. and Zhuang, Y. (2000), 'The Technology Acceptance Model and the World Wide Web', *Decision Support Systems*, Vol. 29, pp. 269–282.

Lo parco, S. (2000), *Pianeta PMI*, Ipsoa, Milano.

Mate (2001) Osservatorio Net Economy 2001: Summary of Main Results, second year, second semestre, Mate, Milano.

Mate (2003), Osservatorio Net Economy: Osservatorio PMI, quarto anno, Mate, Milano.

Michela, J.L. and Burke, W.W. (2000), 'Organizational Culture and Climate in Transformations for Quality and Innovation', in N.M. Ashkanasy, C.P. Wilderom and M.F. Peterson (Eds.), *Handbook of Organizational Culture and Climate*, Sage, Thousand Oaks, CA, pp. 225–244.

Moon, J.W. and Kim, Y.G. (2001), 'Extending the TAM for a World-Wide-Web Context', *Information & Management*, Vol. 38, pp. 217-230.

Moore, G. and Benbasat, I. (1991), 'Development of an Instrument to Measure the Perceptions of Adopting an Information Technology Innovation', *Information Systems Research*, Vol. 2, pp. 192–222.

Rogers, E. (1995), *Diffusion of Innovations* (5th Edition), The Free Press, New York.

Schein, E. (1985), *Organizational Culture and Leadership*, Jossey Bass, San Francisco.

Schneider, B. (1990), 'The Climate for Service: An Application of the Climate Construct', in B. Schneider (Ed.), *Organizational Climate and Culture*, Jossey-Bass, San Francisco, pp. 383–412.

Schneider, B., Bowen, D., Ehrhart, M. and Holcombe, K. (2000), 'The Climate for Service: Evolution of a Construct', in N.M. Ashkanasy, C.P. Wilderom and M.F. Peterson (Eds.), *Handbook of Organizational Culture and Climate*, Sage, Thousand Oaks, CA, pp. 21 – 36.

Sparrow, P. and Gaston, K. (1996), 'Generic Climate Maps: a Strategic Application of Climate Survey Data?', *Journal of Organizational Behavior*, Vol. 17, pp. 679–698.

Straub, D., Keil, M. and Brenner, W. (1997), 'Testing the Technology Acceptance Model Across Cultures: a Three Country Study', *Information and Management*, Vol. 33, pp. 1–11.

Venkatesh, V. and Davis, F. (2000), 'A Theoretical Extension of the Technology Acceptance Model: Four Longitudinal Field Studies', *Management Science*, Vol. 46, pp. 186–204.

Weick, K. (1995), *Sensemaking in Organizations*, Sage, Thousand Oaks, CA.

West, M. and Anderson, R. (1996), 'Innovation in Top Management Teams', *Journal of Applied Psychology*, Vol. 81, pp. 680–693.

Zohar, D. (1980), 'Safety Climate in Industrial Organizations: Theoretical and Applied Implications', *Journal of Applied Psychology*, Vol. 65, pp. 96–102.

Zohar, D. (2000), 'A Group-Level Model of Safety Climate: Testing the Effect of Group Climate on Microaccidents in Manufacturing Jobs', *Journal of Applied Psychology*, Vol. 85, pp. 587–596.

Chapter 4

Changing Leadership Cultures in e-Commerce Service Industry

Mikko J. Ruohonen

The Nature of e-Commerce Service Industry Change

The information and communication technology (ICT) applications that support e-commerce services have the potential not only to improve cost-effectiveness but also to boost innovations (Rogers, 1983; Swanson, 1994). Examples include mass-customized products (Pine, 1993), industrial service innovations (Ruohonen *et al.*, 2003; Warkentin *et al.*, 2001) and, more recently, product and service based innovations (Pine and Gilmore, 1999). E-business and e-learning is starting to change operations models, organizational processes, ways of meeting and serving the customer and how knowledge is shared within industries. The goal of new e-business designs is for companies to 'create flexible alliances that not only off-load costs but also make customers ecstatic' (Kalakota and Robinson, 2001, p. 24).

The new business potential is increasingly across borders. Different collaboration and outsourcing strategies will become more important (Shepherd, 1999; Stabell and Fjeldstad, 1998). Kalakota and Robinson (2001) have collected a variety of names for the third generation of outsourcing alliances such as e-business webs, venture keiretsu, clusters, and coalitions. They are using outsourcing to create reputation, powerful economies of scale, cumulative learning, and preferred access to suppliers or channels.

Network competence theories suggest that innovative business potential is not based solely on transferring transactions between companies. It also entails sharing knowledge, integrating processes and developing joint measures for operations (Dyer and Singh, 1998; Larsson *et al.*, 1998; Warkentin *et al.*, 2001). We can call this phenomenon the era of knowledge networks or k-business (Ruohonen and Salmela, 1999). The rationale for this argument is that when e-business becomes more widely adopted, company and industry service models become more alike and standard. Hence, e-business systems will become prerequisites for doing business and competitive advantage will be derived from the exploitation of knowledge to gain customers' attention (Davenport and Beck, 2001; Pine and Gilmore, 1999). Enterprise information systems, routine-based supply chain management and basic customer relationship management applications need to be effective in order to achieve an integrated unity through the whole supply chain community (SCC) to meet unique needs of every customer.

The management of co-operation between organizations is a challenge. Contracts between organizations are just a first step. The building of knowledge networks demands new qualities (Stabell and Fjeldstad, 1998; Wenger *et al.*, 2002; Norris *et al.*, 2003). Kalakota and Robinson state that in order:

> to swim the unknown and often treacherous waters of technology ... true leaders know that they cannot manage e-business conversion at a distance by hiring consultants or other so-called experts and giving them adequate resources. e-Business methods and its supporting technology must not be a black box to managers. If it remains so, they will lose their ability to position the company, respond to market changes, and guide the internal innovations required for success (Kalakota and Robinson, 2001, p. 31).

Management of Interorganizational Competitive Advantage

The current challenge that faces many SMEs in Europe is how to drive or even adjust to this kind of evolution. Organizations are networked, competition is increasing, processes are shared and people need to learn very quickly how to accommodate the changes. The latest development in collaboration-based organizational theories has proposed that competitive advantage should also be derived from inter-organizational relationships. In the current e-business alliance-based organizational structure, this means that both customer and service companies need to possess new qualities. The following four qualities have been identified as important sources of competitive advantage between organizations (Dyer and Singh, 1998):

1. relation-specific assets i.e. investing in the specific relationship of partners;
2. knowledge-sharing routines and processes between partners;
3. complementary resources supplementing this core competencies of each partner;
4. effective governance of the collaboration relationship.

Knowledge business companies should manage all of these qualities. For example, when a company either co-operates within an ICT project or has an outsourcing service relationship with a customer company, knowledge creation is necessary. This is reflected, for example, in the building and maintenance of electronic marketplaces, in the administration of communication network services or in the management of intranets.

The co-operation relationship between organizations is not only reflected in formal agreements but also in a commitment to long-term co-operation. The service provider must be able to learn the business model of the customer organization. Service outsourcing begins the co-operative relationship with many options. Pricing, cost control and exit provisions only provide a skeleton for a tighter co-operation relationship. It must be possible to evaluate the outsourcing operations and at the same time to make selective outsourcing possible. The outsourcing which produces added value leads to changes in models of co-operation and strategies that rely only on cost cutting become rapidly outdated (Lacity and Hirscheim, 1993; McFarlan and Nolan, 1995; Kern and Willcocks, 2002).

Currently many businesses organize their services behind common web-based business portals. However, business portals are too often only cyber-crossings, hyperlink lists, or a bulletin board that is full of advertisements and notices. If the portal is created for problem-solving it requires a common knowledge shared practice between the portal partners and customers. The transfer of customer knowledge is difficult because the knowledge is context-related. Many organizations have developed their services continuously for a long time in order to become more proactive, with the right pricing of services and anticipation of customers' needs (El Sawy *et al.*, 1999; Turban *et al.*, 2002). Added value is thus not based on control of the transaction costs but is sought beyond the control of the traditional value chain (Stabell and Fjeldstad, 1998).

The resource-based theory of the firm (Barney, 1991) suggests that it is necessary to identify resources that are valuable, rare, difficult to imitate and effectively organized (VRIO-approach). The core competence has often been created over time (Prahalad and Hamel, 1990) and the interaction with customers provides a foundation for this success – a knowledge creating relationship. However, these competencies may become obsolete if competitive or technological changes affect the business environment. The competitive advantage of knowledge networks is created through the clustering process in which two or more organizations with complementary competencies begin to compete against other competitors' clusters having similar interests. The complementary competencies can open up new markets and technology areas. Traditionally such situations are avoided in which espionage or theft of corporate core competences is obvious. On the other hand, external competencies should be produced in the hyper-competitive businesses (D'Aveni, 1995; Matusik and Hill, 1998).

Competitive advantage is not achieved if the costs of the cooperation exceed the level of other competitors. Thus a project, such as the e-service portal, must be governed effectively with respect to both the technical infrastructure and the contents (i.e. services). The rules of co-operation must be created while different stakeholder groups control their own interests. A mediating organization may be useful as an official broker functioning either formally or based on partner relationships. Both modes of action dedicated to some individuals and the processes must be clear and explicit to every partner. The broker must be able to operate fast without the constant arrangement of meetings when the cooperation and customer interface changes. Situations in which this customer setting has to be evaluated and checked will be continuously created.

Changing Leadership Cultures in ICT Services

All this has effects on human resource management in e-commerce service firms. While service and knowledge creating relationships are constantly changing and trying to fit with the current situation, we need to know more about how e-commerce customer projects are managed. In general, the ICT industry is characterised by having a strong employee turnover, especially in the metropolitan areas of industrialised countries. At times, this can reach an annual level of a 20–30 per cent change in the labour force. Knowledge workers look for more inviting jobs and are more aware of new work opportunities. Many knowledge workers feel themselves to be part of the new economy with better salaries and share options, creating a kind of 'worker capitalism' (Kühl, 2003).

A number of these companies, particularly new start-up e-commerce firms, are at the forefront of the first phase of an ICT leadership culture. In this phase, the 'rules of the game', if not completely absent, were extremely flexible and often invented on a company by company basis. This was very evident in late 1990s in the so-called dot. com companies. An enormous lack of human resources was one of the reasons. Greed was other. The search for experts of 'the new economy' ended up with acceptance of poor quality management and productivity practices. Project management and business know-how were not really appreciated while it was more interesting to strive for venture capital, Initial Public Offerings, and a sky-rocketing rise of shareholder value (Kühl, 2003). Most of the companies were very small in size, with very young personnel, narrow qualifications and no business management experience. Some dot. com-companies recruited personnel by offering additional attractions ranging from free soft drinks to, say, diving or flying courses. Professional management practice and well-designed working processes were rare. The companies were more like bunches of good friends or families. This management model can be very attractive but also holds the risk of severe organizational limitations. Social systems which focus exclusively on promoting verbal communication through direct, face-to-face contact have not proven to be particularly successful in addressing complex tasks.

The term 'exit-capitalism' (Kühl, 2003) applies because the growth company founders, the venture capitalists who back them and the small stockholders on the exchange are not interested primarily in receiving regular dividends on a capital investment. Rather, their main goal consists of selling the shares they hold for a high exit profit. The logic is not based on an investment made for the long haul, but is dictated by the orientation of venture capital investors whose earnings depend on the difference between the purchase price and the sale price of their shares. Since offering stock for sale implies selling a piece of the company itself, interest therefore focuses on a purpose behind the actual product (Kühl, 2003).

Following the dot.com crash, ICT companies now try to create other sources of value in addition to the economic attractions. In the Finnish Business Journal *Talouselama* the managing director of one of the fastest growing and profitable new media companies says: 'Overgrown personnel benefits are no more appreciated. Free coke and Friday afternoon wine parties are not any more a clever way to attract personnel' (Tenhunen, 2003). The economic advantages are a kind of hygiene factors as such but in addition to them the character of the work community, the culture of the organization and management style and the general attractiveness of the business sector are now taken into account. Knowledge management has also emerged as an important factor in the evaluation of the quality of a firm's management.

New start-up companies enjoy the advantage of quick implementation of new practices compared to more established businesses which have often created organizational rules which are slow to change. There were lessons for firms to learn from the dot.com crash but e-businesses are still very young and business models and management systems are still evolving. It is difficult to say how much a firm should change its processes and agreed business models in order to boost its quality, image or growth in sales (Tenhunen, 2003). Kühl (2003) observes that it is possible to end up with a centralised structure even though it was originally intended to be decentralized:

> Even if it is preferable to replace the negative connotations of 'hierarchy', 'department', 'regulations' and 'job descriptions' by substituting 'information channels', 'team', 'value creation process' and 'task profile', in the final analysis it always remains a question of determining who should have less to do with whom in the organization and in which areas an intensification of a verbal communication is at all meaningful (Kühl, 2003, p. 140).

Many lucrative start-up companies are now either merged with larger firms or they have become bankrupt due to the closure of venture capital or loss of customers. However, some of them have survived and it would be interesting to examine what are the success or survival factors behind them. Instability of labour markets

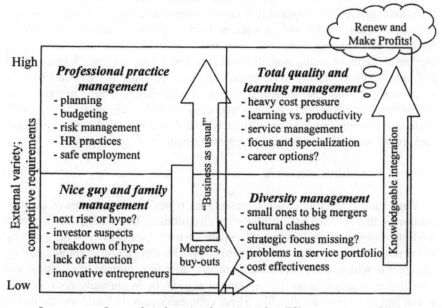
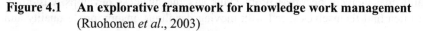

Figure 4.1   An explorative framework for knowledge work management (Ruohonen *et al.*, 2003)

and people feeling unsafe in their jobs have also led to unionization (Kühl, 2003). In Finland, for instance, trade unions have conducted large, and in many cases successful, campaigns to attract ICT workers.

Our research group has been working on a 3-year research program on emerging knowledge work and leadership cultures at the University of Tampere (Ruohonen *et al.*, 2003; Ruohonen *et al.*, 2004). The group has conducted action research investigations with three e-commerce service companies in Finland. Those companies represent different businesses, from internet service provision to ICT infrastructure business and shared enterprise systems services. The framework, shown in Figure 4.1, has served as a proposition or theoretical lenses to examine what has happened in the ICT service sector over the past five years.

For an e-commerce service company it is important to position itself within the following dimensions:

- external variety, i.e. growing competitive pressures in the ICT industry with more complex business models and more effective product and service demands;
- internal variety, i.e. increasing differences of ICT labour force in more demanding service situations and merging of ICT companies.

The dimensions for categorizing different contextual leadership approaches are defined by external variety (competitive business forces) and internal variety (personnel differences). Competition makes companies aware of good quality and project deadlines and has put pressure on knowledge organizations, especially on the glamorous dot-com companies. Personnel differences refer to those emerging challenges which are rising from differences in age, culture, job career, professional and cultural backgrounds, even gender and race in some societal contexts. As an example, it might be challenging for a 30-year female project manager with management degree to coordinate her team consisting of a 22-year, single male self-made web-programmer, a 50-year divorced mainframe specialist with engineering background and a 40 year bohemian graphic designer with arts degree.

Nice guy and family management

This quadrant of the framework represents the typical start-up company. In these companies, there is often a close intimacy with customers. Knowledge sharing is easy while the company is small in size. All people can participate in joint problem solving and in project sessions. However, in these companies recognition of complementary resources is seldom done explicitly. Normally, there is a shortage of resources and governance of projects, such as e-commerce projects, is normally poor. Quality is low and timetables are flexible. These companies provide value mainly due to market inequalities. When markets develop and customers learn to demand more, quality management becomes problematic. As the business develops, customers can often find themselves faced with moving deadlines, inappropriate quality and missing service processes. This is due to the focus of technology enthusiasm instead of on finalizing service processes.

Kühl (2003), citing Stephan Jansen, calls this style as 'management by Enid Blyton'. This children's book author sends her protagonists off on adventures exhorting them to be 'five friends'. Company founders seem to adopt such advice as a management philosophy. Sense of friendship, family or communality extends not only to individual employees but to the company's entire staff. Typical start-up firms are face-to-face organizations in which:

> everybody knows everybody else from working together on day-to-day basis, and ... every person has direct access to every other member of the firm. An employee in a start-up with a group-like structure can approach the chairperson of the board directly, without causing an annoyance, let alone breaking protocol (Kühl, 2003, p. 131–32).

Management of people is based on 'nice guy feelings', normally managerial structures are avoided and there are no systematic administrative processes. Office hours are very flexible and people like to use their free time with their colleagues or even overnight in the office. Management follows the guidelines of how to do with friends or even family members.

Diversity management

This describes a typical situation for some of the growing or grown dot-com companies. They have increased their size by buying smaller companies and at the same time achieved public listing on a stock exchange. Usually the rapid growth has created problems in communications and management routines and eventually a clash of cultures. A number of small 'family management' companies have been 'destroyed' by their acquisitions. Projects are diverse in nature and demand variety of personnel competencies. Knowledge sharing might become problematic due to rapid growth and different learning styles of personnel. It is increasingly more difficult to gather complementary resources for a larger customer project. Governance can still be poor and that affects the quality levels of service. Fragmentation of service and customer accounts creates a situation which makes customers unpleasantly aware of project management problems.

The challenge is diversity management, both projects and human resources become more diverse and managers need to know more about the different psychological, social and cultural phenomena reflected in their daily work. E-business is also a global issue. Many companies buy services from providers that can maintain the same level of quality in every part of the world. Small companies need to be part of an international business network which might put pressure to renew their e-commerce systems.

Professional practice management

This quadrant is for professional communities in tougher competitive situations. If companies can create more systematic approaches, improve their strategies, structures and processes in line with customer demands, they might survive. Customers usually find this change as a more systematic, but maybe also more bureaucratic, movement to provide e-commerce services. Very often pricing structures change, too, and customers usually start to compare between competitors.

There is a potential danger that interminable discussions will ensue, blocking important decisions (Kühl, 2003). Furthermore, this may also mean that some of the workers become unhappy when they cannot do what they want. Project managers need to be aware of project deadlines, strong enough to resist last minute changes and very authoritative when people are producing over-quality. Also, Tenhunen (2003) confirms that it is not impossible to shape the company in a way that it is both a good place to be and profitable, but profitability should not be sacrificed for having fun.

The opportunity is for long lasting customer relationships that educate both parties to do their best. Professional rules, patterns and even support systems can help knowledge sharing inside the company and within customers. Constant review of service quality is done and governance is more systematic but enables freedom when necessary.

Total quality and learning management

This is the most challenging quadrant as it requires both the management of business competition and also diverse personnel management approaches. These companies are normally the big players which provide variety of services to customer companies. They normally have very diverse personnel working also abroad. These businesses need to take care of both 'old economy' systems and emerging new economy systems. They analyse, support and consult strategy making. Many of these take care of outsourcing and application service provision. They hire people for customer companies. Projects and customers are categorized. They have initiated both formal (ICT-based) and informal (face-to-face) knowledge sharing practices with information systems support. Companies normally use their visibility and brand for marketing their services to customers. Customer trust to these companies is higher but in the same time customers need to be prepared to pay for 'a big player fee' for their e-commerce services.

Complementary resources are developed through team building, task forces and evolving organizational arrangements. Governance uses total quality management and critical chain reviews. Quality is defined either by excellence criteria or through meeting customer demands. At the same time, these companies face a clear threat of becoming too bureaucratic, therefore active learning management processes are also needed. Processes which support reflection and socialization are especially needed. Managers have to take into account, from one side, costs and schedules and, from the other, creativity, freedom of ideas and professional learning. Managing director

Jari Mielonen (2003) observed that well-designed organizational structures and cost control are important things which need an increasingly competent staff to keep in balance.

Concluding Remarks

This chapter has raised the need to take into account increasing competitive pressures and emerging business models when analyzing the changes in e-commerce service firms. These findings are particularly applicable as the e-commerce service industry expands. Strategic re-orientation is needed in focusing the shift from pure software development towards a portfolio of service provision and even further, to the holistic management of customer experience through information systems. Networked ICT business is increasingly dependent on alliances, clusters and especially on refocusing on key competencies placed in an inter-organizational setting.

This has inevitable implications for human resource management practices in ICT companies. The challenge is to change leadership practices for a more service-oriented and knowledge network-based business. New hybrid leaders need to be aware and to balance the changing evolutionary shifts from one culture to another. 'Happy family' culture was first a lucrative way of work and of doing business. Now, it seems that only a few companies can continue with this leadership approach, mainly those innovative firms with emergent technology opportunities. Many of them have had to grow to become more professional (and maybe also more boring). However, ignoring the 'who needs strategy' question might be lethal in a turbulent environment.

Complexity of digital economy systems is also driving companies to be more diverse. Diversity management means both skills and knowledge to listen to customers more carefully and organize valuable, rare and non-imitable resources in a corporation or even in a nexus of companies. Finally, in order to make progress, firms need to maintain both safe, efficient core processes and at the same time leave freedom for environment scanning and new competence building. However, this is an organizational learning process and no 'quick fix'. Eventually, emergent e-businesses are shaping a new genre or culture of knowledge work.

References

Barney, J.B. (1991), 'Firm resources and sustained competitive advantage', *Journal of Management*, Vol. 17, pp. 99–120.

D'Aveni, R. A. (1995), *Hypercompetition: Managing the dynamics of strategic manouvering*, Free Press, New York.

Davenport, T.H. and Beck, J.C. (2001), *The attention economy: understanding the new currency of business*, Accenture, Harvard Business School Press, Boston.

Dyer, J.H. and Singh, H. (1998), 'The relational view: Cooperative strategy and sources of inter-organizational competitive advantage', *Academy of Management*

Review, Vol. 23, pp. 660–679.

El Sawy, O.A., Malhotra, A., Gosain, S. and Young K.M. (1999), 'IT-Intensive Value Innovation in the Electronic Economy: Insights from Marshall Industries', *MIS Quarterly*, Vol. 23, pp. 305–333.

Kalakota, R. and Robinson, M. (2001), *E-Business 2.0*, Addison Wesley Longman, Reading, Massachusetts.

Kern, T. and Willcocks, L. (2002), 'Exploring relationships in information technology outsourcing', *European Journal of Information Systems*, Vol. 11, pp. 3–19.

Kühl, S. (2003), *Exit – How Venture Capital Changes the Laws of Economics*, Campus, Franfurt a M., New York.

Lacity, M.C. and Hirscheim, R. (1993), *Information systems outsourcing myths, metaphors and realities*, Wiley, Chichester.

Larsson, R., Bengtsson, K., Henriksson, K. and Sparks, J. (1998), 'The interorganizational learning dilemma: Collective knowledge development in strategic alliances', *Organization Science*, Vol. 9, pp. 285–305.

Matusik, S.F. and Hill, C.W. (1998), 'The Utilization of Contingent Work, Knowledge Creation, and Competitive Advantage', *Academy of Management Review*, Vol. 23, pp. 680–697.

McFarlan, F.W. and Nolan, R.L. (1995), 'How to Manage an IT Outsourcing Alliance', *Sloan Management Review*, Vol. 36, pp. 9–23.

Mielonen, J. (2003), 'A Reporter Interview', in Talouselämä, the Finnish Business Journal 'Kooditaituri tarvitsee tiukan pomon', by Sami Rainisto 13.6.2003, ('Code nerd needs a tough boss').

Norris, D., Mason, J. and Lefrere, P. (2003), *Transforming e-Knowledge – A Revolution in the Sharing Knowledge*, Society for College and University Planning.

Pine II, B.J. (1993), *Mass Customization: The New Frontier in Business Competition*, Harvard Business School Press, Boston, Massachusetts.

Pine II, B.J. and Gilmore J.B. (1999), *The Experience Economy: Work is Theatre and Every Business a Stage*, Harvard Business School Press, Boston, Massachusetts.

Prahalad, C.K. and Hamel, G. (1990), 'The core competence of the corporation', *Harvard Business Review*, Vol. 68, pp. 79–91.

Rogers, E. (1983), *Diffusion of Innovations*, Free Press, New York.

Ruohonen, M., Kultanen, T., Lahtonen, M., Rytkönen, T. and Kasvio, A. (2003), 'Identity and Diversity Management for New Human Resource Approaches in the ICT Industry', in F. Avallone, H. Sinangil and A. Caetano (eds), *Identity and Diversity in Organizations*, Guerini Studio, Milano.

Ruohonen, M., Kasvio, A., Kultanen, T., Lahtonen, M., Lehtonen, J.M. and Vanne, T. (2004), Tietoyritysten muuttuvat työkulttuurit, Tampere University Press, Tampere.

Ruohonen, M. and Salmela, H. (1999), *Yrityksen tietohallinto (Information Management)*, Edita, Helsinki.

Shepherd, A. (1999), 'Outsourcing IT in a Changing World', *European Management Journal*, Vol. 17, pp. 64–84.

Stabell, C.B. and Fjeldstad, Ö.D. (1998), 'Configuring Value for Competitive Advantage – on chains, shops, and networks', *Strategic Management Journal*, Vol. 19, pp. 413–437.

Swanson, E.B. (1994), 'Information Systems Innovation among Organizations', *Management Science*, Vol. 40, pp. 1069–1092.

Turban, E., King, D., Lee, J., Warkentin, M. and Chung, H. (2002), *Electronic Commerce – a Managerial Perspective*, Prentice Hall, New York.

Tenhunen, T. (2003), 'A Reporter Interview', in Talouselämä, the Finnish Business Journal 'Kooditaituri tarvitsee tiukan pomon', by Sami Rainisto 13.6.2003, ('Code nerd needs a tough boss').

Warkentin, M., Sugumaran, V. and Bapna, R. (2001), 'E-knowledge Networks for Inter-Organizational Collaborative E-Business', *Logistics Information Management*, Vol. 14, pp. 149–162.

Wenger, E.C., McDermott, R. and Snyder, W.M. (2002), *Cultivating Communities of Practice: A Guide to Managing Knowledge*, Harvard Business School, Boston.

Chapter 5

e-Business and Small Firms in London

Jane Tebbutt

Introduction

This chapter is based on two survey waves carried out in late 2002 and 2003 into SME adoption and exploitation of e-business in London (Business Link for London, 2003, 2004). The work was commissioned jointly by Business Link for London (a large business support organization, providing assistance to the 300,000 or so small and medium enterprises (SMEs) as they are often called in policy documents, which make up roughly half of London's business population of public and private entities) and 'UK Online For Business' (a national programme, sponsored by the Department of Trade and Industry (DTI) to promote awareness and uptake of ICT). In 2002, 5,000 firms were interviewed. In 2003, the sample consisted of 4,000 firms. Although the surveys were conducted in 2002 and 2003, both reports were published in the year following the fieldwork; thus, results are reported by referring to publication date. The surveys examined e-business adoption rates, barriers and enablers, technology preferences, and impacts. The outputs were used to inform e-business support delivery programmes and the wider economic development landscape in London.

This chapter is written from the perspective of a business support organization seeking to make sense of micro-level marketplace data and to understand its implications against a changing macro-level policy environment. This issue will be facing many different policy and delivery agencies across Europe. Although the specific point of reference in this chapter is London and the behaviour of its SMEs with regard to ICT, the experiences, conclusions and actions which result, may serve as useful idea generators to other cities or regions.

Background

London is a massive market, with over 600,000 SMEs, large firms, and public corporations. The entrepreneurial spirit is strong. Start-ups are running at a very high rate; there were 36,600 new VAT registrations in 2003 (Small Business Service [SBS], 2004a), the highest number in any UK region. There are 62 new starts per 10,000 head of population aged 16 or over, so it is also the most active of any region. Business ownership is diverse. Black and Minority Ethnic (BME) owned firms account for around 22 per cent of the business stock, and women-owned firms for around 20 per cent. In both cases this is under-representation of their presence in the population as a whole.

However, not all the indicators of growth are strong. VAT de-registration rates are also the highest of any region in the UK – 34,600 firms de-registered in 2003, equivalent to 58 per 10,000 head of population aged 16 or over. The 3 year business survival rates are the lowest in the UK, 63 per cent, and London has made the least progress of any region in driving up this rate since 1993 (SBS, 2004b). The region is not as powerful a user of innovation as might be expected given the strength of the knowledge base (there are 40 Higher Education Institutions in London, accounting for 25 per cent of national research council funding). Around 75 per cent of firms have not introduced either product or process innovation during 2004 (London Development Agency and Business Link for London, 2004). Despite having the highest UK Gross Value Added per head of population, the averaging that this involves masks variations in performance between sectors. Some are large, and internationally competitive, such as financial services, whilst others are struggling. Most SMEs are not growing, they are either static or in decline. In 2003, the turnover of 61 per cent of firms either stayed the same or declined. During the same period the staff productivity of 71 per cent of firms either stayed the same or declined. The vast majority of firms are very small. Although London contributes 15.2 per cent of the entire UK business stock, it is dominated by microfirms: 89 per cent employ 10 or less people, 78 per cent employ 5 or fewer people; only 1 per cent employ more than 100 staff (Business Link for London, 2003). The majority of firms (59 per cent) have a turnover of less than £100,000 (145,000 €); only 4 per cent turnover more than £5m (7.25m €).

Survey Rationale

Business Link for London provides business support services to all of London's SMEs. The market, as described, is large but diverse and fragmented. It has particular characteristics – a strong supply of new starts but a seemingly weak ability to sustain them, very small firms dominate, and most firms operate in the service sector – many more than in other UK regions. Despite this, and the acknowledged general growth of the service sector, many of London's firms have not grown during the period under observation. Although business owners remain optimistic about future growth, current performance leaves room for improvement.

The aim of the survey was primarily to inform business development activities to create appropriate ICT related products and services, differentiated by size, sector, ownership or location as appropriate. However, a secondary aim was to build a picture of the use of ICT by 'ordinary' firms; to see if it was possible to understand what difference it was making to their businesses – were the firms adopting ICT reporting improvements to productivity or other benefits. In other words, could ICT be a way of delivering business growth?

The term 'e-business' is used relatively loosely to cover any or all of the processes involved in running a business, which may be set up or managed using ICT. It is not constrained to e-commerce or to transactions.

Methodological Points

There were some differences between the two waves, as well as differing sample sizes (due to budgetary constraints). The second wave attempted to interview more BME firms and more firms in certain geographic regions; although this ambition was not always realised. The second wave also concentrated more on the impact of ICT adoption rather than connectivity and use. It produced specific market segmentation and internal programme development and design ideas for Business Link for London.

Common features between the two survey waves were the equal division of the sample between the five sub-regions which make up London (i.e North, South, East, West and Central). The surveys were both carried out using CATI, by the same independent market research firm. The sample was weighted to represent the SME population of London, but there was a slight over-sampling amongst larger SMEs. Overall the confidence rate for both reports is ± 1.4 per cent.

Connection

Although pure connectivity is becoming increasingly outmoded as a point of reference for the emergence of the digital economy, we believe it still provides useful data, particularly concerning the uptake of newer digital technologies.

Computer ownership and internet access is becoming ubiquitous in London. In 2003, the survey showed that 81 per cent of SMEs used computers, 72 per cent had internet access (and less than 1 per cent of the remainder planned to go online – which was shown to be a large underestimate in the 2004 survey) and 17 per cent used broadband. Comparable internet and broadband access figures for 2004 are 77 per cent and 43 per cent respectively. In 2003, the Office of National Statistics (ONS) estimated the national SME broadband connection rate to be around 14 per cent, rising to 26 per cent in 2004. It can be seen that SMEs in London have been, and continue to be, ahead of the broadband connectivity curve. This is probably because the underlying infrastructure in London is good; with ADSL available to 99 per cent of the population, broadband take-up is rising sharply.

However, these headline figures mask significant variations. For example, in 2003 only 64 per cent of firms in Objective 2 areas (those areas with socio-economic structural difficulties including depressed areas dependent on fishing, areas undergoing significant change in services or industry, declining rural areas and urban areas with extreme difficulties) were on-line, and 10 per cent had broadband access. Very small firms (1–5 employees) regardless of location, were also disadvantaged, with just 65 per cent having online access, and 8 per cent using broadband. This

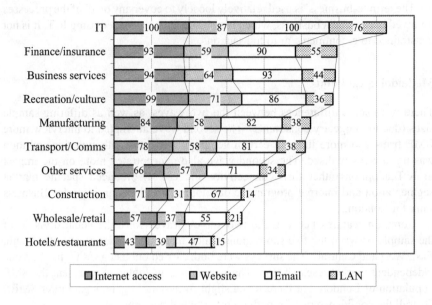

Figure 5.1   ICT adoption by sector
Source: Business Link for London (2004)

pattern of low adoption for small firms is confirmed by the ONS study which showed that only 56 per cent of firms with 0–9 employees had internet access, although 13 per cent had broadband; which is close to the average for all sizebands.

In 2004, technology adoption in very small firms continued to lag. On average, for very small firms, there were adoption levels of 61 per cent across internet access, website, LAN and email, compared to average levels of 71 per cent in firms with between 5 and 9 employees and 92 per cent in firms with more than 50 staff. There is also some evidence that the ethnicity of business ownership has an effect on ICT adoption; with non-white owned businesses lagging, although there are quite high levels of non-response to the survey concerning ethnic origin. For example, 70 per cent of non-white owned businesses have internet access, and 48 per cent have a website, compared to 79 per cent and 56 per cent respectively for white-owned businesses.

There are also sectoral differences in the spread of ICT take-up (see Figure 5.1). The hotels and restaurants sector, and the retail and wholesale sector both lag. Their broadband take-up is also weaker than all other sectors, running at 19 per cent and 26 per cent respectively, compared to 79 per cent for IT businesses – the strongest performers. The former two sectors account for 27 per cent of firms in London – their underperformance is important.

Curiously, given the slightly lower adoption rates for ICT for non-white owned, and very small firms, the same pattern of lower broadband adoption is not repeated.

Both have broadband adoption rates close to, or at, the average (i.e. 42 per cent and 43 per cent respectively). Overall, the survey indicates that if all those who say they are going to adopt broadband in the next 12 months actually do so, then adoption rates for London will be around 60 per cent in 2005.

Emerging Technologies

In 2004, businesses were asked about their use of wireless technologies as a proxy for their engagement with newer technological developments. Just 4 per cent of firms use wireless technologies – ranging from a high of 10 per cent in the recreation and culture sector to a low of 0.5 per cent in the hotels and restaurants and wholesale/ retail sectors. Seven per cent of IT firms use wireless technologies, although 41 per cent say they will adopt them during the next 12–18 months. The average figure for firms saying they will use wireless technologies within the next 12–18 months is 17 per cent.

There appears to be a relationship between awareness of e-business support and propensity to adopt wireless technologies; with twice as many current adopters being aware of sources of assistance as unaware of sources. It is not clear which is the driving element in the relationship – does technology take-up mean a firm needs to find out about support, or typically is it an increased awareness of support which stimulates ICT adoption?

Buying and Selling

Enabled by the relatively high connectivity levels in 2003, 31 per cent of SMEs ordered supplies online and the same percentage allowed customers to order online. In 2004 the picture had changed. Ordering from suppliers increased to 40 per cent, but allowing customers to order online had decreased to 22 per cent. The reason for this may be explained when we look beyond measures of e-business readiness (i.e. connectivity) to assessing its impact. In 2003, two thirds of e-tailers failed to make any online sales. Again, the picture was worse for very small firms (68 per cent failed) and those in Objective 2 areas (69 per cent failed). Comparable figures for 2004 are, unfortunately, not available, but as there is a downward trend in both allowing customers to order and allowing them to pay online (down to 13 per cent on average), it would seem sensible to surmise that volumes of orders and hence values of orders would also be curtailed. However, this downward trend is not supported by the *International Benchmarking Study* (IBS) of the DTI, which shows that on average 37 per cent of firms accept orders online, up 5 per cent from last year. This may possibly be explained by the fact that the IBS interviewed far fewer firms and they tended to be larger.

For these e-commerce metrics, firm size does not seem to be a particular barrier, with activity levels for very small firms close to the average; although those firms

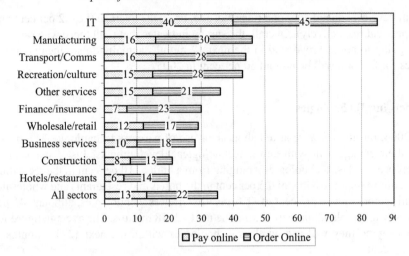

Figure 5.2   Online customer transactions
Source: Business Link for London (2004)

with zero employees lag slightly. However, there are wide sectoral variations (see Figure 5.2). Hotels and restaurants are not keen on customer online ordering with only 14 per cent active; and only 6 per cent allowing online payments – which may be considered odd given the popularity of consumer on-line holiday and short-break booking. IT firms are stronger advocates, with 45 per cent offering online ordering and 40 per cent online payment facilities. Thirty per cent of manufacturers offer on-line ordering – which may be a legacy of previous EDI systems which encouraged supply chain interaction – but only 16 per cent accept online payments. Financial services are particularly weak at accepting online payment (only 7 per cent do this), which also seems a little counter-intuitive, given the rise of online banking, although there may be some security or regulatory barriers. Overall, the service industries, with the exception of the IT sector, are a weaker transactional user of IT than might be expected given their technology adoption profile.

Figure 5.3 shows that transactions with suppliers are running at much higher rates than transactions with customers, although in most cases somebody's supplier must be somebody else's customer. On average, 48 per cent order from suppliers online, with 34 per cent making online payments.

For example, 29 per cent of hotels and restaurants order online from suppliers; with 19 per cent paying them online. This is much higher than the same sector's propensity to interact with customers. It is possible that it is the hotels which are interacting electronically with customers, and that restaurants are interacting electronically with suppliers. In more e-commerce-active sectors, supplier interaction levels are also much higher than customer interaction levels. The IT sector leads the way, with 83 per cent ordering supplies online and 67 per cent making online payments. Business

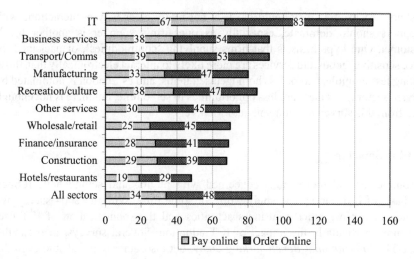

Figure 5.3   Online supplier transactions
Source: Business Link for London (2004)

services is also a heavy supply-side interactive user with 54 per cent ordering and 38 per cent paying on-line – again much higher than the equivalent figures for customer facing interactions.

It is possible that the preference for buying supplies on-line rather than allowing customers to purchase on-line may be due to the nature of the product or service being unsuited to online transactions, or that the firm does not have the right technology in place, or simply that customers prefer to purchase using different channels.

The 2004 survey also asked about SMEs propensity to interact with Government (ahead of its self-imposed target of 100 per cent of services being capable of being accessed electronically by the end of 2005). On average, 16 per cent of firms have some form of interaction with Government, rising to 24 per cent for firms with more than 50 employees. Gender and ethnicity of business ownership were not important performance parameters, although family owned firms were slightly less likely to interact electronically with government. Certain sectors predominated: IT (28 per cent), business services (22 per cent) and recreation and culture (22 per cent). This performance level is weak, particularly given the statutory nature of some interactions – such as the completion of tax returns – although they can still obviously be filed manually. The *International Benchmarking Study* (DTI, 2004) confirms this weakness. Firms in Greater London are less likely than any other region to interact with government to pay tax, and in fact their general communication rates with Government via either email or website have fallen dramatically between 2003 and 2004.

So far, SMEs are not realising the full financial benefits of their ICT investments and are under-exploiting opportunities, particularly the chance to become as fully customer focused as they could be. It is not really clear why e-interactions with suppliers should dominate, especially as one firm's supplier is another firm's customer. One hypothesis is that firms supplying 'commodities', or packaged, or price sensitive, goods and services are more likely to interact electronically than those selling less tangible, and/or less homogenised items; and as London is dominated by service sector firms there are less opportunities to sell online, but there is not enough data from this survey to comment authoritatively.

Getting Smarter

E-commerce, and transactions concerned with buying and selling have formed the basis of ICT survey and study work for some time. With the 2004 survey, we wanted to explore other e-business activities and the sophistication of ICT use, and more particularly the impact of ICT adoption. Several surveys, in particular the DTI's *International Benchmarking Study*, but also other regional studies in the UK, are also progressing towards using a number of different metrics as a measure of ICT sophistication. Research projects such as the trans-national and EU-funded *SIBIS – Statistical Indicators for Benchmarking the Information Society* – are also helping drive forward the way that the e-economy is measured and described.

One way in which the 2004 survey moved forward was to examine the degree to which firms had IT-enabled processes, and the extent to which these were integrated with each other and/or with other business processes. This can be used as a partial indicator of IT appreciation and sophistication, and as a way of beginning to understand what IT firms actually use in the day to day running of a company. Results show that the depth of IT-enabled processes in London is strong. Seventy-two per cent of firms have at least one IT-supported process. Larger firms are more likely to have adopted more IT-enabled business processes: 80 per cent of firms with 50 or more staff have between 4–8 IT-enabled processes compared to 25 per cent of firms with no staff and 35 per cent of very small firms with between 1–4 employees.

There are also large sectoral variations, with the IT sector most likely to have the highest number of IT-enabled processes, and hotels and restaurants the least likely. In fact, over half the hotels and restaurants sector have no IT-enabled processes at all.

The business processes supported by IT, and reported in Figure 5.4, also vary, with finance the most usual function, and human resources the least developed. This may just be a function of the widespread and long-term availability of finance packages, coupled with the mandatory nature of keeping financial records. Businesses seem to recognise the power of IT in maintaining customer relationships, even if, as shown earlier, they are not directly interacting with firms by making or receiving payments electronically.

Asking about the degree of integration across IT-enabled processes gives some approximation as to the likely effectiveness of IT investment or internal process

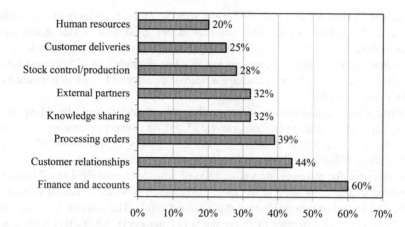

Figure 5.4 IT-enabled business processes
Source: Business Link for London (2004)

efficiency. Almost half (49 per cent) of firms have some degree of IT integration across business processes, with 28 per cent intending to expand this – indicating it must be giving them some benefits, although only 11 per cent of firms have fully integrated all their business processes using IT. This is similar to findings in the *International Benchmarking Study* which show that 36 per cent of UK firms already have integrated internal systems with a further 14 per cent currently integrating them.

The more IT-enabled processes there are in a business, the more likely it is that they are integrated. Sixty-seven per cent of firms with 6–8 IT-enabled processes have integrated them, compared to 33 per cent of firms with 2–4 IT-enabled processes. It is not clear if this is an indicator of an efficiency seeking firm, or whether it is just a by-product of the supply side. In other words, it either means that firms that have decided to 'automate' business processes have also decided to integrate them – indicating a forward looking firm, not averse to challenge – or it may merely be an indication of applications being purchased as a suite of packages; with integration built in. A minor indication of the former is apparent with almost one quarter (24 per cent) of fast-growing firms (self-defined) claiming to be fully integrated.

Bad Attitude?

Both the 2003 and the 2004 survey investigate owner-manager attitudes to planning for investment and use of IT. They show similar conclusions. Organizations with a strategic approach tend to be higher adopters of IT and are more likely to report benefits – they are twice as likely to have a website and also are twice as likely to report a benefit from IT as non-strategic planners. A strategic approach may be defined as having at least one of the following: a budget for IT, a budget to develop e-business, a director or head of IT, or a specific IT or e-business business plan. However, the number of strategic planners is not great, and in fact it has fallen slightly from 30 per cent in 2003, to 27 per cent in 2004. The adoption levels of individual strategic planning elements are low. For example, only 15 per cent have a specific budget for IT, 13 per cent have a head or director of IT and 10 per cent have an IT/e-business plan.

Once again, certain sectors are more likely to operate strategically. Most strong technology adopters also plan for strategic IT growth – except manufacturing. Very small firms are only half as likely to plan strategically as firms with 50 or more staff. This less disciplined approach may be due to factors such as lack of time or other resource for planning, or a more relaxed attitude to running a small business. However, in the 2004 survey, we specifically asked whether a lack of e-business skills and knowledge was holding the business back. The answer, unfortunately, was 'Yes' for over a quarter of respondents (27 per cent). Again, this finding was heightened in very small firms with 1–4 staff (29 per cent), and for certain sectors, i.e. hotels and restaurants (41 per cent). Non-white owned firms were also more likely to state they had a skills-related issue with a third of them stating this was the case; family businesses are also suffering, with 34 per cent lacking the relevant skills and knowledge. Unfortunately, 18 per cent of all businesses (and a quarter of BME-owned firms) believe that the help they need is not available.

Investigating this further, qualitative research (carried out as part of the project) indicates that firms often rely on an in-house 'guru' or champion. This 'super-user' is often called upon to sort out anything from fixing cabling, to helping users with application queries, to ordering new kit; they are primarily a practical source of help. It is not clear the extent to which this person is familiar enough with the strategic aspects of IT and e-business to provide clear help and direction to the people making 'big picture' (and/or 'big ticket') decisions about IT purchase, training or exploitation.

These hypotheses are being examined by other projects as well. For example, in London, the Framework for Regional Employment and Skills Actions (FRESA, 2004), concluded that strategic IT management skills were a key weakness for SMEs in the capital, in other words owner/managers were not sufficiently aware of the potential of ICT. This is a supply side issue in terms of not enough of the right support and training being available, compounded by weak expressed demand on the part of SMEs. A similar hypothesis is currently being investigated in the North West for a subset of SMEs, i.e. digitally dedicated firms. Here, data from the *National Employer Skills Survey* indicates that the acquisition and display of management skills by IT professionals is not particularly highly valued.

Support for e-Business

In London, only two thirds of SMEs know of any sources of help and advice on e-business. This figure has fallen very slightly from 2003 to 2004. Awareness levels vary amongst sectors, with manufacturers the most savvy (45 per cent are aware of sources) and the hospitality sector the least aware (19 per cent). This may be due to manufacturers long-term awareness and use of business support, most recently via the national Manufacturing Advisory Service. Finance and insurance firms, although relatively sophisticated users of technology and e-business, are not very aware of sources of help.

Users of support tend to be stronger technology adopters and users. Roughly 20 per cent actually use e-business advice, and the preferred sources are consultants and software firms, i.e. the private sector. However, there is an unfulfilled, expressed, demand for IT and e-business support. Broadband, e-marketing and website design and navigation are the most popular topics, although some sectors are less interested than others. Hotels and restaurants have the lowest expressed interest in business support concerning IT adoption and use, yet they are also one of the lowest performing sectors in virtually all aspects of e-business. This may be because they believe e-business is less relevant than do firms in the IT, business services and recreation and culture sectors. In these more forward looking sectors, between 79 per cent and 93 per cent believe e-business is important, very important or essential. For the lagging sectors (which also include construction and retail and wholesale as well as hotels and restaurants) the figures are between 40 per cent and 55 per cent. This question of relevance is also effected by size – just over a third (34 per cent) of very small firms believe e-business is irrelevant to them, compared to just 7 per cent of firms employing more than 50 people.

The belief that e-business is not relevant is driven not just by internal business needs, but by some consideration of the external environment. For example, hotels and restaurants are more likely to believe that their customers, suppliers and competitors are not using e-business (45 per cent think this) than other sectors such as IT where only 10 per cent have this understanding. Hotels and restaurants are also more likely to believe that the cost of e-business investment is more likely to outweigh the benefits than other sectors, 45 per cent think this compared to 27 per cent of the IT sector. Attracting the interest of hotels and restaurants in e-business is obviously a tough task. Is this a good use of finite public sector resources?

Is e-Business Beneficial?

There is not a clear endorsement of the benefits of e-business in general. Although 68 per cent of firms overall believe that e-business is essential, very important or important, and 60 per cent state that they have experienced some benefit from their activities; 12 per cent stated it has been of little or no benefit, leaving a rather large proportion of firms which either did not or could not respond to the question.

Interestingly, those sectors with the highest IT adoption levels (IT and finance) were both the least satisfied in terms of non-financial benefits. This is probably because these firms are the most sophisticated and critical audience; they know about the potential of ICT but are frustrated by its ability to deliver in demanding applications or situations; particularly as they are more likely to be dependent on it for the smooth and profitable running of their firms than some other sectors. Construction, although a low IT adopter, was also a critical sector in terms of the benefits brought by IT as it reports slightly lower than average satisfaction in terms of the financial benefits generated by IT. Very small firms were also highly critical, despite not being the highest adopters. In these two cases, it may be that the sectors lack the technical or skills capabilities and knowledge to get the most from their investment.

This picture is further complicated when we look at responses to a question which asked about cost savings enabled by the adoption of IT. Here, IT firms were the most satisfied sector (54 per cent) in terms of saving money, despite recognising relatively few benefits from IT, whereas only 35 per cent of finance firms felt they had made financial savings (as well as not recognising benefits). It is not immediately clear why this behaviour should be so. Larger firms were also more likely to report cost savings than very small ones (56 per cent and 30 per cent respectively).

On the positive side, there are other tangible benefits to be gained from e-business, but even here there are mixed messages – the level of enthusiasm is not high, with the most frequently cited benefit (increased efficiency) benefiting less than a quarter of firms (see Figure 5.5). Taking a longer term view, efficiency gains should in turn lead to increased productivity. It is even possible that increased turnover or profitability may result; which is good for the individual company, and collectively would be good for London.

Another positive impact is that 80–90 per cent of firms with IT-enabled processes are happy with them (the precise figure changes depending on how many IT-enabled processes there are in a firm), although IT and manufacturing firms are less satisfied.

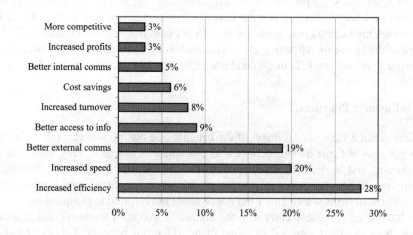

Figure 5.5   Benefits of e-business adoption
Source: Business Link for London (2004)

The process which generates the lowest satisfaction rates is customer relationship management (with an average of 88 per cent), the best performing process is stock control/production (94 per cent).

ICT and Growth

It is not clear if a positive attitude towards e-business is merely held by active, growing businesses or whether there is a more causal relationship between the two factors, i.e. the acquisition of technology is causing the growth. This could be the subject of another piece of research.

However, it is clear that there is a divide between different types of firm. Analysis of e-business attitudes in 2003 showed that 93 per cent of 'fast adopters' (high levels of ICT adoption, high awareness of support, high fast growth expectations) believed e-business to be essential, whereas only 29 per cent of a 'low interest' group (low levels of ICT adoption, low awareness of support, low fast growth expectations) believed this. As previously shown, very small firms and SMEs in Objective 2 areas are more likely to be in this latter group. It is important for business support providers not to exacerbate this divide.

The same trends prevailed in 2004, when a further relationship was discovered between firms expressing general business optimism and their propensity to invest in and use ICT. For example, firms which perceive themselves to be 'growing very fast' have an average ICT adoption level (across internet access, LAN, email and website) of 77 per cent. Firms which think they are 'staying the same size' have adoption rates of 50 per cent. Unfortunately in London, we know that most firms, when measured by turnover or productivity, are in fact staying the same size or decreasing; not growing. This means that despite the many encouraging signs on ICT adoption in London, policy and delivery bodies cannot afford to relax their efforts to offer ICT-related business support. There is a distinct danger that left untended, this is an area where a current competitive edge may become blunted.

Conclusions

Technology take-up not uniform

There are a number of interlinked conclusions arising from these two survey waves. E-business adoption by SMEs in London is increasing, but there are still patches of disadvantage. Very small firms and those that are BME-owned are lagging in their take-up, use and exploitation of ICT. Women-owned firms are also slightly disadvantaged, particularly in ICT take-up. There appears to better news on firms in Objective 2 areas, ICT take-up for them has increased markedly, although as the sample sizes are not consistent between the two waves, this is still an area which could be investigated further. There are clear sectoral differences in the take up of technology, with some sectors consistently lagging on virtually all metrics; particularly hotels and restaurants.

Costs and consumers driving business use?

The emergence of new technologies which are used in consumer and 'private life' may be a way to drive business technology adoption (email use and broadband access have rocketed); coupled with the decrease in costs. New wireless technologies are still in their infancy. Future work should track their take-up, although it seems clear that many firms prefer to use their technology supplier to get information, so perhaps the strength of demand for emerging technologies is partly dependent on the strength of supplier support.

Adoption, satisfaction and benefits

Unsurprisingly, levels of ICT awareness are related to online transactions; with higher technology adopters more likely to transact online. However, the benefits of ICT adoption are not always felt most by the fastest adopters, or most intense users of ICT. It is not clear if this unease is to do with early adoption or the sophistication of adoption and the uses to which ICT is put in these expert environments. For example, the IT sector is the most intensive user of ICT but it is not the most satisfied. Overall, the majority of firms are more satisfied with their ICT adoption than dissatisfied. Benefits include increased efficiency, faster work, and enhanced external communications, but firms are quite vague about the precise nature of these benefits, few are able to quantify them.

Business support could do better

Generally awareness and take-up of e-business support is low. Two thirds of firms are not aware of any sources of assistance; although 50 per cent admit they have problems that need solving. This lack of awareness, coupled with skills problems, and low rate of engagement with the potential of e-business in some sectors, means that a continuation of the strong take-up of ICT is not guaranteed. The prospect of a real 'digital divide' between sectors is also apparent; with the danger that the uninformed and/or the disillusioned will just 'switch off'.

To avoid exacerbating disparities between firms, it is clear that *targeted* information and support is vital according to the needs of different groups. Low e-business adopters still need awareness raising, and practical assistance on the benefits of using ICT and security issues. More sophisticated users need to help them measure and maximise the return on ICT investment by applying e-strategies to turn their current e-business facilities into true e-business capabilities.

But it's a tough problem to crack ...

It will be a 'hard sell' trying to convince certain firms and certain sectors to change their behaviour. There is active resistance to change in some sectors. This either stems from an understanding that change is not necessary or from a belief that the right help is not available. In the UK at least, there are significant changes occurring as national government has decided to disperse major business support funds regionally instead of centrally – this should mean that business support services are better aligned with regional priorities. Across Europe there are certainly competing demands on tightening budgets, so this is perhaps the time to clarify the objectives of publicly funded business support.

Should public resources be spent on assisting 'weaker' firms to embrace the advantages of ICT or would monies be better spent on helping stronger firms become even better? Although much public business support policy is moving away from the old idea of 'picking winners'; it is not clear how agencies, particularly regional agencies, can balance the needs of those firms facing higher barriers to achievement than the 'norm', with their usual aspirations to promote growth, productivity and economic or other forms of success. A related question in some regions is the extent to which policy should be focused on 'disadvantaged' firms or business owners, to meet diversity, community, and social exclusion targets and programmes, or whether it should concentrate on the mainstream. This is an extremely difficult public policy area.

In London, for instance, the Regional Development Agency (the London Development Agency) seeks to balance its traditionally very strong social inclusion and regeneration-led strategy with its new responsibilities for business support. Its new strategy for economic development (London Development Agency, 2004) maintains the inclusive approach by specifically highlighting the needs of certain groups of business owners, specifically women, BME entrepreneurs, disabled people or other 'equalities groups' such as young entrepreneurs. It does not, however, specifically highlight the needs of firm by size, location or age, and it is apparent that sector-based solutions will only be used when there is a compelling need to do so.

At the delivery level, should we continue the 'drip, drip' approach to continually raise awareness of ICT and demonstrate its use, benefit and value to an ever changing pool of businesses; or is the time for something new and radically different? Difficult decisions are compounded by the need to meet stretching targets. For example, Business Link for London aims to reach 100,000 SMEs by the end of 2005–06; one third of the entire business population of the capital. To do this it has developed an award-winning online service (see www.bl4london.com) alongside traditional personal service delivery to reach far more SMEs than it could do on a one to one basis. Most services are free, others are usually subsidised.

Alternative Scenarios

One new idea being considered for London, although it may already in use elsewhere, is the provision of 'vouchers' to allow SMEs to purchase whatever help they require from approved suppliers. Whilst this may encourage the supply side to deliver whatever is being demanded, a drawback is that many firms are constrained by their inability to see the potential of ICT. In the somewhat hackneyed phrase of experienced business support professionals 'business often don't know what they don't know'; so demand for assistance is inarticulate. Coupled with the survey finding that some sectors are either indifferent or actively hostile to change, then it seems likely that the demand for ICT support will be weakly expressed at best, and fundamentally weak, at worst.

Another idea is to promote diagnostics as a way of helping a firm uncover where its strengths and weaknesses lie. This is a good idea but needs careful execution. Self-assessment diagnostics can be self-limiting if the firm undertaking the diagnostic is not overly-familiar with the topic under discussion – and as the survey has shown, many sectors are unaware of the potential or even the strategic imperative to adopt ICT. Managed assessment is usually far more effective, but can be resource intensive.

Then there is the question: 'What exactly is being diagnosed'? Is it IT user skills, the strategic use of ICT in a firm, its technical capabilities, the optimal alignment of its all IT-enabled systems, or its potential to make money from online sales for example? And how does this link into the rest of the business? Remedying ICT problems without understanding the rest of the business can be disastrous, particularly given the costs often associated with capital investment and training.

Lastly, an embryonic and emerging idea is the investigation of the viability of a new advisory service dedicated to ICT issues. This would be available to any SME; accessible via phone, web or face to face interaction. In London such a service is provisionally entitled the 'IT Advisory Service'; its ultimate aim is to join up sources of learning support, i.e. skills development, and business support which are currently funded via different channels and presented separately to employers.

Overall, there is no quick fix to these questions. But given the steep decline in large scale public promotion and awareness programmes, the transfer of the delivery of personal business help on ICT from in-house at Business Link for London to a network of external professionals; and the transfer of control of business support funding to the London Development Agency it seems clear that there is a great opportunity to make a difference and strengthen ICT-related business support in the capital. The corollary of this, unfortunately, is that there is also a chance of a hiatus in the delivery of ICT support to the mainstream of SMEs.

References

Business Link for London (2003), *Analysis of VAT-Registered Businesses in Greater London and its sub-regions*, Business Link for London, London.

Business Link for London (2003), *E-business in London*, Business Link for London.

Business Link for London (2004), *E-business in London*, Business Link for London.

Department of Trade and Industry (DTI) (2004) *International Benchmarking Study*, Department of Trade and Industry, London.

FRESA (2004), *Information and Communication Technologies for Small and Medium Sized Enterprises in London: Research Report*. FRESA, London.

London Development Agency (2004), *Sustaining Success: Developing London's Economy, Economic Development Strategy*, London Development Agency, London.

London Development Agency and Business Link for London (2004), *London Annual Business Survey*, London Development Agency, London.

Small Business Service (2004a), *Business Start-Ups and Closures: Vat Registrations and de-registrations in 2003*, Small Business Service, London.

Small Business Service (2004b), *Survival Rates of Vat Registered Businesses 1993 – 2001*, Small Business Service, London.

Chapter 6

The Value of Internet Forums to Small Rural Businesses

Robert Mochrie, Laura Galloway and David Deakins

Introduction

There is an extensive body of literature on the effects of rural location upon business behaviour in Britain. Roberts (2002) and Smallbone *et al.* (2002), for example, focus on barriers to SME growth and the public policies that attempt to overcome them. They reflect concerns about the deteriorating financial and employment performance of rural SMEs relative to urban ones through the late 1990s, detailed in Cosh and Hughes (2000). One possible cause of this relative change is a decline in the rate of innovation within rural areas, although as North and Smallbone (2000) argue, innovation rates are generally more strongly determined by sectoral influences than by rurality itself. With the increasing use of information and communications technologies (ICTs) in business, the decline in the rate of innovation could be related to low rates of ICT adoption across rural businesses.

In this chapter, we explore some of the links between ICT adoption and business growth and relate them to the current policy debate on the adoption of ICTs. It begins with a review of conceptual arguments. In this, various causes of slow adoption of ICTs are classified according to their effect on the supply of ICTs in rural areas, or else upon rural businesses' willingness to use ICTs. We suggest that the problems of supply can be remedied through public intervention, but that demand side issues will often result from profit maximizing behaviour. The review concludes by arguing that SMEs have the capacity to develop (independently or in conjunction with other businesses) the physical and human capital necessary to undertake effective adoption strategies.

We then suggest reasons for collaborative strategies being more effective than individual implementation of ICT adoption. It is suggested that collaboration might take place in either industry based or local groups Such groupings could behave in a variety of ways and so there is discussion of the possible effects of different types of organizational form upon behaviour. This leads into a presentation of the results of our survey of ICT use in rural Scottish businesses, and a review of the behaviour of five emerging internet forums.

Adoption of ICTs by Rural Businesses

Roberts (2002) and Smallbone *et al*. (2002) provide an extensive overview of the literature documenting the effects of rural location upon business behaviour within the UK. They list many barriers to SME growth and review the public policies designed to overcome them. Although they draw on similar sources, in analysing the apparently slower adoption of ICTs among rural SMEs, they offer quite different explanations. Roberts (2002) emphasizes the importance of limited access to communications networks and technology, high usage costs and limited relevant content. This is the supply side argument, in which slow e-commerce adoption results from competition from other ICTs that provide adequate services and are more effective in enabling SMEs to meet their business goals. This emphasizes the role of additional public support in relation to networks into rural areas, and the development of content relevant to potential users.

The alternative case is made in Smallbone *et al*. (2002). While acknowledging the importance of access issues, this concentrates upon gaps in labour force skills and the reluctance on the part of rural business owners to adapt to the changing environment, identified by Freshwater (2001). It also emphasizes the role of industry mix examined by Mitchell and Clark (1999) and North and Smallbone (2000). In these papers, rural SMEs are presented as being slow to understand the benefits of ICT adoption. Low demand is then a result of information failure among potential users. Policy has a role in providing information, training support and disseminating good practice.

Justifying this position, Mitchell and Clark (1999) distinguish between locally and globally oriented businesses. Locally oriented SMEs operate close to suppliers and customers, while the suppliers and customers of globally oriented SMEs are much more dispersed. They argue that global orientation is the best predictor of rural SMEs' growth. Rapid ICT adoption is most likely within globally oriented businesses (if only) because adoption is necessitated by 'external dependency'. While recognising that characteristics of business owners, such as age or education, also affect adoption decisions, global orientation is treated as an important exogenous factor driving business strategy in this model.

We treat this argument as a refinement of the well-developed literature that studies innovative behaviour in rural SMEs and which emphasizes growth rather than global orientation. North and Smallbone (2000) summarize the findings of these papers, noting that growth oriented SMEs exist in all industries and localities, and that they are distinguished by their relatively high rate of innovation. Linkages between global and growth orientation can then be justified by the argument of Vaessen and Keeble (1995) that growth oriented SMEs in peripheral regions have small local markets that they can tap, and so require to 'export' beyond their home region at an earlier stage in their development than SMEs in core regions. This suggests that businesses in remote rural regions might adopt ICTs especially quickly because SMEs in such localities are more likely to adopt a global orientation at an early stage of their development than businesses in other areas.

The similarity between growth and global orientation could also be understood in terms of the nature of the underlying business. We suppose that local orientation is consistent with businesses relying upon strong personal relationships between customers and suppliers, or facing significant costs of operating some distance from their customers. In contrast, external orientation is consistent with strategies in which relationships with customers are based on the efficient execution of business activity. External orientation then drives the adoption of ICTs because they reduce business costs significantly, increasing market opportunities. However, Smallbone *et al.* (2002, citing CRE, 2000) also argue that it is important to support locally oriented SMEs, 'concentrated in highly embedded sectors such as transport and construction serving local markets'.

It has to be considered, however, that orientation might also constrain business objectives, for orientation seems to be determined by a combination of technology and the structure of the business environment. Thus successful locally oriented businesses might be considered to exploit well-defined market niches in which they exert monopoly power, while avoiding competition from other businesses. Business risk emerges through technological change eroding monopoly power. Such businesses accept limited growth of sales, employment and profits in exchange for a relatively stable and predictable trading environment.

By definition, SMEs have only limited power to transform the environment that they face. For many service businesses, capital exists in the skills and knowledge of employees, and the costs of providing services at a distance can be very high. Smallbone *et al.* (2002) argues that this is likely to have an adverse effect upon the quality of service provided in rural areas. The establishment of strong relationships with both customers and suppliers, facilitated through face-to-face meetings and the use of older ICTs, such as telephones and faxes, is also likely to be important. Understood in this sense, local orientation is almost a necessity, but one that limits the opportunities for growth. The relatively small potential client base also lowers the probability of businesses undertaking rapid innovation and novel or risky developments. In contrast, externally oriented businesses do not have a well-defined local market, and so face a more competitive environment. Business risk comes from the possibility that other businesses might be able to undertake product or process innovation, rendering the firm uncompetitive. To the extent that external orientation leads to a greater tendency to innovate, as suggested by Mitchell and Clark (1999) and North and Smallbone (2000), the adoption of ICT is likely to be especially rapid in such businesses.

These explanations of SME performance work together. A rural SME, in implementing an innovation, experiences a period of growth that necessitates a change in spatial orientation. In much of the literature, there is an implicit presumption that all SMEs define success in terms of their ability to achieve such outcomes. But local orientation and slow growth can be understood as emerging from the ability to satisfy business owners' objectives which might include generating a sufficient income to continue to live in the location where the business is situated. Local orientation ensures high quality services within that community and profitability comes from the ability to exert a degree of monopoly power.

We regard local orientation and slow growth as being the normal state for a rural SME. Innovative behaviour and planned growth are then anomalous for most businesses and so we follow Galloway and Wilson (2003) in arguing that they might be expected to occur in recently established SMEs, or else only sporadically during the typical SME's life. Assuming that local rural markets will already be serviced by locally oriented incumbent businesses, the entrant innovators need to look further afield for sales, and thus global orientation emerges in many cases. For example, among rural SMEs that are typically externally oriented, we count high value-added food processing businesses. These tend to compete against other regionally based producers, but rely upon national or international sales to survive, and their external orientation is simply a result of the business environment. As suggested above, remote delivery suggests that customer needs and wants should be met through the efficient execution of routines. Competition based on efficiency then drives innovation, creating at least the appearance of growth orientation.

There is, however, an alternative explanation of the effects of locale, for it can be used in developing and promoting the product. Product differentiation is then achieved through tying the perceptions of quality to the place of origin. Such branding reduces the importance of process, increases linkages with customers and leads to the establishment of monopoly power similar to the local power exploited by locally oriented firms. Businesses that achieve a degree of location-based brand identity seem likely to be under less pressure to adopt a growth orientation. But since external orientation is always dependent upon relationships between physically distant partners, this by itself seems likely to promote ICT adoption.

Many previous studies report that ICT diffusion has been very slow among rural SMEs. Smallbone and North (1999) report very low levels of take-up of web based marketing, results echoed by Sparkes and Thomas (2001) and Baourakis *et al.* (2002) with respect to the food industry. The results of Sparkes and Thomas (2001) are particularly relevant, since they surveyed businesses producing high quality, high value-added food products that benefit from strong brand and product differentiation, often based upon the locality in which production takes place. They found that such businesses seemed likely to have a strong global orientation, but that relatively few appeared to have developed effective strategies for integrating web-based technologies within relationship marketing processes, either at the business-consumer or the business-business level.

The conventional model of SME behaviour underpinning rural policy interventions treats innovation as the driver of employment and income growth. It is argued that ICT adoption, as a form of innovation, deserves support because of its potential impact on the health both of individual businesses and the rural economy more generally. For this claim to be justified, SMEs' use of ICTs has to be innovative, at least at the level of the firm, and this cannot be guaranteed. For this reason, within the policy literature, Fuller and Southern (1999) criticize government policies based on 'technology push' as being unlikely to engage with the business development needs of many rural SMEs. Warren (2000) examines in some detail the response to such policies within the farming sector, and, as noted above, Smallbone *et al*. (2002) note the need for policy to support internally oriented, low growth SMEs on the grounds that their presence is essential to the continued functioning of rural communities.

Despite their concerns about the form of government intervention, Fuller and Southern (1999) recognize the value of imaginative ICT adoption for rural businesses. The lack of engagement is noted by Mitchell and Clark (1999), in one of the few recent studies that considers the use of stand-alone, rather than networked, ICTs. They found that the majority of locally oriented SMEs make very limited use of computing facilities, typically using computers for 'word processing, financial management and producing accounts'. This limited usage of ICTs is consistent with businesses simply treating computers as office equipment that reduces the costs of secretarial and clerical services. Such attitudes limit the possibility of ICTs being used in innovative ways, such as e-commerce. However, Warren (2000), argues that for micro-businesses in particular, limited use of ICTs can be a rational response to the business environment. A counter to this anti-development tendency may the localised support advocated by Smallbone *et al*. (2002) in which control of training is located within local communities and industrial clusters The alternative that we explore in this paper involves locating this training within networks established and controlled by local communities with the objectives of providing easy access and ensuring content relevance.

Community Based Support Services

An internet forum is a locally controlled organization designed to promote the use of web based technologies among businesses operating in some specified locality, whether in a particular sector of activity, or more generally. A minimum requirement for such for a forum is the establishment of a common web portal that publishes information about members and include links to members' websites. A forum brings together businesses and provides them with an entry in a virtual business directory. For community based forums, membership might be expected to support the emergence of e-commerce activity, with additional sales and promotion channels developing. For sector based forums, the emphasis might be on business-to-business linkages, and the development of supply chains.

A forum must provide other services to distinguish it from an online directory. For example, a community based forum might provide a local news service, information about social events, or information of use to visitors to the area. An industrial sector forum might offer consumers general information, or be associated with a trade body engaged in activities such as quality assurance schemes and representation of members at trade fairs. By increasing content, additional services encourage visits to the forum website, from which will come visits to members' websites. Additionally, as suggested by Sparkes and Thomas (2001), registering forum websites with a range of search engines, and including keywords and meta-tags that lead to the sites being placed high on the listing from relevant searches, leads to the forum emerging as the virtual front door to the community, enhancing its reputation further.

The development of such forums does not appear to have been advocated anywhere within the rural policy literature. Nonetheless, as an organizational form, it appears to meet many of the criteria for potentially successful intervention identified by Fuller and Southern (1999) and Huggins and Izushi (2002).

Control of the organization is embedded within the local community. In situations where low take up rates can be addressed by a 'supply-push', a forum can encourage the development of locally provided services, in conjunction with other public authorities. But where low take-up rates result from demand-side failures, a forum, like any other public intervention, faces substantial challenges. There is the potential for members' attitudes to constrain the forum, ensuring that their limited engagement with new technologies continues. Nonetheless, if the staff of a forum are willing to engage with members and help them to address their needs, they should be able to meet the challenges of demand side failure very well. Our expectation is that successful forums will be formed by groups of businesses that are open to process innovation, possibly dependent upon external linkages, and willing to enter into a period of growth. In other words, among the proponents of a local internet forum, we expect to find many globally oriented businesses.

Methodology

A telephone questionnaire explored many aspects of the ICT adoption behaviour of the sampled businesses, which were drawn from across various regions of Scotland, and also from a wide variety of industries. As well as identifying membership of internet, there were questions on use of stand-alone IT and web based technology, the effects of these technologies upon business activity, and the business' perceived need for training and other resources to make more effective use of existing technology.

The sample was constructed through a random selection from databases held by various local development bodies in remote rural areas of Scotland (from the south of Scotland near the English border to the Orkneys in the North Sea). Five internet forums were also identified, two in Orkney, one in Caithness, and two in the South of Scotland. To ensure comparability of firms within the sample by geographical area, businesses were added from the Yellow Pages. Altogether, 324 rural business were identified with a response rate of 35 per cent, a final sample of 113 firms.

Questionnaires were administered by telephone between April and July 2003, following the successful trial of a draft version with a small number of businesses in a focus group in March 2003. Respondents were typically the owner of the business or else its manager. In addition, qualitative analysis of the behaviour of five internet forums, whose members had been sampled within the telephone questionnaire was undertaken. Information was obtained through a series of extended on-site interviews arranged with the managers of the sampled forums. These were designed to elicit a fuller, deeper understanding of the forums' operating environment, the motivation for establishing them, their organizational structures and histories, and, most importantly, the challenges that they face, especially problems of long-term sustainability.

Such a case study methodology has been shown to be effective in obtaining this type of information because it afford us 'experiential understanding' (Stake, 1995), while still allowing for comparison (Yin, 1994). Indeed, according to Yin (1994) case studies are used when it is recognized that phenomena and context are inseparably linked. This is relevant to the current study since being based within a locale and using the locale as a focal point, a local rural forum can only function and be understood within the context of local circumstances.

Triangulation of research is particularly important due to the inevitability of subjectivity when data is based entirely on one to one open-ended interviews (Cassell and Symon, 1994; Stake, 1995; Yin, 1994). Fortunately, for the current research triangulation was possible by simply visiting the 'forum' anonymously on-line in order to corroborate much of that which had been learnt from interviews. Other triangulation materials were made available, such as internal forum reports, and public sector research documents that included the forum in the remit.

Findings

Telephone survey

The characteristics of the business owners in the sample were very similar to those found in other research. There were slightly fewer aged over 45 and more under 30 than is usual, two thirds were male, and two fifths had lived in the area for the whole of their lives. A large majority were microfirms, with the average number of employees (including the owner) 8.08 and the median annual turnover, of those reporting turnover (a relatively small fraction of the sample) £85,000. Median turnover shows some signs of recovering from the levels of 2001-02, when many rural businesses experienced difficult trading conditions following the outbreak of foot and mouth disease. The majority of the businesses were also well established, with 61 per cent more than 10 years old, and only 18 per cent formed within the last three years. As expected, firms were most frequently engaged in providing personal and business service, with just over 75 per cent undertaking such activities. Growth was not an important objective for most businesses (only for 14 per cent of the sampled firms). Table 6.1 shows that the most important constraint on business growth was perceived to be consumer demand. This might consistent with growth orientation requiring an external trading orientation.

Further evidence on the role of external orientation and growth is presented in Table 6.2. This shows that businesses tend to rely upon local and regional sales and suppliers (though, part of the sample, drawn from Southern Scotland could respond

Table 6.1   Importance   of   perceived   constraints   on business growth

	Percent
Consumer demand	57
Competition	39
Environmental factors	24
Appropriate and qualified staff	23
Accessing resources	21
Change in business concept	41
Other factors	31

Table 6.2   Average sales to local markets and use of local suppliers (percentages)

	Customers	Suppliers
Local	25	23
Regional	26	17
National	32	30
International	17	31

that English suppliers, are international). The sales into international markets of 17 per cent suggest only limited export capacity.

Thus, there appears to be rapid catch up in e-commerce related activities on the part of small firms in rural areas. No less than 89 per cent of all respondent firms were using a computer and, of these, 94 per cent claimed to use their computer at least once daily for business purposes. Use of the Internet was also reported as being nearly universal among these businesses. However, access to more advanced communication hardware such as ISDN/ADSL was still relatively low, with only 30 per cent reporting ISDN access, and none reporting ADSL access. Over 99 per cent had access to printers, 72 per cent had access to scanners and 50 per cent reported using laptops in the business.

It is helpful to distinguish the use of stand alone PCs, and associated applications, from e-business and access to the Internet. Respondents almost invariably used PCs for word processing (99 per cent), and very frequently for record keeping (84 per cent), accountancy (79 per cent) and database management (70 per cent). Important other uses were design and related activities such as web design, graphics and desk-top publishing. This appears to reflect the relatively high proportion of businesses in the sample providing ICT support services, possibly a feature of the sampling method. The important point is that almost all businesses have found a role for computer-based support in their activities.

Table 6.3 Effects of adoption of stand-alone PCs on business performance (percentages, N = 99)

	Some effect	Ranked 1st	Ranked 2nd	Ranked 3rd	Sum of Ranks
Improved information processing	84	30	12	10	51
Improved planning	67	4	12	5	22
Increased sales	65	11	9	10	30
Increased profit	65	11	11	5	28
Entry into new markets	59	5	5	8	18
Reduced costs	59	4	10	9	23
Increased diversification	53	4	8	6	18
Increased employment	13	1	2	3	5

Table 6.4 Participation in e-business (percentages, N = 113)

	Percent
Business having their own website	60
Providing information about the business and its products	57
Enabling customers to pay on-line	37
Enabling customers to print off order forms	19
Other	13

As shown in Table 6.3, businesses most frequently report that stand-alone ICT has improved processing of information. The frequency with which improved planning, sales and profit were reported were similar, but stand-alone ICT effects improved sales and profits more than planning. Again, this is consistent with previous reports of the use of stand-alone ICTs.

There was also a relatively high level of use of networked technologies, with 80 per cent of the full sample of 115 having access to internet technologies. In spite of this high level of access, a significantly higher proportion of firms reported beneficial effects on their business performance from ICT-related technologies, using stand alone PCs or related software applications rather than networked technologies and e-business. This suggests that networked applications are not yet integrated into the businesses' processes in the same way as stand-alone technologies. Table 6.4 reports on some of the uses of networked technologies. We noted earlier that 99 per cent of computer owners reported having access to the Internet. E-business adoption was, however, rather lower. Some 60 per cent of the total sample reported that the business had its own website. However, most firms only use their website to provide customers with information, rather than offering more advanced services such as on-line sales or printing off order forms online.

Table 6.5   Expected effects of changes in website (percentages, N=33)

	Percent with 'Some effect;
Increased sales	94
Increased profit	88
Entry into new markets	79
Increased diversification	67
Improved planning	61
Improved processing of information	57
Increased employment	36
Reduced costs	27

Only a minority of 33 firms had plans to use their websites over the next two years to improve business performance. Table 6.5 reveals that the expected effects are concentrated upon sales and profits; the impact of internet on developing new markets, diversification and planning is expected to be more substantial than the improved processing of information. Given the low numbers, it is difficult to assess the importance of the expected positive effects of increasing internet presence.

Of the 115 businesses sampled, thirty one (27 per cent) reported that they were members of Internet forums. Among the businesses that reported that they were forum members, 61 per cent gave increased sales as the main motive for joining, compared to 39 per cent that reported the need for a holistic package with ready access to a web site. It appears that forum members mainly seek to use the forum to increase sales, already having begun to engage with e-business practices through their own website.

Previous research suggests that members of internet forums should tend to be more growth-orientated, have more diverse markets and sales, be more innovative in using ICTs and possibly also utilize sources of assistance, such as support agencies. The results regarding these issues are now examined in more detail. Respondents valued membership of forums because they contribute to their ability and potential of increasing sales and profits. No less than 80 per cent of firms agreed that membership increased profit, while 60 per cent of firms claimed that membership increased sales. Respondents also frequently mentioned the value of internet forums in providing business support and benefits flowing from participation in networks, as shown in Table 6.6.

There were statistically significant differences in perceptions of the effect on business performance of ICT adoption between forum members and non-members. Table 6.7 shows that members were more likely to believe that ICT usage had led to increases in sales and profitability, and hence on business growth. There were no significant differences in perceptions on the effect of ICT usage on information processing, entry to new markets or diversification. This suggests that forum members

Table 6.6   B2B services used by internet forum firms (percentages)

	Percent
Industry support	50
Business networking	46
Business advice	41
Other contacts	38
Sourcing suppliers	32
Other service	10

Table 6.7   Membership of internet forums and ICT adoption effects (percentages)

	Firms in Internet Forum	Firms not in Internet Forums
Increased sales*	81	56
Increased profits*	83	56
Entry to new markets	65	60
Increased diversification	45	60
Improved information processing	87	85

* $p < 0.05$ for chi-squared statistic

are still using e-business as a communication channel and a selling mechanism, but have not yet started to use it to improve their marketing efforts.

Forum members seem to have a higher external orientation than non-members. They tended to report higher levels of international sales than non-members, with 22 per cent of members reporting that more than half their sales were international, compared with 14 per cent of non-members, a statistically significant difference. We did not investigate the direction of causation here, so cannot say whether membership leads to an increased international presence, or whether businesses that are dependent on exports are more likely to join forums.

These were the only statistically significant differences that we were able to identify between forum members and non-members. Among non-members, 69 per cent stated that the firm had developed a website, with 82 per cent of these being the business's own, rather than part of a larger domain. Firms in rural areas appear to recognize at least some of the advantages of having an Internet presence for accessing markets, given the dispersed markets in which they trade.

Table 6.8   Summary profiles of internet forums

Case	Age (yrs)	Base	Funding at start	Decision makers	Original focus	Formal evaluation
A	3+	Locality	Private	Proprietor	Business	No
B	3+	Industry	Public	Members	Business	No
C	2-3	Locality	Private	Proprietor	Community	No
D	1-2	Locality	Public	Committee	Community	Yes
E	1-	Locality	Public	Committee	Business	Yes

Qualitative analysis of internet forums

Of the five forums studies, four simply used locality as the focal point, while the fifth was based upon a distinct industry specific to the locality. Table 6.8 summarizes a number of key features of the forums.

Table 6.8 shows that each forum has emerged through a different process. Forums B, D and E were publicly funded at the start, with Forums B and E starting as a result of a community (industrial and local respectively) seeking public funding, while Forum D emerged from of a public sector initiative.

Case A was a privately owned concern originally designed as a portal and services provider to a specific industry within the locale. It has since developed its remit to include any business within the locality. Upon development local public sector agents became involved at a strategic level via funding, as it was believed that the facility could have the potential to be of local economic benefit.

Case B was created by local public sector agents as a means of supporting a specific industry within the locale. While several forms of collaboration and communication were possible via this facility, and had been considered by members, the forum served mainly as a common marketing tool, using the locale and the industry as a branding mechanism. Inclusion in the forum, however, also implied quality, as in order to become members, businesses were judged with respect to quality of product offered. The forum was maintained by membership subscriptions eventually replacing public funding.

Case C was developed as a perceived business opportunity that embraced the founder's loyalty and attachment to the locality. It was a for-profit privately owned company, which originally aimed to serve community groups, but had developed subsequently to provide local businesses with an Internet portal, web-site development and services.

Case D was originally created in response to three needs. The local training agency faced demands from the community for ICT training; the LEC and local authority were keen to promote social inclusion; and the local branch of a business support agency was required to address the national remit to provide an online business directory. The resulting facility, while having a business directory, was actually intended for community use as an aid to increase awareness, interest and participation in ICT. Having become operational shortly before the interview, it was included because its plans include expansion of business services.

Case E was developed as part of a wider community regeneration scheme. It was linked to the established community web-site, and was created in response to local demand for improved business services, support and partnerships. The forum is part of a holistic business promotion project, funded by public sector grants, and is directed entirely by the community via committee.

In cases A and C, decisions about content and strategy were taken by the owner manager, with some consultation with the community in Case C. In cases B and E, strategy and content were decided via an iterative process involving forum members (case B) and the community (case E). Case D appeared to lack structure and decisions seemed to be taken in an ad hoc manner.

The organizational structure that had emerged in Case D had proven to be problematic since inception. Content about the area existed on a draft website, but had not been incorporated into the online version. There was considerable confusion about the division of responsibility for developing the facility between local staff and the commercial contractor that was building, hosting and maintaining the site. Forward planning was limited. Although better organized generally, other forums also had experienced considerable strategic and structural difficulties. For example, in Case A, public sector agencies had not always provided promised support as they sought to maintain an element of control.

All of the forum co-ordinators were asked why they thought businesses would seek inclusion. The co-ordinator of Case B claimed that businesses perceived the advantages of joint marketing. The others claimed that businesses joined in order to obtain internet presence. Further questioning elicited quite varied beliefs about the nature of benefits from participation. The co-ordinator of Case B claimed baldly that she could not define any specific benefits, and the co-ordinator of Case D claimed that potentially it would give businesses access to markets, but that there are no plans to develop this potential. The others identified local development and economic benefits. The co-ordinators of Cases A and E argued that ICT skills and ICT participation rates will improve locally as a result of the existence and use of the forum. Co-ordinators of Cases A, C and E also believed that inclusion facilitated increased orders, partnership building, and opened up additional marketing channels for businesses.

Exploring the role of forums further, co-ordinators were asked about the range of services that they were trying to provide to members. In Cases A and E, a long term aim was to have subscribers hosted by the forum. In the short-term, links between businesses, and provision of services to increase businesses involvement in on-line activity, such as web-site building, and skills development, were seen as core provision. Forums C and D provided similar services, with a view to making advertising and Internet linking available on the forum web-site. The co-ordinator of Case B claimed that the forum did no more than include members' details of, and links to their sites, with inclusion on the forum site implying quality of product.

Business support information and advice was only available in Cases A and E. Case E, which had emerged from local development efforts had the capacity to provide the widest range of support to businesses. The appropriate range had been identified following discussions with the local business community. It included schemes to raise awareness, such as PC lending, and access to bespoke ICT training and consultancy. In terms of networking facilities, only Case C, which provided an on-line bulletin board, had anything appropriate for business use.

For a forum to be effective, it must be able to communicate its presence, so that membership leads to virtual visits by potential customers and suppliers, and possibly other businesses. It is therefore important for the forum to establish itself as the most widely recognized domain for the area, since locale will generally be its main selling point. All of the forums studied included at least part of the local area's name within the forum's domain name and this helped to ensure that the forums appeared in prominent positions in on-line search engine and directory listing. Indeed, two co-ordinators described the maintenance of high hit rates in this way as an important priority.

Content on the forum website is also important if visitors are to explore it sufficiently. Many visitors will have specific reasons for visiting the front page. Through tradition and aesthetic appeal, rural Scotland has strong attractors, supporting a relatively healthy tourist industry and a high profile worldwide. This is, no doubt, linked to some extent to a long history of emigration, and the idealisation of rural areas (referred to abstractly by, for example, Aitken, 1984). Internet forums can attract repeat visitors by recognising these specific demands. All of the co-ordinators appeared to be aware of the value of creating an on-line community of potential customers by using external perceptions of their locality. The co-ordinators of the two rural forums which used hit counters for evaluation purposes noted that hits had increased (in one case 'tripled overnight') after uploading a photograph gallery.

Reynolds (2000) argues that this bundling together of commercial content with more general information is relatively well established on the internet, with Amazon.com, for example, hosting reviews and suggestions to support and enhance its core selling function. People visiting a community through an internet forum may also be potential customers of a range of local produce, and may also be encouraged to visit the locality as tourists. Encouraging traffic to a forum should increase members' sales.

Through these means, forums might increase members' access to non-local markets. Such access should be maximized where businesses have integrated e-business activities fully within their operations, enabling, for example, on line sales. The interviews corroborated the telephone survey findings that a very small proportion of businesses had reached this stage of development, suggesting that growth orientation is not an important driver of rural business activity.

Contrary to the authors' prior expectations, the ICT skills possessed by co-ordinators and staff were highly variable. While Cases A, C and E had staff with specific ICT skills, Cases B and D did not. Only in Case A was the forum hosted by the co-ordinator, with a third party responsible for site maintenance in Cases B and

D. In these two cases, local co-ordinators were responsible for attracting members and sourcing content for the remote provider to upload. While some staff involved with Case D had some ICT skills, the sole staff member for Case B claimed neither to have nor to need any. Unsurprisingly, Case B did not provide ICT services for members in the form of web-site building, Internet-based business advice, etc., instead referring enquiries of this nature to the hosting business.

The widely variable scope of the forums' activities led to large variations in the numbers of salaried staff directly involved with the forum. The largest had several staff with specific remits (ICT development, marketing, and outreach), while the smallest had one part-time employee. The extent of out-sourcing of technical development was an important factor in determining staffing levels. In addition, some forums relied heavily on volunteers, or had partnerships with local support agents or community groups. The interviews did not suggest the existence of an optimal organizational form for a forum.

None of the forums studied had developed a strategy for maintaining participation rates. The co-ordinator of Case A claimed that at its creation, during the dot.com boom, local firms had been very interested in the forum, but that subsequently interest had been waning. It may also be that a lack of perceived benefits from membership has led to this falling away in interest. For other forums which had started more recently a similar effect might be observed either if free membership cannot be sustained or if only limited benefits can be found. Maintaining participation amongst businesses seems to be the key to sustainability. The case studies suggest a schematic model of the sort shown in Figure 6.1.

On the left side of Figure 6.1 are inputs necessary for the successful operation of an internet forum. This requires an identity and purpose in order to be able to define the scope of its operations. A local focus, perhaps of local history or other attractions of the area, helps to attract initial visitors to the site. Concentration on the

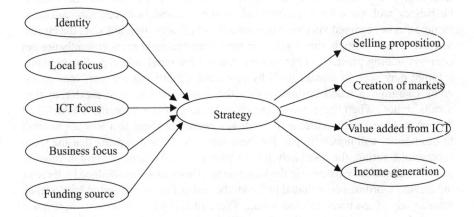

Figure 6.1   Elements of internet forum operation

ICT services that members are likely to require should enable the forum to develop additional services, encouraging more members to join. A business focus, being able to provide research about possible markets, might also prove attractive to potential members. Lastly, since the forum is unlikely to be profitable initially, a source of long term funding, together with clearly defined means of revenue generation will be required.

These strategic inputs will help the forum establish a successful business proposition, attracting members, and also promoting the local effectively. This provides opportunities for businesses to target new markets. The forum can also encourage the adoption of an e-business orientation among members, enabling them to develop value adding ICT facilities within their operations. Lastly, the forum will be able to charge for services, through such means as paid advertising on the website and consultancy fees. It appears that only Case C had attempted to most of these issues. Although the staff of all five forums were committed to their successful development, operational difficulties and strategic failings were widespread. This was most apparent in Cases D and E where no strategy to ensure sustainability has emerged, other than applying for further grant funding.

It may be that sustainability is almost impossible to achieve. For a forum to be effective, a virtual marketplace – or at least the potential for one – has to be created. Initially, much of a forum's resources and time must be spent on building a site and generating wider interest through the inclusion of content. Businesses will choose to join the forum if they believe that this site will attract substantially more visitors and potential customers than if the business hosts a site independently. Correspondingly, forums can often enjoy the additional revenue stream of web-site building for businesses. However, within a rural locale, with a limited number of businesses, this revenue stream has a finite life span. It is diminished further in the long-term if the forum provides ICT training, as the add-on market (site maintenance, hosting, etc.) will decrease as businesses become more sophisticated in using e-business. Eventually, an Internet forum may only be required to provide on-line links to businesses' web-sites. Revenue from links can be limited, however, although some income can be regained via charging a percentage of sales from links. As the current research shows, though, direct sales via the Internet in rural areas currently are not common trading practice. Other income streams are unreliable also. For example, a forum may seek to sustain itself by providing advertising for local businesses, or by charging included businesses (whether hosted or linked to the forum site) a subscription. The experience of the co-ordinators of the three most established forums included in the current research has been that there is a low upper limit to businesses' willingness to pay for these services. Thus it appears that the more successful a forum, the less likely it is to have income streams of enough value to allow for continued existence in the longer term. This was acknowledged by three of the forum co-ordinators included in the study, and is further supported by evidence from a study of one urban Internet forum, where alternative (and innovative) revenue streams had to be created to allow for continued forum provision (Galloway, 2001).

Conclusions

While the data does not contradict our hypothesis that a forum is a learning organization accelerating the dissemination of good business practice within a locality or an industry, the small sample size limits our ability to draw conclusions about the extent to which forums accelerate such tendencies. Businesses that are members of internet forums do seem to have greater external dependencies and to have started to experiment with more advanced online services than other businesses.

These data also demonstrate the extent to which the use of ICTs within rural SMEs is expanding. All businesses, irrespective of whether they are members of forums or not, now appear to use IT as an integral part of their business. While this use of IT is often purely to improve business efficiency, processing information more efficiently than in the past, the increasing use of applications such as databases suggests that the dissemination process might be slower in rural areas than in urban ones, but that it is definitely occurring.

In this context, it is possible that our investigation of internet forums is slightly premature. While constructing our sampling frame, it became clear that there are not many forums in Scotland. The forums that do exist are also very different in form. Thus in our qualitative study of emerging forums, we have tried to identify a range of critical success factors. Our initial findings indicate that successful forums tend to have clearly defined objectives that are broader than the promotion of a group of businesses or a locality. Where they do not, then their business model is unlikely to be sustainable over time, the forum will be unlikely to attract and retain the professional staff who are necessary to drive forward such a venture, and there will be no strategic plan for the development of the project. These failings are likely to reduce the attractiveness of the forum to potential members, prevent it from developing a portal that can act as the sort of virtual gateway identified above, and keep it from reaching the size necessary to be able to change the behaviour and attitudes of its members.

We believe that internet forums and other business networks have an important role to play in the diffusion of ICT in rural areas, enhancing the rate of innovation in member businesses. Given the importance of this objective in public policy, and the barriers to the successful emergence of forums that we have already found, there is an argument for public support of the establishment of these organizations. Appropriate policy might provide initial funding to permit the employment of staff who can build an attractive portal that enables the development of the forum. Beyond this, forum members would be required to develop a plan to ensure its sustainability in the medium term.

References

Aitken, A.J. (1984), 'Scots and English in Scotland', in P. Trudgill (Ed.) *Language in the British Isles*, Cambridge University Press, Cambridge.

Baourakis, G., Kourgiantis, M. and Migdalas, A. (2002), 'The Impact of e-Commerce on Agro-Food Marketing: The Case of Agricultural Cooperatives, Firms and Consumers in Crete', *British Food Journal*, Vol. 104, pp. 580–590.

Cassell, C. and Symon, G. (1994), 'Qualitative Research in Work Contexts' in C. Cassell and G. Symon (Eds.) *Qualitative Methods in Organizational Research: A Practical Guide*, Sage, London, pp.1–13.

CRE – Centre for Rural Economy (2000), *Rural Microbusinesses in North East England: Final Survey Results*, University of Newcastle on Tyne.

Cosh, A. and Hughes, A. (2000), 'British Enterprise in Transition: Growth, Innovation and Public Policy in the Small and Medium Sized Enterprise Sector 1994–99', ESRC Centre for Business Research, University of Cambridge.

Freshwater, D. (2001), 'Delusions of Grandeur: the Search for a Vibrant Rural America', TVA Rural Studies, University of Kentucky, Staff Paper 01–07.

Fuller, E. and Southern, A. (1999), 'Small Firms and Information and Communication Technologies: Policy Issues and Some Words of Caution', *Environment and Planning C: Government and Policy*, Vol. 17, pp. 287–302.

Galloway, L. (2001), *Virtual Scotland*, unpublished teaching case, University of Strathclyde.

Galloway, L. and Wilson, L. (2003), *The Use and Abuse of the Entrepreneur*, Heriot-Watt University, Discussion Paper DP2003–M03.

Huggins, R. and Izushi, H. (2002), 'The Digital Divide and ICT Learning in Rural Communities: Examples of Good Practice Service Delivery', *Local Economy*, Vol. 17, pp. 111–122.

Mitchell, S. and Clark, D. (1999), 'Business Adoption of Information and Communications Technologies in the Two-Tier Rural Economy: Some Evidence from the South Midlands', *Journal of Rural Studies*, Vol. 15, pp. 447–455.

North, D. and Smallbone, D. (2000), 'The Innovativeness and Growth of Rural SMEs during the 1990s', *Regional Studies*, Vol. 34, pp. 145–157.

Reynolds, J. (2000), 'E-commerce: A critical review', *International Journal of Retail and Distribution Management*, Vol. 28, pp. 417–444.

Roberts, S. (2002), *Key Drivers of Economic Development and Inclusion in Rural Areas*, DEFRA, London.

Smallbone, D. and North, D. (1999), 'Innovation and New Technology in Rural Small and Medium-Sized Enterprises: Some Policy Issues', *Environment and Planning C: Government and Policy*, Vol. 17, pp. 549–566.

Smallbone, D., North, D., Baldock, R. and Ekanem, I. (2002), *Encouraging and Supporting Enterprise in Rural Areas,* Middlesex University Business School.

Sparkes, A. and Thomas, B. (2001), 'The Use of the Internet as a Critical Success Factor for the Marketing of Welsh Agri-Food SMEs in the Twenty-First Century', *British Food Journal*, Vol. 103, pp. 331–347.

Stake, R.E. (1995), *The Art of Case Study Research*, Sage, London.

Vaessen, P. and Keeble, D. (1995), 'Growth-Oriented SMEs in Unfavourable Regional Environments', *Regional Studies*, Vol. 29, pp. 489–505.

Warren, M. (2000), 'Farmers, Computers and the Internet in Contrasting Areas of the UK: Implications for Rural Development', University of Plymouth.

Yin, R.K. (1994), *Case Study Research: Design and Methods* (2nd ed), Sage, London.

Chapter 7

e-Business and the Work Organization in Craft Enterprises

Sabine Wendt, Tatjana Grek and Lothar Lissner

e-Business in Craft Enterprises: Optimization of Work Organization

Craft enterprises introduce e-business applications mainly for two reasons. Firstly, they have to meet business requirements of large customers, who increasingly apply e-business solutions for more and more business processes with their suppliers. Secondly, e-business solutions might lead to mid-term and long-term reductions of costs.

The implementation of e-business procedures requires restructuring of office work in craft enterprises. All aspects such as quality, competence, flexibility and effectiveness of the office work are tackled. The introduction of e-business applications generates a restructuring of work contents and work flow. These changes directly affect the situation of the persons employed in the craft enterprises.

On one hand, it opens the chance to extend the individual scope of employees and to support their competence development. E-business solutions might offer the chance to promote the employees' motivation and performance as well as to make full use of their abilities and creative potential. On the other hand, there is a significant risk of more stress, less flexibility and in an overall reduction in skilled work tasks. Recent studies have confirmed that psychological stress will grow (Ritter *et al.*, 2003). This is likely to be particularly acute in very small craft enterprises, which have a very little division of labour. Indeed, only one employee often carries out most tasks and the process of restructuring can quickly lead to permanent excessive demand.

The Air-Craft Project

'Air-Craft' was a three years project, financially supported by the German Federal Ministry of Education and Research. Project partners were the Chamber of Crafts Hamburg, Airbus Hamburg, the National Institute for Standardization DIN, the Kooperationsstelle Hamburg and several craft enterprises in the building sector.

The aviation builder Airbus is running electronic order systems for different types of products. Airbus intended to introduce a similar order system for the supply of services in the repair of buildings based on an electronic catalogue. The focus of the new process was on common repair services, not on regular maintenance or occasional emergency repairs. E-business in this sense meant electronic ordering or procurement, electronic selection of services via a catalogue, complete electronic communication in planning and performing the service and finally electronic billing and paying. This e-based system significantly influences the business communication with the suppliers – small or medium craft enterprises from the building sector.

The main objective of the Air-Craft project was to develop the Airbus e-business application in a way that the work organization in the SMEs was improved – or at minimum not worsened. Consequently, the main operational objective in Air-Craft was to consider all aspects of work organization in craft enterprises while developing and implementing the electronic order of handicraft services. That should help to avoid errors, which cause excessive demands, frustration, stress and consequent health complaints.

In Germany in 1996 a new safety and health legislation came into force and extended the legal framework.[1] It required much stricter ergonomic organization of work activities and workplaces.[2] Scientific insights concerning the ergonomic organization of workplaces are summarised in the European standards series DIN EN ISO 9241 'Ergonomic requirements for office work with visual display units (VDU)'. This standard describe principles for the organization of work tasks, working environment, workplaces and hard and software.

For the planning and implementation of new VDU-supported data processing systems it is recommended to consider the following dimensions:

1. aspects of organization: this level includes dimensions as workflow, organizational structures, work content and development of skills;
2. aspects of working materials and physical working conditions: this level includes in our case mainly requirements on hard- and software, on system support and the design of the physical work environment;
3. aspects regarding personnel resources: this level includes dimensions as personnel planning and company regulations (instructions, prescriptions), criteria for selection and placement of personnel and training programmes.

During the planning and implementation phase and even afterwards users should be encouraged to point out existing and possible problems that can occur.

All dimensions mentioned above needed to be considered during the introduction of the e-business solution planned by Airbus.

Survey in Craft Enterprises

The implementation process of catalogue-aided (or assisted) electronic ordering basically needs a comprehensive analysis of existing working and business conditions

---

1 Arbeitsschutzgesetz (1996), § 5 (1) (German Occupational Safety and Health Law).
2 Bildschirmarbeitsverordnung (1996), § 4 (1) (German ordinance for VDU's).

Table 7.1   Distribution of trades in the study

Metal/Pipe Engineering	6
Sanitary/Ventilation equipment	5
Masonry	4
Painting/Building protection	2
Electrical engineering	4
Joinery	2
Cleaning	2
Total	25

Table 7.2   Company size according to number of employees

1 to 10 employees	3
11 to 25 employees	5
26 to 50 employees	6
51 to 100 employees	3
More than 100 employees	8
Total	25

in craft enterprises. The Kooperationsstelle Hamburg performed a survey in craft enterprises. The survey contained a set of questions about issues such as VDU-equipment, business processes related to repair work and special practical knowledge of employees referring to the use of computers and electronic catalogues.

A sample of craft enterprises, already delivering services for Airbus and all dealing with the repair of buildings, were drawn from 7 trades. The distribution of trades in the sample is reported in Table 7.1.

The sample included both small crafts enterprises with less than 25 employees and medium sized enterprises with up to 200 employees (see Table 7.2).

The survey was divided into two separate parts and conducted in the period from June to December 2002. In the first one, the managing directors of the 25 craft enterprises were personally interviewed. The questionnaire for the managing directors included questions about the company, about their EDP-equipment and its use, about the procedure concerning procurement and the processing of orders, and finally, about co-operation and joint-ventures with other enterprises.

The second survey concerned the employees and was focused on work content, individual experiences in using EDP and catalogue systems and stress situations as well as on job-related qualifications and the qualification demands. The questionnaire included sections on current occupations, working conditions, training and further education.

**Table 7.3   Distribution of the trades in the employees'
survey** (Percentages)

Metal/Pipe Engineering	41
Painting/Building protection	35
Electrical engineering	17
Joinery	7

The commercial operations necessary to handle the orders of repair services were in the centre of the project. Consequently the survey involved those employees who dealt with the administrative transactions and business processes. This involves such steps as receiving of orders, ordering of materials, issue of delivery notes, bill issue, supervising of payment receipts, and so on. Thus, the number of clerks, occupied in offices, came up to 106 persons. Clerk employees were not interviewed; they answered a questionnaire, and a return ratio of about 53 per cent was obtained.

Clerk employees showed a very balanced distribution of age; they worked for at least 5 years full-time in their craft enterprises and had completed a commercial or industrial education. One third of those interviewed were female. Table 7.3 reports the distribution of employees according to trades.

The Situation of Airbus Suppliers Before Changing to e-Business

EDP equipment and use

Against common prejudices, the craft enterprises were very well equipped with EDP-technology. They worked with efficient and up-to-date PC's, which are connected by servers to – mostly internal – networks. Internet access is standard. The operating systems were predominantly based on Microsoft® products and all enterprises used Microsoft® Office Software. Furthermore, the enterprises were also working with different trade and branch specific software for order processing including, occasionally, some self-programmed solutions.

With two exceptions, all enterprises were equipped with different versions of the German standard interface GAEB (Common Committee for the Use of Electronics in the Construction Industry).[3] The GAEB interface facilitates the electronic import and export of construction data as describing the building as drawings, dimensions, materials, installed equipment etc. It allows further processing of construction data in the calculation software or other specific trade software, so that they are available for electronic order processing.[4] Thus the craft enterprises were technically well prepared for the implementation of the catalogue-based electronic order of services.

---

3   GAEB DA 1985, GAEB DA 1990, GAEB DA 2000.
4   See for further information about the GAEB Data Exchange: http://www.gaeb.de/.

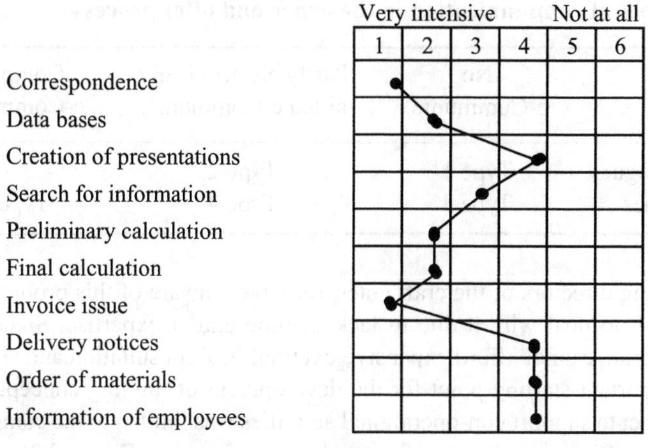

	Very intensive				Not at all	
	1	2	3	4	5	6
Correspondence	●					
Data bases		●				
Creation of presentations				●		
Search for information			●			
Preliminary calculation		●				
Final calculation		●				
Invoice issue	●					
Delivery notices				●		
Order of materials				●		
Information of employees				●		

Figure 7.1   EDP use in order processing at the start of the Air-Craft project

	Very intensive				Not at all	
	1	2	3	4	5	6
Presentation of enterprise			●			
Marketing				●		
Price investigation				●		
Customer contact			●			
Customer acquisition					●	
Personnel acquisition					●	
Purchase				●		
Distribution/sales					●	
Online Banking				●		

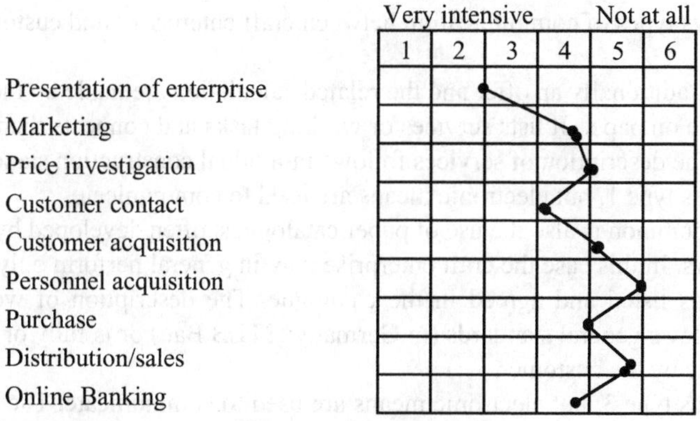

Figure 7.2   Internet use at the start of the Air-Craft project

The firms were already well developed in their use of computers to support internal business processes. Figure 7.1 shows the level of use of some typical activities in the order processing.

However, the majority of enterprises, irrespective of their size, did not have a comprehensive e-business strategy. Many single process applications operated in isolation from the total process and were not co-ordinated. Despite the potential benefits offered by technology and software, very few firms had integrated data streams. Because of multiple input of the same data and numerous medium breaks, the processes were error-prone and showed a high optimisation potential.

Table 7.4   Types of communication in the order and offer process

	No e-Communic.	Partly electronically aided e-Communic.	Complete e-Communic.
No use of catalogues	Type 1	Type 2	–
Use of catalogues	Type 3	Type 4	Type 5

The managing directors of the craft enterprises were aware of this problem, but found it difficult to deal with it due to lack of time and/or expertise. Since craft enterprises as a rule cannot afford expensive external ICT consultation and support, this was an important starting point for the development of training concepts. The use of the Internet to support non-operational activities was limited to the company's homepage presentation as well as the financial transactions (see Figure 7.2).

Experiences in the work with catalogues and electronic order procedures

Table 7.4. shows types of communication between craft enterprises and customers.

- Type 1: traditionally an offer and the related calculation are made by the craft enterprise on paper. It lists services or working tasks and connects them with prices. The description of services follows individual construction standards.
- Type 2: as type 1, but electronic means are used to communicate.
- Type 3: common is also the use of paper catalogues, often developed by large customers. In this case the craft enterprise may in general perform only work operations listed and agreed in the catalogue. The description of working tasks follows general standards (in Germany: STLB Bau) or is fully or partly self-made by the customer.
- Type 4: as type 3, but electronic means are used to communicate. The use of dynamic construction data (in Germany: STLB BauZ) is possible.
- Type 5: the use of electronic catalogues represents the latest development. It allows, in comparison to paper catalogues, that all business communication during the process can be performed electronically. There is no gap in electronic communication.

The basis of ordering in Type 3, 4 and 5 are catalogues accepted by the contractor and the customer. They describe products or services clearly and precisely. In this sense electronic catalogues do not differ from paper catalogues. In electronic catalogues the single services can be clearly identified with help of search function or an article number. The catalogues can both contain all usually requested services (demand catalogue) and represent the service spectrum of a craft enterprise (offer catalogue).

In the maintenance of buildings, it is usual to arrange frame contracts between customer and crafts enterprise. These frame contracts fix prices on small construction, repair and restoration services for a certain period. For the description of construction

Table 7.5   Employees' positive expectations and fears about implementation of electronic catalogues

Positive expectations	Doubts and fears
Processes are shortened, time is saved. The work in the order processing is facilitated. Business processes are simplified.	More time needed to process an order. Completion of tasks becomes more complicated. Connection to practical work is lost. Repair services cannot be standardized, thus cannot be reflected in catalogues. Prices become transparent; orders are in the future given to the cheapest offerer only.

works (VOB[5]), suitable standard texts have been prepared by GAEB. They are traditionally available in book form or electronically on CD-ROM or online and distributed in form of dynamic construction data on CD-ROM or online.[6] The essential information is compiled by specialists from all areas of the construction industry in over 70 working groups, guaranteeing compliance with exiting legislation.[7]

The managing directors of the interviewed enterprises knew the service catalogues for their trades but, according to current figures, only one third of enterprises in building maintenance use catalogues. Of those that do use catalogues, most were paper catalogues developed by large customers such as large housing associations or industrial companies. Some craft enterprises were already working with electronic catalogues. Generally, the craft enterprises needed to purchase a special software solution to exchange data with this customer.

The majority of the managing directors avoided using catalogues, mainly because of the inaccuracy of current catalogues. They argue that the catalogue specifications incompletely reflect the repair and maintenance services to be done. Two-thirds of the managing directors could, however, imagine covering the maintenance services for Airbus in self-prepared catalogues. The standard texts of the STLB BauZ were found as principally suitable to support the creation of such a catalogue. Also the employees of the craft enterprises were sceptical about working with service catalogues in the maintenance and repair area. Only one third of employees, those that already had experience in using service catalogues, saw a clear facilitation of work. The positive expectations, as well as doubts and fears of the employees are reported in Table 7.5.

---

5   VOB (Verdingungsordnung für Bauleistungen) is the general legal ordinance for the performance of construction works in Germany.

6   STLB-Bau is prepared by GAEB and published by the German National Standardisation Institute DIN.

7   http://www.beuth.de/php/frame.php?rub=12881&_artid=10386.

It became clear that the doubts and fears of the employees refer not to the use of the new technology or lack of technical know-how, but to the procedure of the order processing between craft enterprises and Airbus. They were sceptical about the feasibility reflecting repair services in catalogues. To overcome this scepticism, the involvement of employees in the development of e-business applications is particularly necessary.

Traditional procedure of the order processing

The craft enterprises in the Air-Craft project form a very heterogeneous group. They represent different trades, are of various sizes and have partly very individual business relations shaped by personal contacts with Airbus. Consequently, their internal operational processes are differently organized. However, all enterprises are connected by frame contracts with Airbus, which regulate the small repair and maintenance work. Currently, major contract conditions are agreed between Airbus and each craft enterprise. These included a yearly order with an upper limit, a demand limit per individual order and hourly pay rates.

The first call of the service and/or the error message is made by an employee of the responsible Airbus department by telephone, fax or via personal appeal to a member of the craft enterprise. In the next step, the craftsman and the Airbus employee together inspect the damage, in order to agree upon the repair extent and estimate the costs. If it can be foreseen that the order upper limit is exceeded, it is necessary to co-ordinate the matter with the central procurement department of Airbus.

On the basis of experience and know-how and/or the different types of catalogues and standard service specifications, the craft company compiles a list of the prospective tasks and material costs and forwards it to the Airbus special department. Compiling the list of services can demand up to one hour time, since scrolling the different catalogues is often laborious and time intensive.

The accepted list of work to be done is the basis of the order from Airbus. In addition, the employee of the Airbus department prepares an order sheet, which also contains an estimate of the needed working time. This order sheet, with a rough description of the order, is delivered by post office or fax to the crafts enterprise. Afterwards, the enterprise prepares the documents to start the work (clarifying dates, organizational questions, employees, tools and materials needed).

It is not unusual in the repair sector for the real costs to exceed the costs calculated in advance. In this case, the Airbus department and the craft enterprise negotiate a supplement. After the work has been performed, the craftsman documents the work (time and material) on time sheets and special notes.

The craft enterprise collects the time sheets and notes according to hours and material expenditure, examines and submits them to the Airbus department for further check and confirmation. Finally, the craft company calculates its costs and sends the invoice to Airbus by post. Airbus audits the price and material calculation and afterwards releases the order to pay.

It is helpful to visualize the process in order to find options for a better organization and optimization. To illustrate the order process in craft enterprise graphically, the Service Blueprinting, a method for process visualisation (Kleinaltenkamp, 2000), was chosen. This kind of presentation shows the activities of the craft enterprise as well as the interdependencies and interfaces to customer's activities. The Service Blueprinting plot shows the relevant process sequences from the service ordering till accomplishment. The service is seen from the customer, in this case Airbus. This procedure helps to consider the needs of the customer. Central aspect of Service Blueprinting is the distinction of the actions of the customer and the enterprise. These are arranged within different action areas, separated by interaction lines:

- the *line of visibility* separates activities into those which are directly noticed by the customer and those which are not directly noticed
- the *line of external interaction* distinguishes the area of the activities of the customer from those of the service provider
- the *line of internal interaction* divides the activities of different internal departments of service provider from each other (Hoeth and Schwarz, 1997; Kingman-Brundage, 1991).

The model of the traditional order process, shown in Figure 7.3, was developed as a result of the survey and of the several workshops and discussions with craftsmen and Airbus employees. It illustrates the necessary operational sequences in completing repair orders in the craft enterprise and shows at the same time the interfaces to the process of Airbus as well as necessary support instruments.

According to Figure 7.3 many different tasks in order processing need special software developed for craft enterprises. The background processes undertaken by Airbus, and not reported in the Figure 7.3, are to a large extent conducted over the ERP (Enterprise Resource Planning) system in the case of Airbus SAP R/3.

In order to design the entire process completely with computerised data exchange, the implementation of a mutually accepted electronic service catalogue is an essential pre-condition. Additionally, the interfaces between the activities of the craft enterprise and the Airbus must be adequately computerised.

Reorganization through e-Business Applications: The Case of Airbus Suppliers

Organization of the work-flow

Based on the model of traditional order processing, an exemplary process of electronic ordering of craft services was developed step-by-step in co-operation between craft enterprises from different trades, employees from Airbus and the Chamber of Crafts in Hamburg. The electronic process was implemented, tested and optimised in a pilot enterprise for floor covering services. The electronic process shows some major

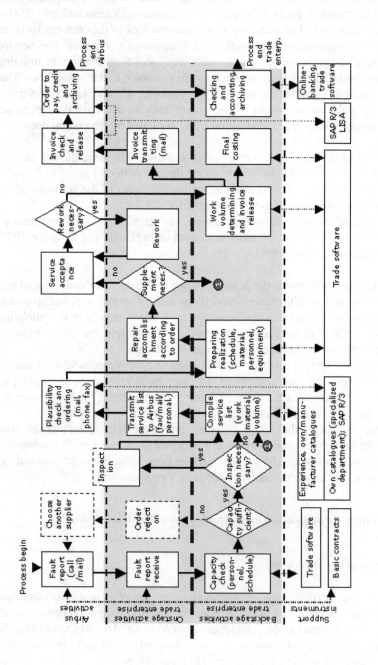

Figure 7.3 Current processes of the order processing of repair services on the basis of frame contracts

differences and innovations in comparison to the traditional process of the order processing. Such differences concern the following four points.

Use of electronic catalogues   The use of electronic catalogues is of crucial importance for a consistent procedure of the electronic order processing. Electronic catalogues represent the individual services of the craft enterprise on the one hand and correspond to the regular repair demand of the customer on the other.

The tasks and services contained in the electronic catalogues must meet the following requirements:

- technical and factual correctness as well as clarity of the performance/service specifications,
- adherence to the legal basic conditions,
- definition of standard prices for the catalogue entries,
- classification and coding for the definite identification of the positions by the ordering and calculation systems.

In addition, the electronic catalogue must contain interfaces, to ensure a smooth embedding in the existing software for task performance. In the catalogue solution that has been developed in Air-Craft, the description of the craft services for building repair follows the standard service specifications of the GAEB.

This solution guarantees conformity with German construction laws, technical and factual correctness as well as clarity of the service specifications. The GAEB software is wide spread and functions as an interface for a variety of programs in the building trade. The data in standardized data exchange formats can be imported, exported and/or processed into calculation software.

The production of an electronic catalogue and its co-ordination with the customer is usually very complicated and requires either professionally trained employees or the support by external consulting service. However, it is inevitable within an electronic procurement process.

Development of complete electronic process by solving interface problems   The basic pre-condition for a complete electronic operational mode of the order process was created by the installation of the data exchange tool *Win*GAEB®[8] and its integration into the software system used in craft enterprises. *Win*GAEB® converts incompatible data exchange formats of the Airbus order system[9] and the software system of craft enterprises into a suitable format.

A demand for a service can be reported also by telephone or fax, if the special circumstances (e.g. time pressure, explanation demand) require it. As a rule, the message should be sent by e-mail.

---

8   *Win*GAEB® is a product of Schnittstelle Bau (http://www.schnittstellebau.de).
9   SAP R/3® BUYSIDE.

Personal inspections and the assessment of the work to be done gained a greater importance in the re-modelled process. The electronic order, which is released on the basis of the service list conveyed by the craft enterprise, represents an obligatory order. The list of services cannot be extended later, even if the work to be done slightly deviates from the order. Additional work services have to be subsequently added as a new and revised order. A very detailed determination of the repair requirements is desirable and necessary, before the work starts.

Modified accounting procedure   In the traditional procedure, the invoice was issued according to the data of the working documentation. A slight deviation from the estimated and ordered services was tolerated and paid after examination. The electronic process requires an invoicing exactly related to the order released by the customer. The basis of the order is the list of services with provided catalogue positions and amount specifications, which is handed over by the craft enterprise to specialists of Airbus to be examined for plausibility.

Subsequent inclusion of more material or more working time into the invoice is not possible. In case of an excess of the estimated expenses and demanded works, the additional services have to be subsequently ordered. In this case, a new order procedure has to be released. The invoice is generated by the trade software and transmitted electronically over *Win*GAEB® to Airbus. For tax law reasons Airbus prepares a collective invoice per company. This collective invoice has to be checked and hand-signed by a craft enterprise.

Accelerated invoice clearance through process shortening by Airbus   In this new procedure, Airbus only checks whether the factual work and the invoice match. The price examination, as in traditional process, is not necessary because provided catalogue positions are settled with standard prices against an order generated by, the BUYSIDE order system. The entire sub-process of accounting is obviously accelerated in comparison with the traditional procedure.

Organization of the work tasks

The seven criteria for well organized work, defined by the standard DIN EN ISO 9241-2 (1993), are reported in Table 7.6.

Traditionally, the work in a craft enterprise meets the criteria of versatility, holistic approach, clarity and scope of action, due to its special organizational structure with flat hierarchies and low work fragmentation. This aspect was also confirmed by the survey carried out in Air-Craft.

Organization potential was seen particularly within the areas of user orientation and personal development. The employees were involved already at an early stage into the concept of the e-business solution. Their individual experiences, abilities and skills, their desires and suggestions, also their fears and doubts about the implementation of the new e-business solution were taken into account. These

Table 7.6   Criteria of well organized work tasks

Ergonomic criterion	Characteristic: A well organized work task is ...
User orientation	... to consider the experience and abilities of the user group
Versatility...	... to use an appropriate variety of skills
Holistic approach	... to guarantee that the tasks are recognized as holistic work instead as fragments
Clarity	... to guarantee that the tasks fulfil an important, for the user understandable contribution for the overall function of the system
Scope of action	... to plan an appropriate scope of action regarding reasonable order of work, work speed and individual approach
Feedback	... to give sufficient feedback how the task has been fulfilled
Development potential	... to give an opportunity to develop existing skills and to acquire new skills

factors have been reflected in the development and design of necessary adjustment concepts. Moreover, the electronic order processing is connected to an extension of the task spectrum for the employees.

Secretary workplace   Traditionally a technical fault or malfunction is reported verbally or by fax. The person in charge is informed personally by a written notice about the error and the customer demands. The faxes or telephone notes are stored chronologically or/and systematically in a folder. In the new process, the error message should arrive at the craft enterprise in form of an e-mail. In the same way, the secretary receives the catalogue based order from Airbus by e-mail with attachment. The tasks of secretary are broadened by electronic post and electronic filing.

Two working situations are common. In the first, the secretary has a particular e-mail address for receiving data and has access rights to the network, where the order specifications are stored. The transfer of the data to the person in charge works via electronic folders. Based on these technical preconditions, the following work procedures are necessary:

- opening the e-mail and printing of the e-mail text;
- filing of the message into the respective electronic folder of the person in charge (construction supervisor, foreman, accountant);
- filing of the e-mail attachment (message or order) in a particular directory and/or a file;
- filing of the return/response in a paper file folder;

- *Win*GAEB® does not have to be installed at this place, the qualification to use it is not necessary.

In the second situation, the secretary and all specialists involved in the process, each have separate e-mail access. The secretary has access right to the network server, where the order specifications are stored and used by authorised staff. The transfer of the data to the person in charge works via e-mail. The following work procedures are necessary:

- opening of the e-mail;
- filing of the e-mail attachment (message or order) in a particular directory and/or a file;
- selection of the e-mails and forwarding them to respective persons of charge;
- *Win*GAEB® does not have to be installed at this place, the qualification to use it is not necessary.

In the second process speed of data transfer is increased and error rate reduced.

Workplace of site manager/person of charge   The site supervisor in general has a separate e-mail access. For the following description of working tasks *Win*GAEB® must be installed on his/her workplace. He/she has access right to the network drive on which the order specifications are stored. Traditionally the site manager based his assessment of necessary working tasks on a site inspection. The message from Airbus department was not standardised. A detailed investigation of the situation on site was necessary. Afterwards the site manager developed an offer using standardised service or task descriptions and calculated a price. This offer might include 'open' and not finally fixed tasks. This offer was send via mail or fax to the customer.

   In the new process, the site supervisor is informed in the same way as the secretary. The subsequent actions (establishment of contact with the person requesting the service, selection and instruction of employees for the inspection of damage) do not deviate from the existing approach. The main change in the new system is that, through standardisation of the notification (fields in the message system have to be completed), it is guaranteed that all required information is available. The information includes also general data such as sender of the request with name, telephone number and e-mail address, location with house, floor, room number and a description of the required service. It might be that a site inspection is not necessary because the data required are already sufficiently described by Airbus in form of catalogue entries. A personal site inspection is, in general, still performed to check all details of the repair task. A list of services based on the electronic catalogue is compiled and conveyed electronically. A confirmation of agreed repair services by e-mail from Airbus is obligatory.

   A complete determination of required repair tasks is now a strict obligation. All tasks have to be fixed, all must be entries in the electronic catalogue. If during the execution of work additional repair tasks are necessary, both parties – the craftsmen and Airbus employees – need to release a new order. The transmitted repair invoice is to be examined for deviations from the order. All non-ordered services are accounted for separately over the additionally released assignment. The collection of the data for the recalculation and accounting is done by the standard construction software.

Accountant workplace   The accountant has the same system specifications available to the site supervisor, i.e. separate e-mail access, WinGAEB® is installed and access right to the network drive is available. In the traditional paper based process the accountant needed the offer, the report about the work performed by the craftsmen and possibly a report on deviations from the customer. If no deviations came up between offer and the work performed, the calculation of the invoice amount was easy.

Now the amount and items in the invoice have to match the electronic order completely. The data transfer is faster and more reliable, the error rate is reduced. Electronic invoice transmission replaces printing of an invoice and mail. The original file *.ord (order) is opened with *Win*GAEB®, provided with invoice number and date from accounting and sent over the e-mail function to the customer. Only the monthly collective invoice in paper form has to be signed for legal reasons. The employee in accounting adjusts the collective invoice voucher with the sales list of the internal system.

Craftsman/operator   The craftsman generally uses no ICT at the workplace on site. This situation has not been changed by the project. In future, the recording of the repair tasks on the workplace with an organizer will be common. He/she should be made aware that it is impossible to attach additional service positions to the invoice or to increase assigned quantities and that each repair task, completed beyond the order, forces an additional order procedure and should be communicated to the site manager and/or to the other person of charge.

Equipment organization/design

The company Schnittstelle Bau was engaged to program technical solutions of the interface problems between the trade software and the ERP system by Airbus. Schnittstelle BAU develops and distributes the data exchange tool *Win*GAEB ®, that supports the displaying and processing of the standard exchange formats according to GAEB-rules and SAP R/3. The implementation of *Win*GAEB® and its integration into the software of the craft enterprises makes it possible to realize a catalogue-based electronic order processing of repair services. For the adjustment of the solution to the technical requirements of Airbus, the functionality of *Win*GAEB® had to be extended by the FlatFile formats ORD ('order') and INV ('invoice').

New Competence Requirements in the Craft Enterprise

In the course of the project, some qualification fields for the employees of the craft enterprises were identified. These qualification areas form the basis for the training courses developed in the project Air-Craft.

Strategic e-business competence   The experiences in the project Air-Craft showed that the majority of craft enterprises lack a comprehensive e-business strategy integrating all EDP-applications. The development of the e-business strategy is an executive task and should focus on such issues as:

- understanding of contents which are to be realized with the help of e-business;
- criteria for the selection of the functional on the market of e-business solutions;
- criteria for the decision 'make or buy' of supporting EDP services;
- organization options of electronic business processes;
- personnel management and personnel development under the conditions of the e-business.

Technology competence   Using applications of EDP and the Internet are not new for the employees of the craft enterprises. An average level of competence covers more than the pure technical use of the systems. It needs also skills like understanding the special characteristics of communication by e-mail or the reasonable connection of different media with each other.

Work with electronic catalogue systems   The catalogue-based order processing and its integration into the business processes of the craft enterprise is a new task for the majority of the employees and requires comprehensive skills and knowledge in the following complexes:

- administration of electronic catalogues (basic understanding of their contents, structures and classifications of electronic catalogues)
- basic conditions of catalogue use (e.g. interfaces, catalogue formats)
- receiving, processing and generating order sets.

Information technology use in internal and external business processes   In order to fully exploit the advantages of internal and external information-technical networking by e-business, a new integration of technical and economic processes is required. The implementation of an e-business solution in the electronic order processing of repair service demands the following qualification of the employees:

- electronic accounting and cost calculation (e.g. posting acquisition, internal cost calculation, annual account, sales tax summary report);

- electronic ordering (e.g. creation of company related master data, issuing delivery note/calculations);
- electronic personnel management (e.g. human resource allocation, electronic time registration);
- electronic communication (work with date-, address-, and mail programs; electronic correspondence);
- using interfaces to standard programs;
- automatic payment transaction (electronic monetary transaction, electronic signature);
- legal obligations (additionally to the VOB e.g. contract creation with catalogue centres, bases of the electronic payment transactions).

Conclusions: Success Factors for a Human Resource Oriented Implementation of e-Business Applications

General preconditions for the successful introduction of e-business applications, described in the literature,[10] include the following success factors:

- development of a concept of the work flow and the role of each work operation (as pre-condition);
- appointment of a responsible person and/or formation of a project group (as necessity);
- consistent support by the management (as executive function);
- systematic procedure (project management) and if necessary step-by-step implementation (pilot projects);
- informing and involving employees during the planning and implementation of e-business;
- involvement of the customers into the conception phase.

The following success factors were verified in the Air-Craft project.

Development of an operational concept The improvement potential of an e-business solution can be best used if it is merged into a strategic business concept. The modelling of an integrated electronic process takes place in the context of a strategic e-business concept, which includes a clear goal definition, cost and time framework considerations, use expectations (e.g. customer binding, image improvement) and the demand on employee qualification.

Systematic procedure and step-by-step implementation 'A stepwise introduction and expansion of e-business activities reduces the probability of failures and helps to learn from experiences' (Biondo *et al.*, 2001). The e-business solution developed

---

10 See: Die Interaktive Organisation – Methoden und Modelle für gesunde und produktive Arbeit im e-business. see http://www.inter-org.de.

in Air-Craft supports existing e-business attempts in craft enterprises and uses the experiences of the employees. This application represents a milestone on the way to a better e-business acceptance in the craft enterprise.

The craft enterprises tested the practicability with Airbus and selected repair services. In case of success these activities will be expanded to further customers. Moreover, the process saves the potential to extend the e-business activities (e.g. e-procurement, electronic time registration, electronic signature).

Informing and involvement of the employees   The success of the Air-Craft e-business solution depends on the degree of involvement and contribution of the employees. Referring to Biondo *et al.* (2001), the new system can be correctly implemented by employees who are convinced of its usefulness, have the required competence and are assigned by management to the use of the new system.

Two central problems were identified as a result of the field study: 1) the content conception of the catalogues (definition and completeness of catalogue positions, consideration of preparation times, submitted materials, pricing) and 2) the organization of the order process between customer and contractor. These problems were discussed several times in workshops and meetings with craftsmen of different trades and persons of charge from Airbus. During the Air-Craft project a gradually accepted, standardized solution was developed. Opposition and prejudice against the catalogue-supported electronic order in the crafts enterprise was diminished by transparent information and communication. Moreover, valuable experiences and suggestions of the employees contributed substantially to the solution. This provided the basis for implementation and successful adaptation in the crafts enterprise.

References

Biondo, S., Eyholzer, K. and Fux, M. (2001), *e-Business, Leitfaden für KMU-Strategien und Potenziale für den Interneteinsatz in KMU*, Technologiezentrum Wirtschaftsinformatik, Brig/Bern.

Hoeth, U. and Schwarz, W. (1997), *Qualitätstechniken für die Dienstleistung*, Hanser, München.

Kingman-Brundage, J. (1991), 'Technology, Design and Service Quality', *International Journal of Service Industry Management,* Vol. 2, 3, S. 47–59.

Kleinaltenkamp, M. (2000), 'Blueprinting: Grundlage des Managements von Dienstleistungsunternehmen', in H. Woratschek (Ed.), *Neue Aspekte des Dienstleistungsmarketing*, Ansatzpunkte für Forschung und Praxis, Wiesbaden, S. 3–28.

Ritter, A., Schütt, P., Schulte, A. and Weimer, S. (2003), *Innovative Arbeitsgestaltung im Handwerk – Bilanzierung*. Verlag, ITB, Karlsruhe.

Note

The complete report of the Air-Craft project is available in German in:

Fischer, L., Kaiser, S., Rönnau, A., Thiemann, J. and Wendt, S. (2005), E-business Zwischen Handwerk und Industrie. Elektronische Auftragsbearbeitung mit standardisierten Leistungsbeschreibungen in der Gebäudeinstandhaltung. Mit Demonstrationsanwendung auf CD-ROM. (E-business between craft and industrial enterprises. Electronic processing of orders by standardized service specifications in the building maintenance sector. Includes a demonstration software on CD-ROM), Wilhelmshaven, 2005.

PART II
Internet Marketing and Website Effectiveness

Chapter 8

Internet Marketing and the Portuguese Marketplace

Rute Xavier and Francisco Costa Pereira

The Rise of the Internet: New Marketing Realities

With the rise of new, Internet based, electronic media, new realities in mass communication were introduced that revolutionized the process of communication between parts. This caused a new balance of power as the world witnessed a shift from the media to the audiences (McQuail, 2000). While traditional mass communication was done in one direction, the Internet offers bi-directional communication, allowing for interactivity, an unlimited choice of content, diversity of audiences and global communication.

The rise of these new information and communication technologies, and of Internet users, has introduced a new marketing reality.

The consequences of this new 'marketing' change the relations between the different players in the traditional market, especially at the level of consumer relationship. Through this medium, organizations are looking for establishing and maintaining long and stable relationships by the use of one-to-one communication and a customized offer that fulfils the needs and desires of individual consumers. These consumers are different from the ones on the traditional marketplace, and expect to easily find information that can allow them to make informed decisions, in the most comfortable way. They want to communicate with other consumers in order to get better advice, they want to become more independent and more capable of influencing the organizations. This gave rise to the beginning of a new language that is appropriate to this new medium and its users.

As described above, the Internet is a communication medium more interactive and individualized. The one-to-many communication was abandoned and the one-to-one communication is taking over. The Internet and e-mail are considered by many authors as the privileged medium to overcome time and geographical barriers and to allow listener and speaker to quickly exchange roles.

In this way marketing becomes interactive and, following Komenar (1997), it is 'more than multimedia used to entertain or engage a consumer. It is a higher level of strategic marketing, made possible by sophisticated technology and intelligent databases that can respond to interactive relationships' (pp. 87–88).

Due to its specificity, where technology allows for the integration of text, sound and images, the Internet has revolutionized the traditional unidirectional mass communication, making it similar to bi-directional telephone communication, considered by Poster (1995) the paradigm of a democratic structure. Within this new medium it is therefore possible to introduce a new factor that further distinguishes online marketing from traditional marketing: real-time communication.

Real-time communication leads to the time value concept (Aldrich, 1999). The relevance of time has significantly evolved in the past few decades. We all consider that we have less time for ourselves than we did previously. Socio-cultural conditions have changed: more and more women are working, we spend more time commuting and jobs are demanding more working hours. All these conditions imply that in order to find more time for leisure activities, consumers will try reduce the time spent in other activities, such as cooking, shopping or communication. It therefore makes perfect sense to attach an added value to products, the time value, which accounts for the time saved from using this new medium and that, has emerged as the most valuable commodity. This includes for example product delivery where and when the consumer wants it or the automation of shopping lists from product use and previous purchases. There is a wide range of services yet to be delivered in the field of automatic execution of small, essential tasks that require valuable consumer time, while providing little intrinsic enjoyment, such as getting the (snail) mail, taking the car to the workshop or filling the gas tank. Nascimento (2000) has estimated that electronic marketing and online shopping would allow consumers to save about 2.5 dislocations and 1.5 hours a week in domestic supplies shopping, especially since this type of shopping is incredibly inefficient, as the consumer is forced to systematically go through all aisles in the supermarkets, week after week, to get the same products (that represent, on average, over 85 per cent of purchases).

The value of the Internet has led the consumer to be extremely aware of the time spent communicating. The Internet consumer is not willing to wait and is constantly impatient. This makes certain web site characteristics, related to the time it takes to get the relevant information, paramount for the return of consumer.

In a study we conducted during 2003, we analyzed the website of 22 Portuguese firms, drawn from the following sectors: newspapers, e-commerce, search engines, culture and entertainment, public organization and online training and education. The sample includes firms whose website received the JETNET 2002 Prize (a competition where firms from different sectors are proposed by a specialized jury and then voted by cybernauts). Other firms were selected randomly from a Portuguese search engine to add firms in the before mentioned sectors. In that study we analyzed many aspects of Internet marketing, which we report in this chapter.

About website characteristics related to time and ease of use we observed that:

- 95.5 per cent of the companies update frequently the information on their website, but only 45.5 per cent had an update date up to the previous week. Up-to-date information and the existence of a 'last update' date give the consumer the perception that the information is still valid. But 50 per cent of the sites did not have any update date at all. Information dating back to 1998 may still be valid, but if the update date is not given, the consumer may be suspicious of the information provided, may get a negative impression of the firm and decide to look elsewhere. Therefore, there is a clear concern on keeping the information on the websites up-to-date, but this is not done in a way that can be clearly perceived by consumer;

- the site map, that allows users to find what they are looking, is still not in use for many Portuguese companies. We found that only 38.5 per cent of the organizations had this tool;
- navigation tools, helping customers an easy navigation in the site, were present, contrary to the use of the site map, in all the analyzed companies;
- about the download time, Forest Research considers 8 seconds the limit time that consumers are willing to wait for a webpage to download. Unfortunately our study shows that for 77.3 per cent of the observed websites, the first page takes more then 8 second to download and for 22.7 per cent this time is more than 30 seconds;
- an easy to remember URL allows customers to repeat the access without loosing time to find the web company address again and again. From our study we can conclude that the vast majority of the companies (77.3 per cent) have an easy to remember URL, in the form www.name-of-firm.pt;
- the internal search engine significantly reduces the time it takes to look for information. The majority of the websites analyzed do not have an internal search engine, and those who do have one are usually ineffective, as the results of a search are normally a large amount of useless alternatives or no alternative whatsoever. The simple existence of a search engine is not enough, as it has to be effective (returning positive results for searches of simple or complex information), easy to use (with menus, categories and help), searching also in a FAQ list (FAQ – or frequently asked questions – are one of the most helpful tool for consumers) and accessible from any point in the website. Our study shows that for 25 per cent of firms the search engine in the site was not effective, and for 40 per cent was not user friendly. The search engine for most companies (95.5 per cent) does not look in the FAQ list, and it was accessible from any point on the website only for 70 per cent of the analyzed companies.

In conclusion, we can say that the websites of the Portuguese companies we analysed have been adapting quite well to keep up with the 'new order'. However they still have some way to go before they can properly respond to real time demands and attract audiences/consumers for a second visit.

Internet Marketing

Internet Marketing is a result of Internet as the paradigm of information society and also the result of user needs. Users search for information, try to get needs and desires fulfilled, want to communicate, raise questions, find alternatives and accept suggestions from other users. This new reality has lead marketing to adapt itself, building a new grammar capable of responding to this new work logic. Communication must change, and advertisement will adapt a new logic, that is able to respond to different consumer's predispositions (Butler and Peppard, 1998). This leads to the medium changing from broadcast to narrowcast, and from one-to-many to one-to-one communication (Hoffman and Novak, 1996). Targeting can be based on demographic factors, interests, consumer behaviour, buying history, etc. For example, Crayon.net allows users to create their own customized newspaper from articles and news from newspapers throughout the world. Internet marketing also leads the consumer to become less passive and more of an active buyer. New technologies give consumers the possibility to push their needs and desires and wait for someone to fulfil them. Furthermore, advertisement becomes a medium for consumer interaction. Given that this medium is characterized by the possibility of very fast response time, the key goal for marketers is to immediately convert website visitors into customer. This would never be possible with advertisement in a newspaper or with a brochure, because they do not encourage an immediate action from the consumer.

The type of relationship between companies and consumers that is presently established in this new medium will not cause traditional marketing to disappear, but will force it to adapt, as Internet marketing still has limited range.

To better understand Internet marketing it is important to know the differences from traditional marketing; these differences focus in six areas: information, relationship, targeting, communication, accessibility and the consumer.

In relation to information, the traditional marketing has fewer information details and is less available to the customer. In opposition, in the Internet not only there is abundance of information and of better quality, but it is also supplied by different partners: companies, other customers and 'infomediaries' (new intermediaries that in the Internet mediate information by comparing products or listing the companies that sell a specific product or service). Moreover, in the Internet collectioning data on consumers allows firms to create a relationship or personalize an offer. New contents related to firms' main activity appear in the sites with the purpose of incrementing the visits to the company's website, e.g., while we visit a website that sells trousers we can also find information about fashion events or even get to know the international news.

The customer relationship is an area that suffered many changes in the process of moving from traditional to Internet marketing. With the traditional marketing, there is in general no relationship between firms and consumers, and when it exists it is made through intermediaries. In the Internet marketing the relationship tends to be one-to-one and interactive. Therefore consumers talk directly with firms. It is also important to emphasise the appearance of virtual communities that are formed by the similar interests or activities of their members and provide an important means of exchanging information on products and services. It is also possible to witness the appearance of networks of firms and suppliers that are created with the purpose of delivering specific offers to consumers.

In terms of targeting, traditional marketing uses demographic factors, whereas Internet marketing is based on consumer behavioural patterns like patterns of websites search and use, or transactions made.

Regarding communication, while traditional marketing is characterized by mass communication and push advertisement, marketing in the Internet allows for a more personalized and interactive communication with pull advertisement (e.g. via newsletters). In fact, it is the potential consumers that decide to access the websites and receive extra information from the firm on its offers and new products or services. Also, if we look at Internet advertisements they are much more interactive than the traditional ones, and when we access a website it is similar to being in a fair or looking at a big shop window. Stewart and Zao (2000), comparing the Internet and the traditional media, observed that the Internet overtakes the press, television and radio or even the telephone on capacity of commercialization in big areas to a vast public with small costs, interactivity and quantity of information delivered.

In terms of accessibility and comparing traditional stores with websites that sell products, the former are more restricted in their selling activity geographically. Their dealing hours are restricted and delivery is also limited to their physical location. In the Internet, the websites are open 24 hours a day, are available globally which means that any one in any place is able to access them, and the delivery place and time can be arranged by the customer.

Finally, the consumer is changing from being passive in the traditional marketing to becoming much more active, better informed, more demanding and more willing to complain.

Internet in Portugal

Bareme Internet and NetPanel are two regular annual studies conducted by a leading Portuguese audience measurement company, Marktest. The first focuses on the use of Internet in Portugal and the latter on the browsing behaviour of Portuguese cybernauts. The samples used cover about 1200 households or 3000 individuals reflecting the demographic proportion of Portuguese population. Between 1997 and 2003, these studies show that the increase in the number of the Portuguese cybernauts is associated with a better balance between the different social and demographic groups, getting closer to the real structure of Portuguese population. In 2003, 57 per cent of Portuguese cybernauts were men (compared to 71 per cent in 1997) and 38 per cent are between 15 and 24 years of age (compared to 51 per cent in 1997). The major social group (31 per cent) is the middle class (compared to 35 per cent in 1997). It should also be noted that in 1997 20 per cent of Portuguese cybernauts belonged to the upper class, compared to only 14 per cent in 2003 (this class represents 5 per cent of the real Portuguese social structure). Finally, most cybernauts are from Great Lisbon and North Littoral (29 per cent and 18 per cent), although we observe some decrease of their percentage when compared to 1997 (34 per cent and 21 per cent).

The Marktest studies reported as the most relevant reasons for Internet access mentioned by Portuguese cybernauts in 2003, the access for professional purposes, for the news, for self education/improvement, for academic purposes, for entertainment (the most relevant reason for Internet access until 2001) and, finally online banking (a reason mentioned since 2000, and chosen by 9 per cent of interviewed cybernauts in 2003).

The main form of Internet connection is still residential dialup connection (57 per cent), but new broadband connections are becoming more frequent (Cable TV – 27 per cent, and ADSL – 12 per cent).

Internet Marketing Characteristics

Contrary to traditional marketing, Internet marketing focuses on information. In this sense it returns to its primary origins, the elementary information on products or services. Just as advertisement in early newspapers, that described the attributes, characteristics and price of the product being advertised, the website of an organization must have information about the institution, products and services, and this information must go beyond standard brochure contents and encompass deep technical detail.

But above all, Internet marketing represents the creation of relationships between companies and customers and also between customers. As different efforts are made to communicate with potential consumers, these will in turn refuse most offers presented by companies, will want to know more about product or services, to voice their opinion, and to customize services and/or products in a way that they believe will be the best to satisfy their needs.

Furthermore, there are several other characteristics that are important in Internet marketing. Here we briefly describe five of them. First the customization of communication, products and services, prices and placement. The direct relationship between consumers and companies enables companies to identify the needs and wishes of potential and effective customers. Second, the appearance of new contents. The Internet medium allows for the use of new types of content, not necessarily related to the main activity of the companies, that may attract consumers to the website, as we described before. Third, the gathering, integration and analysis of information about consumers. Through the use of transactional databases it is possible to characterize not only the average consumer but also the individual one, in a way that was not possible before. Fourth, the empowerment of Internet users. The cybernaut has different characteristics from the traditional consumer, being more involved, independent and informed. This gives him more power of choice over the products being offered, and also more demanding in terms of individual needs. Finally, the disintermediation and infomediation of channel distribution. In the Internet, with the direct communication between companies and consumers, the need for the traditional intermediary is gone, leading to a process of disintermediation. However, given the vast amount of information available in the Internet, there is a need for some tool (or tools) to facilitate access to the required information and even to summarise the available information which leads in turn to a process of infomediation. In the following we add some details on customization, loyalty and disintermediation.

Customization   With an effective technology it is possible to direct communication to each consumer, either by using personalized e-mail or through the use of customized webpages when access is made by a registered user It is also possible for users to create customized products and/or services on their own image. Let us look for example at the purchase of a personal computer at dell.com: the consumer may buy a standard product but he can also choose a customized system, as different consumers, highly knowledgeable consumers, chose adequate characteristics to their purpose. Some users may decide on different memory configurations, disk drives, DVD readers/burners, leading to an almost unlimited set of choices. But this is not limited to computers: other products can also be customized like music, compilations of films, TV shows or news. There is always something we would like to change or personalize in products and especially in services being offered, such as travel, financial services, mobile operators, and medical services.

Loyalty   Acquiring customers on the Internet is extremely expensive, and creates a need for repeated purchases from the same consumers to allow for profit (Reichheld and Schefter, 2000). In this sense, consumer loyalty is a determining factor in Internet commerce, even more than in traditional commerce. Just as in traditional commerce, the initial cost of earning the trust of consumers is very high, and profits will rise slowly. On the Internet, those initial costs tend to be even higher. According to Reichheld and Schefter (2000), in retail the cost for acquiring new consumers for companies that operate solely on the Internet are 20 per cent to 40 per cent higher than for companies operating on the traditional marketplace. However, in the following years the profit growth for Internet companies is far superior, as repeat customers spend more than twice as much in months 24 through 30 of their relationships than they do in the first 6 months. This can be explained by the fact that online shops can increase and diversify their offer, and that consumer tend to consolidate their purchases on a primary supplier, which turns the access to the company website into a daily routine.

   Another key factor for Reichheld and Schefter (2000) are the referrals, which are already extremely lucrative in traditional commerce, and that have an even greater effect on Internet commerce. It is said that the 'word of mouse spreads even faster than the word of mouth'.

   Loyalty in Internet commerce is also related to trust. For consumers to be willing to give their personal information and financial data (including credit card numbers) it is essential that the consumer considers the company and their website trustworthy. Issues related with security and payment method have therefore an important role in getting the consumer's trust.

   In our study we observed that among companies that use their website as a distribution channel, 57 per cent offer more than one payment method and 87 per cent explain the use of encryption system to safeguard personal data. This means that the analyzed companies are aware of security issues in getting consumer trust, trying to give the consumer various forms of payment and addressing the perception of computer security from the consumers.

Disintermediation In the physical world, the most types of intermediaries in commerce are retailers, wholesalers, middlemen and sales representatives. With the Internet, all of the distribution processes changes, and especially these intermediaries, since their primary functions are replaced by the medium. This is due to the fact that information is increasing in quantity and improving in quality. Information travels simply and quickly, not only to the consumers but also back to the companies. Internet also allows a direct relationship between consumers and consumers, through websites, e-mails, banners, and discussion forums that allow interactivity between companies and consumers, and also between consumers themselves. Internet users have quickly grown used to comparing products and services, especially from the best known brands. Finally, the Internet allows easy access to new markets and the opportunity to escape from geographical boundaries.

As a result, the role of traditional intermediaries is vanishing, in a process known as disintermediation. In our study on Portuguese companies, we observed that all of the analyzed companies provide at least an e-mail address for contact and 14 per cent provide all the contact information (telephone, fax, e-mail, etc.), including e-mail addresses for specific departments and personal e-mail of the person in charge of these area. In 81 per cent of the companies the website motivates the mailing of suggestions, comments and complaints, and from these, 56 per cent already use web forms for this purpose, which encourages the user to send in the information, and helps the analysis of this information, further improving customer relationship.

It should be noted however that, as stated above, the Internet is a vast and immense information repository, and although abandoning intermediaries seems obvious, other needs have appeared and other intermediaries have come forward to fulfil them. In fact it is not enough for a company to have a website; the company must make it accessible for consumers and lead them to it. To that end, new intermediaries are required, the so-called infomediaries, that organize and distribute information, and lead to a new power in the marketplace.

Aldrich (1999) points out that infomediaries may have several roles in this process. Infomediaries attempt to integrate and aggregate services and needs, to create a floating price system based on supply and demand, to manage the flow of products from the initial supplier to the consumer, and to manage an ever changing affinity group composed of vendors, suppliers and customers. Infomediaries also monitor the performance of all players in Internet commerce, and attempt to save them time, to manage operational functions such as warranty, exchange and returns, and to develop new consumers and markets.

These new intermediaries include, for example, search engines, electronic auctions (such as ebay.com), online software delivery, online service and support, outsourcing professional services, multimedia content delivery, online financial services, online market aggregators, and virtual communities.

It is important for the analysis of Portuguese companies on the Internet, to find how they are placed in search engines, since these are the infomediaries that are common to all of them. In this sense, we checked if both the company name and its main services came up as positive results in searches done in the main national and international search engines. The results were the following: 100 per cent of the analyzed companies get a positive result when a search is done for its name in the main national and international search engines and only 14 per cent of the analyzed companies had positive results when searching for the main products and services that the company supplies.

This shows that the analyzed companies did not position themselves correctly on the search engines, as only users that already know the company will be able to find it. This is especially problematic for companies aiming towards the global market, as they are wasting the opportunities that infomediaries give them to overcome geographical barriers.

Internet Advertisement

Advertisement, as a communication tool for marketing, has gained new forms on the Internet to adapt to this new reality. It began in 1995 with banner advertise being placed in between webpage contents, or with companies creating their own websites and assuming a passive posture, waiting for Internet traffic to come to their webpages. In 1996 the start of a second stage, a cooperative one, was witnessed and advertisers began to measure the communication effect and to identify the most creative and effective elements to convey their messages on webpages. Links with press was established, and it was common for newspapers and printed press to try to persuade consumers to get online and access several advertised websites.

Coordinated strategies were developed that made the possibilities of this new medium more visible, and there was a shift from entertainment advertisement to information oriented advertisement. In 1997 we can say that a third stage of Internet advertisement began, which was one of targeted advertisement. This evolution was possible because of the significant technological development that happened in the mean time, such as virtual technologies, that allowed advertisers to a great deal of information in small advertise, e.g. smart banners. Furthermore, this technological development allowed advertisers to offer more options to the sponsors based on a direct marketing model. From 1998 to the present day Internet advertisement continued to evolve significantly, with the appearance of interstitial advertisement, and with a large cooperation with the other media.

However, companies began to realize that this new medium was not the universal panacea for all their communicational problems and, at the same time, negative reactions from consumers in regard to some ethical issues began to emerge. Some of these are still unsolved, and this is why it is urgent to create legislation that is adequate to this new reality.

Presently, advertisers that create Internet advertisement have began to realize that the interactivity in this medium was related to the choices that each and every consumer was able to do online, i.e. when a consumer is surfing the web, accessing portals and websites, the consumer wishes to follow a logical and rational path. Therefore, advertisers must develop a set of creative and original Internet advertisements that will lead consumers to further explore them.

This type of publicity has four main goals: brand building, just like in any traditional medium; the creation of a database of customers or potential customer; to create Internet traffic towards the sponsor website; and finally instant direct sales (Delepine, Hussherr and Levieux, 1999).

We now briefly describe how Internet advertisement is currently working in Portugal and how it is integrated in marketing strategies, whether traditional marketing or Internet marketing. To this end we performed 1034 visits to the Portuguese websites most visited during 2003, and gathered 180 Internet advertises for further analysis. We report here some of the characteristics of Internet advertisement we observed, specifically the advertise size and shapes, the type of access, the behaviours that it induces and types of appeals to consumers. The profile of Internet advertisement that we observed is as follows:

- the shapes and sizes are based primarily on banners, be they standard (horizontal) banners (46 per cent) or vertical banners (19 per cent). Next we have buttons, either rectangular (14 per cent) or square (9 per cent). Finally, with a very low percentage, we have pop-ups (5 per cent);
- Internet advertisement leads the consumer to act by supplying him with a path to reach desired goals. The most common form of call to consumer actions is 'click', whether in the imperative form (28 per cent) or as a request (16 per cent). The remaining calls to action use a plethora of requests, each one adequate to their target audiences. These calls to action were only present in 41 per cent of the ads analyzed;
- if the consumer, by his own initiative, would click on the ad, only 6 per cent of them would not give any access, and in 4 per cent of the cases access would not be possible due to technical difficulties. Therefore, in 49 per cent of advertises the consumers had to discover the way to access to the required information through trial and error;
- in 33 per cent of analyzed advertise some form of Internet commerce/sale was presented. However, in the vast majority of these cases (93 per cent) there was no indication of how the transaction could be performed, or what would be the payment method;
- the appeals that Internet advertisements make to consumers were divided between emotional and rational appeals. Our results show that 63 per cent of analyzed advertise use emotional appeals, emphasising all that brings comfort

or effortlessness and that may attract the consumer. In these advertise we also see reference to fear, alarm and insecurity, namely in 12 per cent of them;

- rational appeals are more frequent in advertise (78 per cent) than emotional appeals, with emphasis on promotions and economic benefits. This show that advertise predominantly target the consumer self interest at the economical level, taking advantage of the fact that the consumer is price sensitive;
- the advertisement message is predominantly informational, with messages in a negative way (65 per cent), rather than transformational, with messages in a positive way (34 per cent) (Rossiter and Percy, 1998);
- when compared with other media, Internet advertisement makes less use of actors and characters to promote their products/services. In fact only 23 per cent of advertise analyzed used such characters. In the Internet advertises we analyzed, male characters represented a 60 per cent; in television this number goes down to 46 per cent and in newspapers to 32 per cent. Finally, on the Internet the dominant character takes the role of an expert and also of someone or something that is associated with the product thus providing it with meaning;
- just like in other mediums, the dominant colour in Internet advertise is blue; it is followed by green and orange as first colours;
- finally, it is in this medium that there is the greatest use of promotional messages (43 per cent) similarly to what happens on radio.

In Portugal, advertisement must still go a long way to adapt itself to the new realities and become an important tool for Internet marketing.

Interactivity: Consumer Benefits

Since consumers are the targets of Internet marketing, it is important to identify the main benefits and the reasons that lead them online. With the development of Internet marketing, the main benefits for consumers are the following: access to information, access to different geographical markets, direct relationship with companies, customization of information and services to the consumer needs, access to virtual communities and to online auctions.

Our study allows to investigate which facts contributed negatively or positively to the above benefits:

- for most companies (64 per cent) there was an excess of information on the home page of the website, which confuses the consumer. One interesting fact is that in spite of the too much information on the home page, 68 per cent of the websites do not have excess information on the subsequent web pages;
- most companies (91 per cent) only use the Portuguese language on their websites, ignoring most of the Internet population and restricting their presence to the national and Portuguese-speaking market;

- only 32 per cent of the companies use the Internet as a distribution channel. Within these companies, we also found that only half of them provided an easy to use online purchase interfaces, which further hinder the advantages of this medium. The key characteristic for online purchase interfaces are: a) the existence of a 'shopping cart' or something similar that allows a consumer to add a product or service to their shopping list; b) the ability to access the current shopping list at any time in order to review the items already selected for purchasing and c) when the payment procedure is initiated, all costs, including additional taxes or expenses, should be displayed and explained in detail. Although the use of the Internet as a distribution channel is not frequent in the analyzed companies, we highlight that for most of them (86 per cent) the online price of products was equal or less than the price of the products in the physical world.

From these results we see that Portuguese firms are still unable to provide consumers with all the benefits provided by the Internet. However, access to information, to other consumers and benefits related with the value time are now common for the Portuguese companies with online presence.

Virtual communities

The virtual communities are socio-cultural groups that emerge on the Internet when a certain number of individuals take part in public discussion on a given subject for a certain period of time. There is a tendency for companies either to create these virtual communities around their brands, or to join existing communities. Companies want to create and take part in these discussion groups in order to benefit their image and their brand (Stopnicki, 1999).

We should however point out that virtual communities represent an unstable medium for marketing. In fact, enriched with the exchange of information and relationship interactions, consumers will use their online activities to evaluate offers, and resist what they consider to be a huge amount of poorly directed e-mail. The more the members of these communities communicate between themselves the bolder they become in challenging marketing and marketers. The right of choice of the new consumer thus develops new social relationships. For example, online consumers will usually only purchase from a given company after getting in touch with some virtual community holding unofficial social information, which will greatly enhance the power of virtual communities as one of the most important referrals. Consumers find the opinion of their peers extremely important. In many cases these communities are the ones giving information on the best website or lower prices. Virtual communities show that marketing is not only about one-to-one communication, but also many-to-many. The global network is populated by consumer groups that communicate with each other, sharing knowledge and experience, and evaluating the quality of products as well as the honesty and integrity of a given company. Thus, to study the needs of online consumers, consumption has to be considered within a social context with multinodal relationships.

In our study we observed that many companies already promote virtual communities, thus providing consumers with a platform for communicating with other individuals and sharing common interests usually related to the activity of the company. One interesting fact is that 54 per cent of the analyzed companies already had some form of virtual community. The predominant type of virtual community is the *newsgroup*, followed by *chat rooms* and *mailing lists*. Most of these communities (72 per cent) are virtual communities of consumption, since they deal with subjects closely related with the company field of work. There are also virtual communities of entertainment where broad ranges of subjects are discussed, but these were only present in three of the analyzed companies.

It is clear that companies understand the importance of virtual communities as separate type of Internet marketing, different from the usual one-to-one model. Several of them already sustain virtual communities, which allows them on one hand to provide information and gain the consumers trust and on the other hand to gather the opinions of consumers that would not normally contact the company outside these communities.

Privacy

The concept of gathering information on consumers is not new, but with the possibilities brought up by the Internet, and the speed at which information can be presently processed, the analysis of consumer information is now more efficient and effective, especially in terms of time and cost for companies. In general three types of information are gathered (Walsh e Godfrey, 2000): 1) basic personal information, usually gathered when the user accesses the website for the first time and registers; 2) purchasing habits are gathered from storing in databases all online user activities, and 3) clickstream information, regarding navigation within the website (which pages were visited, opened, closed, etc.) supplying information about consumer behaviour.

According to Miyazaki and Fernandez (2000) there are several factors that may influence consumer concerns regarding privacy, namely the awareness that information on him/herself is being gathered, and how this information is or will be used by other companies. It is at this stage that consumers begin to feel that they are no longer in control and that privacy related problems start. According to Novak and Phelps (1995) many Internet users would be willing to supply more personal information if they knew how this information would be used.

Our study shows that 95 per cent of the analyzed companies allow consumers to register on their websites. Since this registration is not necessary or essential to access most information on the websites, it appears to be mostly a way for companies to gather personal consumer information. Furthermore, in 41 per cent of the analyzed companies, no official privacy policy is given to consumers about the use of their personal data.

Privacy is always a sensitive area but fortunately a great percentage of Portuguese companies explain consumers their privacy policy, which can strength the trust between consumers and companies and therefore allow companies to know more about consumers.

Conclusions

In our study, we found that the websites we analyzed represent economical benefits for the consumers. Not only for 50 per cent of the analyzed websites it is cheaper to buy the product/service online than on the traditional market but in 60 per cent of them online purchase represents an opportunity benefit for the consumer, since buying on the Internet increases the added value of saving time.

Negative factors that were found in our analysis is that companies are not effectively communicating with consumers and the incentives for consumer-to-consumer communication are still small. The website represents a benefit for consumer-to-company communication in 23 per cent of the analyzed cases. For consumer-to-consumer communication this figure is better (50 per cent), but still low.

We should also highlight that website accessibility and the selling of online adverting on websites influence the communication and information benefits for consumers. We found that most websites can be accessed using the two most common web browsers (Internet Explorer and Netscape Navigator) and that the use of plug-ins is not necessary to access most of the information available. Besides, we found that 50 per cent of the websites have links to other companies and/or organizations, and that 59 per cent of companies sell online advertising on their website. If we assume that the main goal of these websites is to establish communication with the consumer, then we can consider the previous as communication noise. Furthermore, 64 per cent of the websites have internal advertising. Although not as deleterious as external links of advertise, since they highlight products/services or promotions offered by the company, these can also be a negative factor if there is an abuse. Regarding website design, 68 per cent of the companies have appeal website design and in 23 per cent of webpages, video or sound is used. This is an important factor that reflects the evolution and the dynamics of websites in the past few years.

In our study we also analyzed the relation between the several Internet related variables described above and the general characteristics of the companies: activity sector, products and services, dimension, geographical location, company age, online time, and whether websites are developed internally or by outsourcing.

The selling of online advertising on websites is related to strong competition, internal advertising, too many links to other websites and too much information on the home page. We can therefore say that if the sell of online advertising is not aimed to minimise online costs and to offer free services to the consumers, then it represents a negative factor for the webpage, and should not be considered.

Another question raised by our study had to do with computer/software companies being potentially better prepared to explore this medium as a marketing tool. In fact, we found a positive correlation between websites developed by specialized companies and issues like good accessibility, the existence of virtual communities and the presence of an explicit privacy policy.

We also found that having an appealing design is associated with allowing consumers to send suggestions and comments through the website, a smaller online time (younger website) and a negative correlation with having too much information on the homepage. These data points out that younger websites have a bigger concern with general readability and sobriety, as well as presenting information efficiently and providing better navigation. However, websites with appealing design are less likely to support virtual communities and to offer newsletters for consumers.

Furthermore, younger sites have, as mentioned, an appealing design, a site map and belong to the e-commerce sector (financial, travel, bookstores, etc.). Finally we found that longer download times are related to a website belonging to the mass-media sector and not to e-commerce.

We can summarise these results in relation to the activity sectors. The mass media sector is associated with longer download times, excessive information on their websites, the existence of virtual communities, the website being developed and maintained by an external company, and the website representing a communication benefit for consumers. The e-commerce sector is associated with the use of e-mail, shorter download time, younger websites and an economic benefit for the consumer. The cultural sector is negatively related with the existence of an explicit privacy and confidentiality policy, the use of e-mail, and economic benefits for consumers. Finally, websites belonging to other sectors (public companies, etc.) have a low probability of selling online advertising, to have consumer registration and therefore supplying newsletters for consumers. It should be noted that these sectors have very little or no online competition.

Although the firms studied still do not use all the potential tools of Internet marketing, one can say that Internet marketing has been developing in Portugal and has returned to the original functions of marketing: information, customization and relationship. This happens, not only because organizations try to maintain a relationship with users, but also because the information given has the purpose to clarify and inform the consumer, which are two of the most important characteristics of Internet marketing. Looking at marketing in this new medium the mind goes both to the first retailers that personally knew their customers, their needs, supplied them with personalized offers and had with them a friendly relationship, and also to the first advertises that mentioned all the characteristics of products as well as the when/ where they should be used.

The Internet marketing will bear a higher importance in the relationship between consumers and firms. Not only is the Internet affirming itself as the global medium of communication in this new millennium, but also as 'the' new means of doing business. This is a medium that evolves at the speed of the new technologies, forcing marketing and marketers to adapt constantly and to find new tools of communication and promotion.

References

Aldrich, D.F. (1999), *Mastering the Digital Marketplace: Practical Strategies for Competitiveness in the New Economy*, Wiley, New York.

Butler, P. and Peppard, J. (1998), 'Consumer Purchasing on the Internet: Process and Prospects', *European Management Journal*, Vol. 16, pp. 600–610.

Castells, M. (1996), *The Information Age, Vol. I: The Rise of the Network Society*, Blackwell, Oxford.

Delepine, J., Hussherr, F.X. and Levieux, J.P. (1999), 'La Plularité des Objectifs d'une Campagne sur l'Internet', in F.X. Hussherr (Ed.), *La Publicité sur Internet: Comment Tirer Parti Efficacement de l'E-Pub*, Dunod, Paris.

Hoffman D.L. and Novak, T.P. (1996), 'Marketing in Hypermedia Computer-Mediated Environments: Conceptual Foundations', *Journal of Marketing*, Vol. 60, pp. 50–68.

Komenar, M. (1997), *Electronic Marketing*, Wiley, New York.

McQuail, D. (2000), *Mass Communication Theory*, 4th Edition, Sage, London.

Miyazaki, A.D. and Fernandez, A. (2000), 'Internet Privacy and Security: An Examination of Online Retailer Disclosures', *Journal of Public Policy and Marketing*, Vol. 19, pp. 54–61.

Nascimento, J.R. (2000), 'Nova Economia, Novo Consumidor', *Revista de Comunicação e Marketing*, nº 1, Dezembro, ISCEM, Lisboa.

Novak, G.J. and Phelps, J. (1995), 'Direct Marketing and the Use of Individual-Level Consumer Information: Determining How and When Privacy Matters', *Journal of Direct Marketing*, Vol. 9, pp. 46–60.

Poster, M. (1995), *Second Media Age*, Polity Press, Cambrigde.

Reichheld, F.F. and Schefter P. (2000), 'E-Loyalty, Your Secret Weapon on the Web, *Harvard Business Review*, Vol. 78, pp. 105–113.

Rossiter, J. and Percy, L. (1998), *Advertising Communications and Promotion Management*, McGraw-Hill, New York.

Stewart, D.W. and Zhao, Q. (2000), 'Internet Marketing, Business Models and Public Policy', *Journal of Public Policy and Marketing*, Vol. 19, pp. 287–296.

Stopnicki, A. (1999), 'Communautés, personnalisation et cadre juridique', in F.X. Hussherr (Ed.), *La Publicité sur Internet: Comment Tirer Parti Efficacement de l'E-Pub*, Dunod, Paris.

Chapter 9

e-Marketing Adoption in Organizations

Abdel Monim Shaltoni

Introduction

e-Marketing has created a significant impact on organizations all over the world. It is important to understand not only if e-marketing is adopted by organizations, but also why it is adopted. e-Marketing has been defined in several ways; for example, Reedy and Schullo (2004) define it as 'the process of situation analysis, marketing planning, and marketing implementation activities, conducted mostly online, to facilitate electronic commerce'. Another well known definition is the one suggested by Strauss et al. (2003) 'the use of electronic data and applications for planning and executing the conception, distribution, promotion and pricing of ideas, goods and services to create exchanges that satisfy individual and organizational objectives'.

Most of the definitions share the same core: e-marketing is marketing that is accomplished or facilitated via electronic technologies; it is based on ideas and practices that improve, and in many cases transform the conduct of marketing functions. However, the 'e' part of e-marketing is causing some confusion among researchers and practitioners because of the lack of agreement on what is electronic and what is not. Some consider computerized databases and interactive digital television as technologies that enable e-marketing, while others do not. In order to neutralize the confusion, and in line with the aims of this book, the focus in this chapter will be on Internet applications (e.g. World Wide Web and e-mail).

Levels of e-Marketing Adoption

The impacts and benefits of e-marketing have been thoroughly discussed in the literature, and such benefits include, but are not limited to: cost reduction, increased sales and profits, development of domestic and international markets, improved corporate image, improved customer and investor relations, and better communication with stakeholders (Chaffey et al., 2000; Strauss et al., 2003). The seemingly obvious benefits raise expectations that most organizations will be highly involved in e-marketing. However, businesses embrace e-marketing to varying degrees; some use it only for communication purposes while others use it to conduct simple or more complex commercial transaction. In order to understand the causes of such a phenomenon, it is important to begin by identifying the different levels of e-marketing adoption in organizations.

The discussion provided by Strauss et al. (2003) represents a good starting point for understanding e-marketing adoption levels. According to Strauss et al. (2003), organizations have different levels of commitment to e-business; these levels can be viewed as a pyramid. The lowest level of the pyramid affects individual business activities that lead to efficient results (e.g. online purchasing and online advertising). A business process level of commitment means that an organization automates one or more business processes (e.g. Customer Relationship Management). An enterprise level of commitment to e-business means that an organization automates many business processes in a unified system (e.g. virtual malls). The highest level of the pyramid is comprised of Internet pure plays, businesses as, for instance, amazon. com which began on the Internet, even if they subsequently add a brick-and-mortar presence. It is important to point out that Internet pure plays are beyond the interest of this chapter, as they are, by definition, highly involved in e-marketing.

Kierzkowski and McQuade (1996) suggest four key stages for the development of the digital marketing organization:

1. ad hoc activities, characterized by basic online presence with no formal organization;
2. focusing the effort, the organization recognizes the effort as a learning experiment, and few resources are dedicated to digital marketing;
3. formalization, the organization focuses on improving its digital marketing activities;
4. institutionalizing capability, characterized by dedicated experts and managers for the initiatives that ensure the linkage with the core business.

Moreover, e-marketing adoption levels can be viewed as evolutionary stages with newcomers to the Internet starting by developing a basic presence and ending at advanced level of involvement. This view was adopted by authors such as Chaffey et al. (2000) who argue that companies follow a natural progression in developing their web presence beginning with level zero (no web site) till reaching level five (fully interactive web site). However, it is likely that organizations might chose to start their e-marketing experience at a more advanced level.

In this chapter, three e-marketing adoption levels are suggested (Shaltoni, 2003). The first level, the *communication* level, is a simple extension of the marketing communications department. Communications can be classified as out-going (e.g. establishing a simple web site to provide basic information about the company, its products, news, and contacts) or in-going (e.g. receiving customers' enquiries via online enquiry forms or e-mails). The main characteristics of this level are limited interactivity in the communication process, in addition to the lack of financial and human resources committed to e-marketing activities.

The second level, the *transaction* level, concerns organizations which start to conduct marketing transactions using the Internet. Examples of such transactions include selling products and accepting payments via web sites, online customer service (e.g. live chat with customer service staff), Internet advertising (e.g. web site banners), and conducting market research on the Internet (e.g. e-mail survey). Here, the interaction is more complex and personalized than the previous level. Also, e-marketing strategy starts to evolve, and some resources are allocated to e-marketing activities.

The third level, the *transformation* level, is characterized by high interactivity, clear e-marketing strategy, and availability of resources to conduct e-marketing activities. Organizations empower themselves by using e-marketing strategy to drive corporate strategy, and the value chain becomes well interconnected. For example, the Internet plays a major part in Dell Computer Corporation (Dell) marketing strategy. Dell depends heavily on the Internet as a direct distribution channel that allows customers to configure and order computers online according to their specifications. In addition to that, Dell uses the Internet to improve relationships with its suppliers (e.g. allowing suppliers to share real-time information with Dell on their inventories, costs and so on).

Factors Affecting e-Marketing Adoption

Most of the studies that tried to understand e-marketing adoption in organizations employed one dominant approach, which is to identify individual factors that could affect the adoption decision. These factors vary from one study to another depending on the researchers' perspective and the technology investigated. An example of these factors is the perceived complexity of the Internet. When decision makers think that Internet applications are complex and difficult to use, the risk in the adoption decision will increase; therefore, perceived complexity is expected to be negatively associated with e-marketing adoption (Chau and Tam, 1997; Iacovou et al., 1995; Lynn et al., 2002; Nambisan and Wang, 2000).

Another factor which could affect the adoption of e-marketing is the suitability of the product for e-marketing. It is correct that anything can be sold over the Internet; however, not everything can be sold successfully. Firms that produce or sell suitable products for e-marketing are expected to be highly involved in e-marketing and vice versa (O'Keefe et al., 1998; Doherty et al., 2003; Shaltoni, 2003). Well-known examples of suitable products include books (because they are highly standardized) and software (because they are digital products). Tables 9.1 and 9.2 summarize the most established factors from relevant literature that affect the adoption of e-marketing in most organizations, including small firms.

The context of technological innovation framework, suggested by Tornatzky and Fleischer (1990), represents a suitable framework for grouping the factors addressed in Tables 9.1 and 9.2. According to Tornatzky and Fleischer (1990) three interconnected elements of firms' context influence the adoption and implementation of technological innovations. These elements include the organizational context which reflects items such as company size, the external environmental context which includes market conditions such as competitive market forces, and the technological context which relates to the availability of relevant and suitable technologies for the organization. Shaltoni (2003) used Tornatzky and Fleischer framework to classify the factors that impact e-marketing adoption in organizations into factors pertaining to the perceived attributes of e-marketing (relative advantage, compatibility, complexity and cost); organizational context (organizational size, suitability of the product, centralization and formalization) and external environment (competitive pressure and targeted consumers).

Table 9.1   Factors supporting e-marketing adoption

	Brief description	Relevant references
Relative advantage	Organizations are more likely to be involved in e-marketing if perceive that doing so will provide greater benefits than existing methods.	Iacovou et al., 1995; Lynn et al., 2002; Mehrtens et al, 2001; Nambisan and Wang, 2000; Rogers, 1995
Compatibility	Organizations are more likely to adopt e-marketing if perceive that it is compatible with their culture, values, and infrastructure.	Chau and Tam, 1997; Lynn et al., 2002; Nambisan and Wang, 2000; Rogers, 1995
Suitability of the product	Organizations that produce/sell suitable products for e-marketing (books, CDs, etc.) are expected to be more involved in e-marketing.	Doherty et al., 2003; O'Keefe et al., 1998
Competitive pressure	When competitor pressure is high, organizations might adopt e-marketing not for its relative advantage, but on account of competitors who adopted.	Doherty et al., 1999; Iacovou et al., 1995, Tornatzky and Fleischer, 1990

Table 9.2   Barriers to e-marketing adoption

	Brief description	Relevant references
Organizational Size	Smaller organizations are usually found to fewer resources and are therefore less able to adopt e-marketing.	DeLone 1988; Rogers, 1995; Tornatzky and Fleischer, 1990
Centralization	Degree to which power and control are concentrated in the hands of relatively few individuals.	Grover and Goslar, 1993, Robertson and Gatignon, 1986; Rogers, 1995
Formalization	Degree to which an organization defines and emphasizes following rules, authority relations, and procedures.	Grover and Goslar, 1993, Robertson and Gatignon, 1986; Rogers, 1995
Cost	Benefits from e-marketing to be commensurate with the adoption costs.	Iacovou et al., 1995; Nambisan and Wang, 2000

Source: Developed from Shaltoni (2003)

Business Orientation of Organizations

A new approach to understand e-marketing adoption is employed in this chapter. Instead of identifying individual factors, such as those shown in Table 9.1 and 9.2, e-marketing adoption will be analysed from a business orientation perspective. Generally, business orientation is the underlying philosophy held by organizations that influences their strategic and tactical decisions (Miles and Gregory, 1995). The list of business orientations is long, some orientations enjoy widespread acceptance among researchers such as production orientation, sales orientation, and market/marketing orientation (Kotler, 2000; Pearson, 1993). Examples of other established business orientations, but to a lesser extent, include eco-orientation (Miles and Munilla, 1993), customer orientation and competitor orientation (Narver and Slater, 1990), and quality orientation (Miles and Gregory, 1995). Some researchers argue that these orientations are typically mutually exclusive, with organizations normally adopting only one of them (e.g. Kotler, 2000), while others suggest that they should not be regarded as mutually exclusive, and that organizations could have more than one orientation, but with different degrees (e.g. Pearson, 1993).

Organizations with different orientations vary in their strategies, decisions, and the way they conduct business. For example, sales oriented companies assume that consumers will not buy enough products unless aggressive sales and promotional efforts are undertaken (e.g. huge advertising campaigns), while product oriented companies focus on continuous product improvements because they believe that customers prefer high quality and performance products (Kotler, 2000). Therefore, it is expected that companies that vary in their orientation towards e-marketing will have different levels of e-marketing adoption. Based on that, Electronic Marketing Orientation (EMO) is introduced in this chapter as a direct determinant of e-marketing adoption level at the organizational level. But, what is EMO? A literature search and field interviews were conducted to answer this question.

Literature Search

A search for the terms 'electronic marketing orientation' and 'e-marketing orientation' was conducted in two comprehensive databases (Business source premier and SwetsWise) that include academic and industry journals. Surprisingly, only one article by Peattie and Peters (1997) was found to include the term "electronic marketing orientation". In this article Peattie and Peters suggest that the impact of information technology on enabling the marketing function leads to an electronic marketing orientation. Even broader terms such as e-business orientation and e-commerce orientation were hardly found in the search process. In order to overcome the lack of literature, other areas of research could be used as an analogy to explore the nature of orientation towards e-marketing. A suitable choice would be the market orientation domain because it represents a well-established area of marketing research that deals with business orientation.

In recent marketing literature, there has been a marked interest in the concept of market orientation. Having a market orientation is said to be the hallmark of successful organizations because it creates a sustainable competitive advantage (SCA) through providing superior value for buyers (e.g. offering products that meet customers needs at affordable price), and therefore continuous superior performance for the business (Narver and Slater, 1990). Existing research into the study of market orientation has three main themes.

Firstly, a considerable amount of theory concentrates on understanding the theoretical foundation of market orientation (e.g. Deshpande and Webster, 1989; Kotler, 2000). While marketers frequently use a variety of expressions such as marketing orientation or marketing concept to mean 'Market Orientation', few writers explicitly discuss differences between the terms. According to Jaworski and Kohli (1993), the marketing concept represents a cornerstone of marketing thought. On the other hand, the marketing orientation is considered to be the implementation of the marketing concept (McCarthy and Perreault, 1990). Kohli and Jaworski (1990) suggest that the label market orientation is less politically charged than marketing orientation because it removes the construct from the province of the marketing department and makes it the responsibility of all departments in an organization. In contrast, Sharp (1991) suggests that marketing orientation relates to fuller interpretation of the marketing concept than market orientation because the market orientation is biased toward the customer, while the marketing orientation is more than just a customer focus, it also recognizes the organization objectives and capabilities to respond to customers' wants.

Secondly, a number of studies focus on operationalizing market orientation (e.g. Kohli and Jaworski, 1990, Narver and Slater, 1990). Approaches to understand the market orientation concept are made-up from two main perspectives: the behavioral (process) perspective versus the philosophical (cultural) perspective. The behavioral perspective describes market orientation in terms of specific practices. For example, Kohli and Jaworski (1990) define market orientation as 'the organization-wide generation of market intelligence pertaining to current and future customer needs, dissemination of the intelligence across departments, and organization-wide responsiveness to it' (p. 6). Others who adopted the second perspective (e.g. Deshpande and Webster, 1989; Narver and Slater, 1990) viewed market orientation as an organizational culture or philosophy that guides the thinking of organizations. For example, Narver and Slater (1990, p.21) define market orientation as 'the organization culture that most effectively and efficiently creates the necessary behaviors for the creation of superior value for buyers, and thus, continuous superior performance for the business'. Avlonitis and Gounaris (1999) argue that the two dominant perspectives of market orientation reveal significant overlaps between them.

Thirdly, several studies investigated the determinants under which a market orientation could be developed and the impacts of market orientation on business performance. For example, Jaworski and Kohli (1993) argues that the antecedents to market orientation include individual, intergroup and organization wide factors. These antecedents have been labelled as senior management factors, interdepartmental dynamics, and organizational systems, respectively. Also, Narver and Slater (1990) found a substantial positive effect of a market orientation on the businesses profitability.

Based on the literature search, it was concluded that EMO combines the two approaches explaining market orientation in organizations: philosophical and behavioral. The first dimension of EMO is inspired by the philosophical perspective of orientation (Miles and Gregory, 1995; Narver and Slater, 1990) in addition to the intentional based theme which considers attitudes as major determinant of behaviors (Ajzen and Fishbein, 1980; Davis, 1989). The behavioral dimension of EMO is inspired by the behavioral perspective of orientation (Kohli and Jaworski, 1990; Deng and Dart, 1994). However, the need for exploratory empirical work was imperative to gain new insights into EMO and identify any required modifications to the initial conceptualization.

Interviews

Three marketing academics and three marketing managers were interviewed. The marketing academics were selected because of their extensive knowledge in the fields of marketing and e-commerce. Also, the marketing managers were carefully selected from different companies to reflect low and high e-marketing adoption levels. The first company didn't have a web site, however, e-mails were used to communicate with stakeholders. The second and third companies were highly involved in e-marketing: both companies had an interactive web site that provides rich and updated information about each company, its products or contacts, and allows customers to order products and pay for it online using credit/debit cards.

Each interview lasted between 20-40 minutes and was conducted in unstructured format, but generally going through two phases. In phase one, interviewees were briefed about the study subject and the factors which might affect the adoption of e-marketing in organizations. In phase two, the initial conceptualization of EMO that resulted from the literature search was introduced to each interviewee and they were asked to comment on it. In addition to these two phases, only the marketing managers were asked about the e-marketing activities and practices in their organizations (e.g. development of e-marketing plan, meetings about e-marketing issues or evaluation of e-marketing results).

Findings

The comments received by the interviewees were generally in line with the results generated by the literature. All the interviewees agreed that if decision makers appreciate the importance of e-marketing and its potential, they will put emphasis on adopting it. Also the interviewees agreed that emphasis alone is not enough, it should be combined with behaviors that lead to the adoption. These comments confirm the initial conceptualization of EMO. However, one marketing manager said that in his organization they hold several meetings to discuss the plans and issues related to e-marketing, but they rarely take actions to implement these plans. Therefore, the behavioral dimension of EMO was divided into two stages: 'Initiation' and 'Implementation'. Support for this division was found in the literature (Grover and Goslar, 1993; Rogers, 1995; Zaltman et al., 1973).

The initiation stage includes activities such as gathering information about e-marketing from different sources, disseminating information across departments, planning for the adoption, leading to the decision to adopt. The implementation stage includes the activities and decisions involved in putting e-marketing into use such as installing new software solutions, developing or improving the web site, employing e-marketing staff, and discussing e-marketing implementation progress in cross-departmental meetings. The interviewed marketing managers whose companies were highly involved in e-marketing said that they believe in the benefits offered by e-marketing. They also talked about the e-marketing activities within their organizations; some examples include:

- following the developments in e-marketing (news, technologies or regulations) from different data sources (journals or market research);
- monitoring competitors' adoption of e-marketing;
- constant meetings for discussing e-marketing related issues;
- using the latest technologies to conduct e-marketing functions, as, for example, installing advanced security systems to ensure customers' security;
- offering adequate technical and financial support for e-marketing implementation.

Overall, EMO refers to the synthesis of the organizational business philosophy and behaviors towards the adoption of e-marketing. The philosophical component

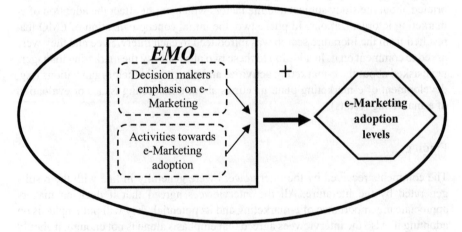

Figure 9.1   The concept of EMO and its relation with e-marketing adoption

of EMO is identified by the degree to which decision makers put emphasis on e-marketing. On the other hand, the behavioral component refers to all activities that lead to high levels of involvement in e-marketing. These two pillars of the EMO concept are interrelated and they are both required for organizations to be e-marketing oriented. The proposed EMO is expected to better explain the adoption of e-marketing in organizations because it covers in an integrated way the degree to which decision makers appreciate e-marketing and the activities which accompany the adoption process (see Figure 9.1).

Organizations which perceive e-marketing as an important part in the way they approach their markets and make efforts to adopt it can be described as having high levels of EMO or 'e-marketing orientation'. Consequently, they are expected to be highly involved in e-marketing.

Conclusion

e-Marketing introduces new methods in most, if not all, marketing functions. Several studies have tried to understand e-marketing adoption in organizations, however, none of them approached this issue from an orientation perspective. Therefore, the concept of Electronic Marketing Orientation (EMO) is introduced here as a direct determinant of e-marketing adoption in organizations. The findings from the literature analysis and the field interviews supported the basic proposition that there is a positive link between EMO and the level of involvement in e-marketing. It was also concluded that EMO represents a synthesis of two organizational dimensions, which are, business philosophy and behaviors.

References

Ajzen, I. and Fishbein, M. (1980), *Understanding Attitudes and Predicting Social Behavior*, Prentice Hall, Englewood Cliffs, NJ.

Avlonitis, G. and Gounaris, P. (1999), 'Marketing Orientation and its Determinants: an Empirical Analysis', *European Journal of Marketing*, Vol. 33, pp. 1003–1037.

Chaffey, D., Mayer, R., Johnston, K. and Chadwick, F.(2000), *Internet Marketing*, Prentice Hall, Harlow.

Chau, P. and Tam, K.Y. (1997), 'Factors Affecting the Adoption of Open Systems: An Exploratory Study', *MIS Quarterly*, Vol. 21, pp.1–24.

Davis, F. (1989), 'Perceived Usefulness, Perceived Ease of Use, and User Acceptance of Information Technology', *MIS Quarterly*, Vol. 13, pp. 319–340.

DeLone, W (1988), 'Firm Size and Characteristics of Computer Use', *MIS Quarterly*, Vol. 12, pp. 51–61.

Deng, S. and Dart, J. (1994), 'Measuring Market Orientation: A Multi-Factor, Multi-Item Approach', *Journal of Marketing Management*, Vol. 10, pp.725–742.

Deshpande, R. and Webster, F.W. (1989), 'Organizational Culture and Marketing: Defining a Research Agenda', *Journal of Marketing*, Vol. 53, pp. 3–15.

Doherty, N., Chadwick, F. and Hart, A. (1999), 'Cyber Retailing in the UK: the Potential of the Internet as a Retail Channel', *International Journal of Retail and Distribution Management*, Vol. 27, pp. 22–36.

Doherty, N., Chadwick, F. and Hart, A. (2003), 'An Analysis of the Factors Affecting the Adoption of the Internet in the UK Retail Sector', *Journal of Business Research*, Vol. 56, pp. 887–897.

Grover, V. and Goslar, M. (1993), 'The Initiation, Adoption and Implementation of Telecommunications Technologies in US Organizations', *Journal of Management Information Systems*, Vol. 10, pp. 141–163.

Iacovou, C., Benbasat, I. and Dexter, A. (1995), 'Electronic Data Interchange and Small Organizations: Adoption and Impact of Technology', *MIS Quarterly*, Vol. 19, pp. 465–485.

Jaworski, B. and Kohli, A. (1993), 'Market Orientation: Antecedents and Consequences', *Journal of Marketing*, Vol. 57, pp. 53–70.

Kierzkowski, A. and McQuade, S. (1996), 'Marketing to the Digital Consumer', *McKinsey Quarterly*, Issue 3, pp. 5–21.

Kohli, A. and Jaworski, B. (1990), 'Market Orientation: The Construct, Research Propositions and Managerial Implications', *Journal of Marketing*, Vol. 54, pp. 1–18.

Kotler, P. (2000), *Marketing Management, The Millennium Edition*, Prentice Hall, Englewood Cliffs, NJ.

Lynn, G., Lipp, M., Akgun, A. and Cortez, A. (2002), 'Factors Impacting the Adoption and Effectiveness of the World Wide Web in Marketing', *Industrial Marketing Management*, Vol. 31, pp. 35–49.

McCarthy, J. and Perreault, W. (1990), *Basic Marketing, a Managerial Approach*, 10th ed., Irwin, Homewood IL.

Mehrtens, J., Cragg, P. and Mills, A. (2001), 'A Model of Internet Adoption by SMEs', *Information and Management*, Vol. 39, pp. 165–176.

Miles, M. and Gregory, R. (1995), 'The Quality Orientation: An Emerging Business Philosophy?', *Review of Business*, Vol. 17, pp. 7–15.

Miles, M. and Munilla, L. (1993), 'The Eco-Orientation: An Emerging Business Philosophy', *The Journal of Marketing Theory and Practice*, Vol. 1, pp 43–50.

Nambisan, S. and Wang, Y.M (2000), 'Web Technology Adoption and Knowledge Barriers', *Journal of Organizational Computing*, Vol. 10, pp.129–147.

Narver, J.C. and Slater, S.F. (1990), 'The Effect of Marketing Orientation on Business Profitability', *Journal of Marketing*, Vol. 54, pp. 20–35.

O'Keefe, R., O'Connor, G. and Kung, H. (1998), 'Early Adopters of the Web as a Retail Medium: Small Company Winners and Losers', *European Journal of Marketing*, Vol. 32, pp. 629–643.

Pearson, G. (1993), 'Business Orientation: Cliché or Substance?', *Journal of Marketing Management*, Vol. 9, pp. 233–243.

Peattie, K. and Peters, L. (1997), 'The Marketing Mix in the Third Age of Computing', *Marketing Intelligence and Planning*, Vol. 15, pp. 142–150.

Reedy, J. and Schullo, S. (2004), *Electronic Marketing*, Mason, Ohio.

Robertson, T. and Gatignon, H. (1986), 'Competitive effects on Technology Diffusion', *Journal of Marketing*, Vol. 50, pp. 1–12.

Rogers, E. (1995), *Diffusion of innovation*, The Free Press, New York.

Shaltoni, A. (2003), 'A Theoretical Investigation into the Factors Impacting E-Marketing Adoption in Commercial Organizations', in S. Zappalà (ed.), *International Workshop on Firms and Consumers Facing E-Commerce, Proceeding*, Rimini, Italy, pp. 45–53.

Sharp, B. (1991), *'Marketing Orientation: More than Just Customer Focus'*, *International Marketing Review*, Vol. 8, pp. 20–26.

Strauss, J., El-Ansary, A. and Frost, R. (2003), *E-marketing*, Prentice Hall, Englewood Cliffs, NJ.

Tornatzky, L.G. and Fleischer, M. (1990), *The Process of Technological Innovation*, Lexington Books, Lexington, Massachussetts.

Zaltman, G., Duncan, R. and Holbek, J. (1973), *Innovations and Organizations*, Wiley, New York.

Chapter 10

World Wide Markets and the World Wide Web: Problems and Possibilities for Small Businesses

Heather Fulford

Introduction

It has long been suggested that for many businesses, one of the most attractive aspects of the World Wide Web is its broad geographical reach, providing an unprecedented opportunity for products and/or services to be promoted and sold in overseas markets (Aldridge, Forcht and Pierson, 1997; Herbig and Hale, 1997; Kiani, 1998). It has been further argued that the web is, in this respect, particularly attractive for small businesses, as its use reduces conventional costs of advertising in overseas markets (Hamill, 1997), and thereby enables small businesses to 'compete more easily in the global marketplace' (Quelch and Klein, 1996). For those small businesses 'offering specialized niche products', the worldwide reach of the Internet makes it possible to find the 'critical mass of customers necessary to succeed' (Quelch and Klein, 1996). However, despite the apparent attraction of the web, it has also been noted that small businesses are struggling to harness the real potential of the Internet as an effective international marketing tool (Haynes, Becherer and Helms, 1998; Schlenker and Crocker, 2003).

The aim of the study summarized in this chapter is to explore possible reasons for this failure by small businesses to capture the web's international marketing potential, and to propose strategies for remedying this situation, in order to help small businesses to compete more effectively in global markets, alongside larger enterprises. The study is focussed on the UK small business sector, but it is envisaged that its outcomes will have wider application to the small business communities of other countries.

The study is divided into four major phases: in the first phase, a review was undertaken of literature on designing web sites for international marketing purposes, with a particular focus on literature regarding the designing and tailoring of web sites to the linguistic and cultural needs of overseas site visitors. This was followed in the second phase by an exploratory investigation of UK SMEs to determine the level of uptake by small businesses of the design guidelines identified in the literature. The findings of the questionnaire survey and semi-structured interviews conducted in this phase of the study (reported more extensively in Fulford 2000; 2003a and 2003b) indicated that very few SMEs were following the linguistic and cultural design guidelines. Arising from the findings of the second phase of the study, as well as from the literature review conducted in the first phase, a staged approach was devised in the third phase to allow small businesses to take an incremental approach to the task of tailoring their web sites to the needs of overseas site visitors. The fourth, final, phase of the study, which is currently underway, involves the evaluation and validation of the proposed staged approach among a number of UK small businesses.

The purpose of this chapter is to present the staged approach to multilingual and multicultural web site development. In order to provide the context and background to the development of the approach, a summary is given in the next section of the pertinent literature on designing web sites for international marketing purposes.

Web Site Design and International Marketing

The literature on web site design is extensive, and growing fast, as lessons are learned from experience, as the Internet era matures, and as good practice principles are becoming established and validated through their practical application. As Hamill and Gregory (1997) have noted, one of the keys to achieving success in Internet marketing is having a 'well-designed site and effective marketing of the site to ensure a larger number of "hits"'. The literature includes general good practice guidelines for businesses, highlighting the principal characteristics of a well-designed web site. Such guidelines tend to emphasize the importance of perceiving the company web site as an 'interface between customers and company' (Wan, 2000). It is further stressed that web sites should be developed with the needs of the web site visitor in mind (Cunliffe, 2000; Rohan, 1999). More specifically, these good practice design guidelines suggest that, for a site visitor, a positive site visitor experience depends on a number of fundamental design issues, the most notable of which are the following:

Web site visitor targeting   Enterprises should identify their intended site visitors, and target the site features and content accordingly (Abels, White and Hahn, 1998; Cunliffe, 2000; de Kare-Silver, 2000; Wan, 2000). Enterprises might, for example, target a specific age group, gender group, special interest grouping, or site visitors based in a certain geographical location.

Web site objectives   The web site should contain a clear statement of the site's purpose or mission. When visiting the site, the visitor should therefore, be fully aware of the intended function of the site. Functions might include: an information provision site, an entertainment site, or a transactional site permitting the placement of online orders with electronic payment facilities (Day, 1997; Lazar 2001; Simeon, 1999).

Web site layout and navigation   The site visitor experience should be kept simple and effortless, by minimizing paths to the completion of a transaction or enquiry, and by ensuring that download times are as short as possible. Site visitors should be able to locate web content with minimal effort. Navigation around and through the site should be swift and clearly 'signposted'. Site should not be cluttered with excessive amounts of information (Aldridge, Forcht and Pierson, 1997; Day, 1997; Herbig and Hale, 1997; Wan, 2000).

Web site appeal and attraction   Web sites should be designed in an appealing way, so that they attract first-time visitors, as well as encourage repeat visits. Overall, web site designers should devote effort to ensuring a quality site visitor experience (Day, 1997; Loiacono, Watson and Goodhue, 2002).

In essence, the emphasis of the web site design guidelines summarized above is on simplicity and ease of use: complex (and hence probably, costly) site designs should be avoided. Such web site design guidelines are applicable to the web site design endeavours of both large and small enterprises alike. One could argue further that they are also equally achievable by both large and small enterprises: the resource implications of following these guidelines are likely to be relatively low. Indeed, as Hamill and Gregory (1997) have noted, the creation of a simple web site comprising an 'online brochure' will probably be significantly cheaper than producing and distributing printed brochures, and is thus a particularly attractive option for the small business. In this respect, it is possible to concur with those researchers in electronic commerce who have suggested that the Internet has levelled the playing field, allowing large and small enterprises alike to compete for custom (see for example, Daniel, Wilson and Myers, 2002). In what follows, it is argued, however, that the situation looks rather different when one examines the additional guidelines for designing international marketing-oriented web.

When designing a web site for international marketing purposes, enterprises are likely to be faced with additional design guidelines to those outlined above, including the recommendation that a decision be made about the country (or countries) to be targeted in order that the web content can then be presented in the languages of the intended site visitors. Likewise, appropriate cultural adaptations for visitors from the target countries should be made to the web content, including where appropriate the adaptation of its graphics, symbols, images, and so on (Hamill and Gregory, 1997; Palumbo and Herbig, 1998; Quelch and Klein, 1996; Simeon, 1999). Cultural adaptations are advocated in order to ensure that web content does not cause any offence in a target country, or contravene any of that country's taboos. This process of language translation and cultural adaptation is often referred to as web site localization (Esselink, 2000; Sheridan, 2001); 'localization' being broadly defined as 'taking a product and making it linguistically and culturally appropriate to the target locale (country/region and language) where it will be used' (Esselink, 2000, p. 3).

A further recommendation found in the literature is that a web site designed for overseas site visitors should, where appropriate, contain relevant 'country specific elements' (Esselink, 2000) for the country, or countries, being targeted. Such elements might include international dialling codes for telephone and fax numbers, overseas delivery details, and the provision of pricing information in the target country currencies.

As with the general web site design guidelines outlined earlier, enterprises are encouraged to follow the site linguistic and cultural localization design guidelines highlighted here in order to improve the quality of the site visit experience for users, and to make site visits as effortless as possible for the site visitor. Tong and Hayward (2001) note, for example, that providing web content in the language of the intended site visitor demonstrates 'at its core a desire to show the consumer that the organization is willing to accommodate his or her needs, showing concern toward the customer'. These authors also found, in their empirical study of both English and Chinese speaking web users, that people develop more favourable attitudes towards, and perceptions of, a company when it presents its web content in their language. This empirical study further found that user perceptions of the design of a company's web site were also more favourable when the web content was presented in their language: users rated such sites more attractive, likeable and informative, for example (Tong and Hayward, 2001). These findings have been endorsed in other studies, covering users from a number of different language groups (see for example the findings of investigations reported in McClure, 2002).

Unlike the general guidelines on web site design, a number of authors within the localization community have noted that adopting the guidelines on web site localization is likely to present enterprises with a variety of difficulties. Maroto and de Bortoli (2001) have noted, for instance, that web site localization entails linguistic, technical and cultural challenges. Poeiras (2004) maintains further that it is particularly challenging for those enterprises presenting 'dynamic content' on their sites, that is to say, web content that either changes automatically (through links to a database, for example), or content that needs to be updated manually on a frequent basis. Elsewhere, it has been argued that managing multilingual and multicultural web content is 'one of the most difficult and least understood, aspects of web globalization' (Lockwood, 2000). This is perhaps best indicated by the fact that the issue of web site localization seems to receive only scant attention in the international marketing literature: those authors that do mention language and culture with regard to web-based marketing, give little or no indication of the complexities involved in designing and implementing web sites that are linguistically and culturally appropriate for overseas site visitors.

In view of its technical complexities, as well as for a number of other reasons, web site localization is likely to be particularly problematic for small enterprises. The first factor that renders it problematic relates to the resource implications of web site localization. To design, create and maintain a multilingual and culturally-adapted web site is likely to require the services of both translators and cultural consultants. A small enterprise is unlikely to have such linguistic and cultural expertise available in-house, and will therefore need to outsource these translation and cultural adaptation tasks. Whilst such expenses might be affordable in a large enterprise, they will probably be beyond the reach of many smaller organizations. In this aspect of web marketing, the playing field on which large and small enterprises compete is certainly not level. In this respect, there has essentially been no change from the more conventional offline business environment, in which only the better resourced enterprises had access to in-house linguistic and cultural expertise, or could afford to employ translators and cultural consultants to produce their paper-based overseas sales and publicity materials suitably tailored to the needs of customers and/or prospects located in specific countries. Findings of the questionnaire survey distributed to UK SMEs in the second phase (the exploratory investigation) of the present study endorsed these points about resource restrictions acting as an impediment to the international web site development efforts of small businesses.

Perhaps more substantially problematic than the issues of cost and other general resource limitations, is the matter of how small businesses typically operate, and how they tend to embark on international marketing ventures, whether in an online or offline environment. The localization of a web site presupposes that an enterprise has devised a strategy for penetrating overseas markets, and has made a decision about which country, or countries, to target. Only when this has been achieved, can the enterprise then engage the services of appropriate translators and cultural consultants to localize the web site for the specific markets being targeted. The design and creation of a localized web site would not, however, seem to represent a viable, or suitable, option for those enterprises that are simply starting to use their web site as a means to explore overseas market possibilities in a tentative way, to test the water, and to determine preliminary indications of the country, or countries, where demand for their product and/or services might be. Evidence from the literature suggests that it is this latter, less formalised, approach that tends to be adopted by many small businesses (Bell, 1995; Chaston and Mangles, 2002).

Literature on SMEs and international marketing seems to contain only cursory mention of the subject of web site localization, and of the technical complexities and resource implications associated with designing, creating and maintaining a multilingual web site. Similarly, little or no indication is given in the existing literature of the fact that these complexities and resourcing issues are likely to place SMEs at a disadvantage, in comparison with larger enterprises, when they seek to use the web to penetrate overseas markets. The study summarised in this chapter aims to address the problem of web-based international marketing ventures in small businesses by proposing ways that small businesses might draw on the techniques of, and thinking behind, web site localization, even when their plans for marketing their products and/or services overseas are somewhat tentative and exploratory in nature. The underlying aim is to help small businesses increase their chances of success when competing in overseas markets.

The specific proposal presented in this chapter is for a staged approach to designing and creating web sites tailored to the linguistic and cultural needs of overseas site visitors. The formulation of this approach takes into account both the informal and incremental way in which many small businesses tend to embark on international marketing ventures. Furthermore, it recognizes the incremental way in which many small businesses develop their web sites and adopt electronic commerce applications. This latter issue of Internet adoption stages has been much discussed in the existing electronic commerce and small business literature (see for example DTI, 2000; Daniel, Wilson and Myers, 2002; Rao, Metts, and Monge, 2003). The stages of the proposed approach to web site design and development are explained in the next section.

A Staged Approach to Creating Web Sites for Overseas Site Visitors

The three stages of web site development outlined in this section begin with a relatively simple site design, and progress through to a more complex site design able to incorporate multilingual web content.

Stage I: A global web site

The purpose of a global web site is for its web content to be as widely accessible as possible. This is important for those small businesses that are, for example, embarking on an exploratory venture in using the web to market their products and/ or services overseas. Such businesses may not have a specific target country, or countries, in mind at this early stage, but which instead to proceed with their venture to expand their geographical reach on a demand-led, or opportunistic, basis. The breadth of accessibility required from a global web site can be achieved in the ways explained below.

First, with regard to site visitor interaction, the web site is likely to contain international contact details for the small business, such as international telephone and fax dialling codes, as well as overseas delivery information. The aim here is to facilitate easy contact between the site visitor and the enterprise, regardless of their respective locations.

Second, with regard to language, the emphasis of a global web site needs to be on neutrality and ease of understanding. So for example, a UK SME might employ a 'controlled vocabulary' to present its web content in English, that is to say, a restricted range of vocabulary involving only commonly used words. The use of this type of controlled language would have the advantage of rendering the web content accessible to site visitors having only a limited knowledge of English. The use of a controlled vocabulary for presenting web content on a global web site is further advantageous for those site visitors who may wish to use an online machine translation system to translate the web content into their own language: the quality of output of such translation systems is likely to be improved if the original version of the web content is presented in clear and simple language. In order to assist site visitors requiring a translation of the site's content, a small business might usefully include on its global web site, a direct link to an online machine translation system. These systems are available online at little or no cost and are typically capable of generating at least a gist translation of web content.

Third, with regard to culture, again the emphasis of a global web site needs to be on neutrality. To achieve this, symbols, icons and graphics should be kept to a minimum, and should be carefully checked to ensure that in other cultures they do not cause offence, break taboos, or may be open to misinterpretation.

Stage II: A semi-localized web site

Designing and developing a localized web site is likely to represent an appropriate choice for those small businesses that have already determined the country, or countries, they wish to target in their online marketing venture. They may, however, have limited resources to commit to the venture, and/or not yet be ready to take the risk of investing considerable resources in creating a web site that has been fully tailored to the linguistic and cultural needs of visitors from the target country, or countries. A certain amount of web site tailoring can nevertheless be achieved without incurring the expense of developing a fully localized web site. To this end, a semi-localized web site is likely to the following features:

Site visitor interaction A semi-localized web site will include the international communication and product ordering features outlined above for a global web site, i.e. international dialling codes, and overseas delivery information.

Language A semi-localized web site will, like the global site, be as widely accessible as possible. Again, the use of a controlled vocabulary might help. As a step towards developing a fully localized web site, a small business might consider presenting some the site's content in the language (or languages) of the target country (or countries). In order to minimize the costs associated with employing translation services, the web content to be presented multilingually should be that which required only infrequent updates (i.e. the web site's static content). Examples of static web content might include the overview, or profile, of the SME, general details of the products and/or services it offers, and information about how site visitors might contact the business. Furthermore, business might consider developing a set of frequently asked questions. To assist site visitors from the country, or countries the SME is targeting, these questions could also be translated into the appropriate language (or languages).

Cultural tailoring of the web content The emphasis should be the same as that for a global web site, i.e. an effort should be made to ensure the content does not cause offence, and so on, in other cultures, particularly in the country, or countries, the SME is endeavouring to target.

A semi-localized web site, then, builds on the design features of a global web site, and includes some basic attempts at rendering the web content specific to a chosen locale.

Stage III: A localized web site

Designing and developing a localized web site would be an appropriate option for a small business that has already 'tested the water' in an overseas market, or several overseas markets, and subsequently decided to proceed with a more concerted effort to target that market (or those markets). Such a business will probably be at the point of being ready and willing to invest more resources in their international marketing strategy, and to be prepared to make a long-term commitment to that investment. Devoting attention and resources to web site localization is likely to yield rewards of increased market penetration in the target country, or countries.

A more fully localized web site will again build on the design features of both the global and the semi-localized web site designs outlined above. The primary addition here will be the provision, not only of multilingual static web content, but also multilingual dynamic web content, that is to say, web content that requires frequent updates. Examples of such content include items contained in databases linked to a web site, pricing information, order tracking facilities, as well as interactive communication facilities, such as online customer enquiry systems. The management of dynamic web content is generally both costly and more involved than managing static web content. This task becomes more complex and more costly if the dynamic web content is to be managed multilingually. Developing and maintaining a web site containing localized dynamic web content is likely to necessitate the frequent use of the services offered by professional translators, cultural consultants, and web site designers, so that web content can be kept up to date as and when necessary, and in order that customer enquiries received in a foreign language can be understood and responded to in the appropriate language. In cases where small businesses do not have in-house linguistic expertise to accomplish this, it may be prudent for them to foster an ongoing relationship with external providers of translation services, and to negotiate appropriate 'retaining' contracts with them so that foreign language customer enquiries received via the web site can be translated, processed and responded to promptly.

Whilst the staged approach to multilingual web site design and development presented here can be followed through sequentially by an SME as commitment to a specific overseas market increases, it should also be noted that the approach allows for entry at any of the three stages, with earlier stages being 'leapfrogged' as necessary.

Next Steps

Having proposed and devised a staged approach to web site development for small businesses embarking on international marketing ventures, the next phase of the study is to test and refine the approach among a number of small businesses. To this end, a series of case studies has been set up involving UK SMEs that are currently seeking to use the Internet as a means to penetrate overseas markets and increase their geographical reach. Preliminary results suggest that participating small businesses are finding the staged approach helpful, and are beginning to reap rewards from their efforts at tailoring their web sites to the needs of overseas site visitors.

References

Abels, E.G., White, M.D. and Hahn, K. (1998), 'A User-Based Design Process for Web Sites', *Internet Research: Electronic Networking Applications and Policy*, Vol. 8, No. 1, pp. 39–48.

Aldridge, A., Forcht, K. and Pierson, J. (1997), 'Get Linked or Get Lost: Marketing Strategy for the Internet', *Internet Research: Electronic Networking Applications and Policy*, Vol. 7, No. 3, pp. 161–169.

Bell, J. (1995), 'The Internationalisation of Small Computer Firms: a Further Challenge to "Stage" Theories', *European Journal of Marketing*. Vol. 29, No. 8, pp. 60–75.

Chaston, I. and Mangles, T. (2002), *Small Business Marketing Management*, Palgrave, Basingstoke.

Cunliffe, D. (2000), 'Developing Usable Web Sites, a Review and Model', *Internet Research: Electronic Networking Applications and Policy*, Vol. 10, No. 4, pp. 295–307.

Daniel, E., Wilson, H. and Myers, A. (2002), 'Adoption of e-Commerce by SMEs in the UK: Towards a Stage Model', *International Small Business Journal*, Vol. 20, No. 3, pp. 253–270.

Day, A. (1997), 'A Model for Monitoring Web Site Effectiveness', *Internet Research: Electronic Networking Applications and Policy*, Vol. 7, No. 2, pp. 109–115.

de Kare-Silver, M. (2000), *E-Shock 2000 The Electronic Shopping Revolution: Strategies for Retailers and Manufacturers*, Macmillan Business, Basingstoke.

DTI (2000) *International Bench Marking Survey for ICT Use, UK*. Department of Trade and Industry, available at http://www.ukonline.gov.uk.

Esselink, B. (2000), *A Practical Guide to Localization*, John Benjamins Publishing Company, Amsterdam/Philadelphia.

Fulford, H. (2000), 'Net Presence: Monolingual or Multilingual? a Study of UK SMEs', *Proceedings of the International Association of Language and Business XXVth Annual Conference*, in K.D. Schmitz (Ed.), Language Technologies for Dynamic Business in the Age of the Media, TermNet Publisher, Vienna, pp. 39–49.

Fulford, H. (2003a), *World Wide Markets and the World Wide Web: a Study of UK SMEs*, HERoBC Final Project Report, March 2003.

Fulford, H. (2003b), 'Using the World Wide Web to Reach Global Markets: Developing a Tool to Support SMEs in Becoming Effective Exporters in the Internet Age', in S. Zappalà (ed.), *International Workshop on Firms and Consumers Facing E-Commerce, Proceeding*, Rimini, Italy, pp. 106–118.

Hamill, J. and Gregory, K. (1997), 'Internet Marketing in the Internationalisation of UK SMEs', *Journal of Marketing Management*, Vol 13, pp. 9–28.

Haynes, P., Becherer, R. and Helms, M. (1998), 'Small and Mid-Sized Businesses and Internet Use: Unrealised Potential?' *Internet Research: Electronic Networking Applications and Policy,* Vol. 8, No. 3, pp. 229–235.

Herbig, P. and Hale, B. (1997), 'Internet: the Marketing Challenge of the Twentieth Century', *Internet Research: Electronic Networking Applications and Policy,* Vol. 7, No. 2, pp. 95–100.

Kiani, G.R. (1998), 'Marketing Opportunities in the Digital World', *Internet Research: Electronic Networking Applications and Policy,* Vol. 8, No. 2, pp. 185–194.

Lazar, J. (2001), *User-Centred Web Development*, Jones and Bartlett Publishers, Massachusetts.

Lockwood, R. (2000), 'Have Brand, will Travel', *Language International,* April, pp. 14–16.

Loiacono, E.T., Watson, R.T. and Goodhue, D.L. (2002), 'WebQual: a Measure of Website Quality', *Proceedings of the American Marketing Association*, Winter 2002.

Maroto, J. and De Bortoli, M. (2001), 'Web Site Localization', *Proceedings of the European Languages and the Implementation of Communication and Information Technologies Conference*, University of Paisley.

McClure, S. (2002), 'Market Survey of Multilingual Websites', *The LISA Newsletter,* January 2002, available at http://www.lisa.org.

Poeiras, F. (2004), 'Localizing Web Content', *Translating Today*, Issue 1, pp. 32–34.

Quelch, J.A. and Klein, L. R. (1996), 'The Internet and International Marketing', *Sloan Management Review,* Spring 1996, pp. 60–75.

Rao, S.S., Metts, G. and Monge, C.A.M. (2003), 'Electronic Commerce Development in Small and Medium Sized Enterprises: a Stage Model and its Implications', *Business Process Management Journal,* Vol. 9, No. 1, pp. 11–32.

Rohan, R. F. (1999), 'Top Mistakes of Business Websites', *Black Enterprise,* March, p. 41.

Schlenker, L. and Crocker, N. (2003), 'Building an e-Business Scenario for Small Business: the IBM SME Gateway Project', *Qualitative Market Research: An International Journal*, Vol. 6, No. 1, pp. 7–17.

Sheridan, E. (2001), 'Cross-Cultural Web Site Design', *Multilingual Computing and Technology*, Vol. 12, No. 43, Issue 7.

Simeon, R. (1999), 'Evaluating Domestic and International Web Site Strategies', *Internet Research: Electronic Networking Applications and Policy,* Vol. 9, No. 4, pp. 297–308.

Tong, K. and Hayward, W. (2001), 'Speaking the Right Language in Web Site Design: Effects of Usability on Attitudes' (Available on web site of Web Usability Laboratory).

Wan, H.A. (2000), 'Opportunities to Enhance a Commercial Website', *Information and Management,* Vol. 38, pp. 15–21.

Chapter 11

Website Usability: Cognitive versus Activity Theory Approaches

Elvis Mazzoni

Introduction

The growing use of the Internet and the evolution of web services is becoming of increasing interest to society and organizations, both public and private. From initially being used to provide and receive information as well as advertising companies and their products, websites have become real 'virtual stores' where things are bought and sold on a daily basis without customers or sellers having to move from their usual seats. Recently, among other things, an increasing number of companies offering free or paid 'services' on the net are being quoted on the stock exchange, so that the number of users of these services is also becoming significant in terms of quotation indexes. The example of Google is well known. Introduced in 1998 in a market that appeared to be saturated and firmly in the hands of two giants which had already been present for some time as search engines (Altavista and Yahoo), Google is currently one of the most famous brands in the world as well as the most used search engine, as confirmed by a survey conducted annually by Interbrand, worldwide leader in brand studies (Interbrand, 2004). On April 29, 2004 Google lodged its official request with the SEC (Securities and Exchange Commission) to go on the stock exchange and be quoted on Nasdaq and the New York Stock Exchange, thus activating the biggest hi-tech stock operation in the United States since 2000. One year later, culminating a year of strong innovation and financial performance, Google announced record profits in the first quarter of 2005.

But what motivates a user to buy a product or use the services of one certain website over another? The evolution of on-line services, ever more attractive and technologically advanced, could be one answer. In most cases, however, users are not aware of the technological features that distinguish various websites offering the same service. Let's take, for example, the three most well-known search engines: Altavista, Google and Yahoo. Most users do not know how the different algorithms operate, which characterize the three search engines; in spite of this, each user prefers one certain search engine over another. One hypothesis could be that users value a certain on-line service uniquely based on the final result obtained. From this point of view, if Yahoo and Google used the same algorithm and thus produced the same search results, it should not matter to the user whether he uses one or the other of the two services. Nevertheless, after a few initial experiences of use, a user chooses only one of the two search engines. What determines this choice? One hypothesis we are proposing is that users construct their preferences on the basis of the effectiveness, efficiency and satisfaction with which they can attain a specific result with a particular web service. In other words, the usability of a web service has a significant influence on users' assessment of its quality and their intentions to use it again in the future. At the same time, usability is also an extremely important aspect for a website's survival in that it increases the possibility that users will return to use it again instead of turning to other websites that offer similar services.

This chapter addresses the issue of website usability: initially the main aspects and critical points of usability according to the cognitive approach of Human Computer Interaction (HCI) will be outlined. Then, a more contextual approach to human-computer interaction, Activity Theory, will be described. Three Activity Theory concepts will be highlighted, as they need to be considered not only by web designers but also by website company managers to improve the usability of websites and web services offered to users and, particularly, clients and consumers.

From Software to Web Usability: Cognitive Approach to Human-Computer Interaction

The concept of usability was used for the first time in the field of traditional ergonomics, and from the beginning has been closely related to cognitive ergonomics and to the improvement of computer products and software. The most well-known definition is probably that of ISO, which in part 11 of ISO 9241 defines usability in terms of 'effectiveness, efficiency, and satisfaction with which specified users achieve specified goals in particular environments' (Çakir and, Dzida, 1997; Jordan, 1998; Faulkner, 2000).

Usability was conceived as a design aid and is specifically applied to the user-system interface, that is, the whole of visual, acoustic and tactile information that mediates the user's interaction with the computer instrument (be it a computer, software or a web tool). It is with an instrument's interface, in fact, that the user interacts to perform a task: if the user clicks on a point with the mouse or types a word on the keyboard, the interface responds, proposing a result or a change of state. Usability thus does not exist in the instrument itself, but takes on significance only within the relationship of use that connects the user to the interface.

The importance of usability in the field of computer science technology has not always been recognized as it is now. Software produced in the early 1970s was used mainly by those who designed it or by persons highly skilled in computer science. This guaranteed with maximum probability that the creator's design model of a system corresponded to the model developed by the user, in understanding how it worked (Norman, 1986), so that usability did not immediately emerge as an important issue.

Usability issues only became evident with the advent of the Internet and the diffusion of websites, although user-website interaction has very different characteristics from those observed in the software field. Indeed, a software program is normally bought without the possibility of actually testing it to know its merits and defects, so that the user-software relationship starts once it has been bought. Internet, on the contrary, gives users the chance to use and test a website before deciding to use it again in the future. From Nielsen's (2000) point of view, the equation is simple:

- in product and software design, customers first pay for the product and only later experience its usability;
- on the web, users initially enter into contact with usability and only afterwards are required to pay for services.
- Considering that many websites offer similar services, we can hypothesize that the usability perceived by the user is one of the determining features when, all services being equal, the user chooses one certain website over another. Design is therefore a crucial phase in that:
- it represents the moment in which interface features determining a website's usability are defined and tested;
- thanks to interfaces, the website responds more or less adequately to users' needs and will thus be more or less likely to succeed on the World Wide Web.

Years of study undertaken in the HCI field have always represented a valid support for engineers in the delicate design phase. In this field different disciplines intersect due to history, culture and the scope of research: psychology and the social sciences on the one hand and informatics and computer science on the other (Carroll, 1997). The main objectives of research and development in the HCI field are the utility and usability of computerized systems, including web tools. To achieve this goal, design should start by comprehending people's needs, as well as what they want to or have to do with the computer, but find difficult. As Nickerson and Landauer (1997) assert, once a function has been identified as useful to the user, calling it up and controlling operations subject to it must be made easy, and it is also necessary to simplify the comprehension, verification and possible modification of such a function's results. In other words, in human-computer interaction a person must be able to easily master the computer, rather than trying to adapt himself to it.

Most of the research on HCI has been conducted in so-called usability laboratories (the main goal of which was to test products before their commercial launch) and was strongly influenced by the cognitive approach. From the cognitive point of view, the human mind is seen as a unit for processing information equal to a computer, and thus is represented in terms of architecture, procedures, information flows, distributed processing, and so on (Kaptelinin, 1996a; 1996b). From this perspective, human-computer interaction is characterized by two information processing units which interact according to an alternate circuit of input and output: the user's motor-output represents an input for the computer and the computer's output represents a sensory input for the user. The interfaces are situated between the person and the computer and are mainly responsible for the input and output between the two entities: the computer keyboard represents, for example, a tactile interface for the user's motor-output and the consequent input of data in the computer, while a web page represents a graphic/textual interface for data output on the part of the computer and consequent visual input for the user.

Research has led to the creation of principles, guidelines and heuristics for the usability of information systems, as well as the definition of operating methods to follow when designing a system. The principles and guidelines regard specific aspects of a certain system (for example color contrast, the maximum number of objects that can be easily memorized, etc.), while the heuristics are more general rules that grant the designer a certain freedom of interpretation (for example the presence on every page of a button to return to the homepage or a tool for navigating and orienteering within the website). These three types of recommendations are often based on research on human processes of analysis and elaboration of information as perceptive processes, such as short and long-term memory, or attention span. Among the authors who have made important contributions to defining recommendations for web design we note in particular, Norman (1988), Shneiderman (1997), Scapin and Bastien (1997) and Nielsen (2000). The main operating methods followed by designers during the design process are the waterfall method, iterative design and participatory design. In the waterfall method, the development process is broken down into various phases, each of which is characterized by an evaluation of usability. Iterative design consists of a continuous process which starts with the creation of a prototype, and from its implementation proceeds to carrying out usability tests, assessing changes to be made, possible intervention to change the prototype, and on to a further testing phase and so on (Wixon and Wilson, 1997). Participatory design, finally, entails the active participation of the user in the development phases of a certain product. The final user of a specific tool can, in fact, offer important information on his point of view and his needs.

Starting in the 1980s, the use of cognitive psychology and the HIP (Human Information Processing) model, foundations of the study of human-computer interaction, were subject to debate. Criticism was aimed, for example, at the debatable 'ecological validity' of cognitive psychology, which does not consider the context in which human-computer interaction takes place, and human beings' passive role in interacting with the computer (Bannon, 1991). We should add that studies carried out in the HCI field had a rather limited impact on the practical design of information systems (Kaptelinin, 1996b). The use of fixed, predetermined standards for design, for example, did not achieve the expected results in terms of usability and utility for actual users. Thus designers had to acknowledge that to understand users' real needs in daily situations and to design really useful and usable systems, they needed to:

- consider a continuous cooperation between designers and final users;
- not restrict the study to single individuals' actions, but to also analyze the cooperative, communicative and organizational aspects, which are often extremely important in successfully carrying out tasks (Bannon, 1991).

Web technologies for communication and cooperation brought about a change in the figure of the user. Instead of the solitary user looking for information on the computer, many people work together in various space-time modalities. There are, therefore, certain aspects that should be adequately considered that have nothing to do with the dual individual-computer relationship, but embrace group and community activities, as well as the management and support that information technology can bring to these activities (Carroll, 1997). Design must take into account how the computer tool can best be adapted to users' natural environments and real social contexts. From this different perspective, furthermore, useful indications could be drawn regarding to:

> the problems users have that technology can remedy, the applications that will promote creativity and enlightenment, and how we can design human technology that ensures privacy and dignity (Nardi, 1996, p. 9).

Starting from theoretical and cultural presuppositions that are radically different from the cognitive approach, contextual orientation attempts to respond to some of these critical aspects. According to this orientation, it is not necessary to start with the assumption that human beings are involved in real life activities that imply the use of the computer. From the contextual orientation standpoint, human beings' relationship with technology can only be understood within the social context in which they are found. This relationship is not static, but dynamic and evolves throughout an historical-cultural process (Kaptelinin, 1996a). One of the most interesting theoretical paradigms of contextual orientation is Activity Theory (AT).

Activity Theory: Contextual Approach to Human-Computer Interaction

Engeström (1996) considers activity theory not as a specific theory offering ready-made techniques and procedures but as a tool for describing and explaining the structure of human activity and its components. Human activity is a broad concept encompassing everything that people do when they are motivated by needs or requirements. Therefore any task is an activity, just like wanting to earn a degree in psychology, organizing a meeting, getting in shape for a basketball game or looking for information on the Internet. Thus Activity Theory:

> is a general, cross-disciplinary approach, offering conceptual tools and methodological principles, which have to be concretized according to the specific nature of the object under scrutiny (Engeström, 1996, p. 97).

In spite of the recent consideration AT has enjoyed in the field of human-computer interaction, its origins are rather remote. Among them we note, first of all, the

German philosophers of the 18th and 19th centuries (from Kant to Hegel), who placed emphasis on history and development, as well as man's active and constructive role. A second important source are the writings of Marx and Engels, which develop the concept of activity. The third source is Russian historical-cultural psychology, the main features of which were founded and developed by Vygotkiy, Leontiev and Luria (Engeström, 1987; 1999; Kuutti, 1996).

The outline of AT proposed by Engeström (1987, 1999) clearly represents the elements and relationships that structure human activity (see Fig. 11.1).

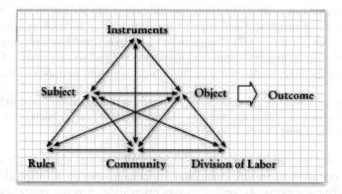

Figure 11.1   Engeström model on the structure of a human activity system
Source: http://www.edu.helsinki.fi/activity/pages/chatanddwr/chat/

The *object* is what the activity is directed towards and should be considered 'as a project under construction, moving from potential "raw material" to a meaningful shape or outcome' (Hasu, 2001, p. 38). Different actors can have different points of view on the object of the activity, as well as dissimilar motivations for participating in such an activity.

People use *instruments* to change and transform the object into a final result. Within themselves, instruments incorporate the historical development of subject-object interaction – in other words the actual instruments have not just suddenly appeared and are not definitive, but derive from a whole series of previous changes that characterized the evolution of subject-object relationship. In mediating human activity, instruments have both an 'empowering' as well as a 'limiting' effect. On the one hand, indeed, they strengthen human capacity to transform the object into a final product, thanks to the competencies crystallized in the instruments. On the other hand, however, the possibilities of interaction are restricted by form, methods of use and the operations allowed by each single tool, making other potentially important and useful aspects of the object 'invisible' to the subject. The first cellular telephone models, for example, rather faithfully reproduced the form and method of use of a home telephone and this probably determined their easy and rapid use by man. At the same time, the interface for typing numbers, similar to that of fixed telephones, but very different from the interface normally used to type a text (for example a computer keyboard), did not offer any input on the possibility of writing brief textual messages, functions which actually dictated the cellular telephone's great success in European countries.

Community of an activity system is made up of 'those individuals, groups, or both who share the same general objects, and are defined by their division of labor and shared norms and expectations' (Barab et al., 2002, p. 78–79).

Division of labor specifies the different power that community members have to define and to influence the object of an activity. This division, within the community, may be observed both on a horizontal as well as a vertical level. For example, in a department of a large firm workers carry out different tasks and are organized in various work teams (horizontal division); furthermore, within each team, the activities are (generally) coordinated by a team leader under the supervision of the manager of the department (vertical division).

Rules, finally, represent 'explicit and implicit regulations, norms and conventions that constrain actions and interactions within the activity system' (Hasu, 2001, p. 57).

This model characterizes human activity as a real systemic whole in which all the considered elements are related to each other (Kuutti, 1996). Instruments, rules and divisions of labor are artifacts (material and symbolic, external and internal) that mediate the reciprocal relationships between the three main elements of human activity: subject, object and community. Instruments mediate the subject-object relationship, rules mediate the subject-community relationship and divisions of labor mediate the object-community relationship.

Activity theory and usability.

Information and Communication Technologies (ICTs) are very present in peoples' lives, during working or leisure time. Thus, if ICTs mediate human activity (Kuutti, 1991), they do not only influence the subject-object relationship but penetrate and transform the entire activity, so that the research and development of these technologies cannot be separated from the research and development of the working activity into which they are introduced. Kuutti stated that:

> When an information system is designed and implemented to serve the needs of some activity, its impact are manifold: there will be new rules – explicit or implicit – for the interaction within the community, the community itself may change, a new division of labour will be established, and even the object of activity may change. And the subject must change in order to learn to use the system. … When a new system is implemented, all the aspects of the corresponding work activity will change – either intentionally or accidentally (Kuutti, 1991, p. 537–38).

Furthermore, the role of any tool is not limited merely to diffusing the operational aspects of human interaction with the world, but also to modeling the objectives of those who use them. Following Kaptelinin (1996a) 'there are implicit goals that usually are "built into" the tools by their developers. The goals achieved by people equipped with a tool ore often influenced by the "tool's goal"' (p. 53).

This means that the features and objectives that the developers have conceived and designed for a certain computerized tool influence users, who may not be fully aware of this influence (for example, the way people communicate by e-mail can be influenced by the nature of the system in use, or a database format can influence the way in which people differentiate and classify elements). The design phase thus turns out to be extremely important in that it influences how a tool will be used. We should thus reconsider usability from a point of view that contemplates, in addition to the immediate aspects of subject-tool interaction as analyzed by the cognitive approach, the more dynamic aspects which characterize the entire system of activity.

In the following part we will focus on three important aspects analyzed by AT which play an important role in the usability of computerized products, and in particular websites: functional organs, action-operation processes and focused attention on the object. In doing this, we will analyze some solutions adopted by the Google website (http://www.google.com) which represent efficient interpretations of such aspects as well as, in our opinion, the main key to this search engine's success.

Functional organs

From the standpoint of AT, human-computer interaction features two levels of interaction: the first level concerns the interaction between the user and the computer, while the second level concerns the interaction between the binomial 'user-computer' and the context in which the binomial is inserted.

Leont'ev defines functional organ as the functional integration between a specific tool and a certain ability on the part of man (Kaptelinin, 1996a). External tools (such as scissors, glasses or a diary) support and complement human's natural abilities, moving towards forming a more efficient system to achieve a better outcome. Scissors, for example, allow one to cut something, 'transforming' the human hand into an efficient cutting organ; glasses improve man's vision; diaries help us to remember by supporting the memory and so on. Functional organs are also characterized by an evolving process: tools that are still not integrated within a functional organ (this happens for example in the first phase of using a new tool) are conceived as belonging to the external world, while when they are integrated within the functional organs, they are treated as an individual's property. The first times we used a pen, or a typewriter, our attention was almost totally captured by the tool and how to use it. After some practice, however, our attention was totally focused on the activity we were doing, that is, writing, and the tool almost 'disappeared' or better yet, was integrated into a functional organ that allows us to carry out that activity. From this standpoint, personal expertise indicates not only that an individual has taken possession 'of knowing how to do a certain thing', but has also taken possession of the tool in use 'to do that certain thing' as part of a functional organ.

To focus on the process of integration of ICT in the structure of human activity, the goals that are intended to be reached with the new tool, the structure of human activity before the assimilation of the tool and users' experience with the not computerized equivalent of the activity have to be considered (Kaptelinin, 1996a).

Briefly, an artifact to be integrated into a functional organ has to satisfy the interests and adequately respond to the needs of the prospective users. Take the example of Google. Google's success is generally attributed to the algorithm at the base of this search engine: PageRank. This algorithm determines the value (importance) of a web page on the basis of two main elements:

1. the preference given it by other web pages (which are also evaluated in turn as more or less important);
2. a textual analysis which does not limit itself solely to how frequently a specific word appears within the page, but thoroughly examines the page's contents, as well as the contents of pages linked to it.

In addition to these important technical features, like other search engines Google offers the possibility to do an advanced, very detailed search which, by defining the 'limits' of the search, increases the probability that the result will be in line with the user's expectations (see Figure 11.2). Furthermore, Google offers other tools for languages which provide ready solutions, albeit rudimentary, for users who find themselves in front of web pages in unknown foreign languages.

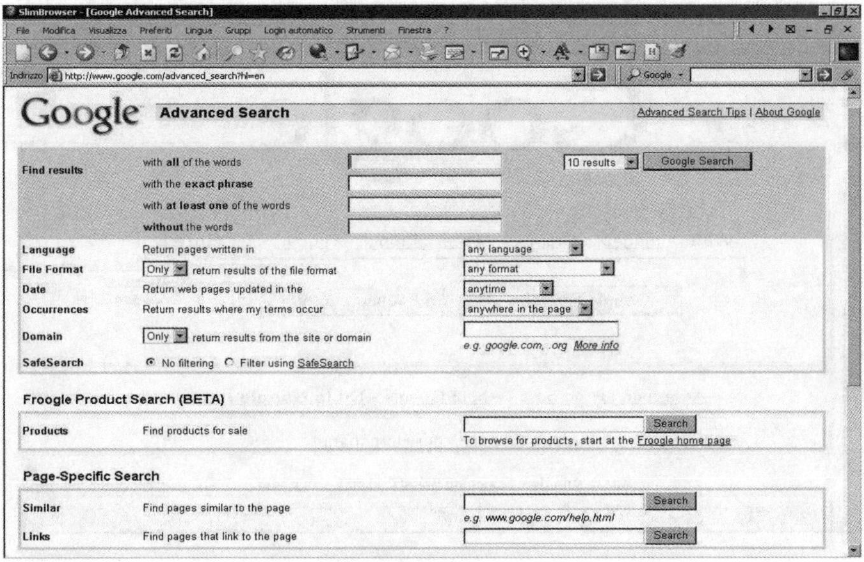

Figure 11.2   Google advanced search page
Source: Google's website page (reprinted with permission)

Google's technological features and the support available to users (modest but well-directed in assisting users to search for information) make the site highly efficient with regard to the user's task and, thus, influence the choice of this search engine. The perception of high efficiency increases the probability that the user will assess Google as a valid response to his/her needs and will integrate it into the tools that can "improve" his performance.

Focusing attention on the object

An artifact 'works well', or is efficient, if it allows the individual engaged in a certain activity to focus the attention on the object of the activity (Bødker, 1996). Two important elements that disturb attention are interruptions and displacements. Interruptions take place when, while using a certain artifact, something interrupts the execution of the work. One cause, for example, could be in the fact that the tool in use causes an inappropriate action or a failure to accomplish adequate operations. In contrast to interruptions, displacements of attention are a more intentional change concerning the object of the action or activity. A displacement of attention can happen, for example, when an Internet expert while teaching a novice how to use this technology, intentionally diverts attention from the object of the activity (for example the search of an information) to the explanation of normally carried out actions which, consequently, become conscious actions.

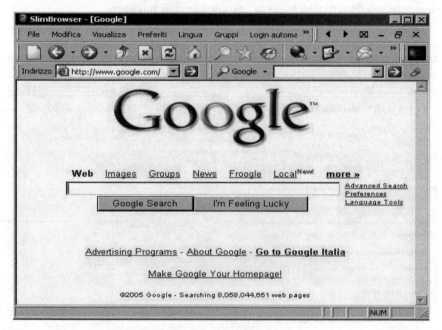

Figure 11.3   Google's minimalist home page
Source: Google's website page (reprinted with permission)

Google's technological features described above, although important and certainly relevant to the success of this search engine, are not immediately perceptible by the user and we can probably hypothesize that most users completely ignore how the search algorithm functions. To carry out a search with Google any user will initially interact with the interface of the engine and only later, having evaluated the attained result, will appreciate the algorithm's power.

Google's interface was and still is in a counter tendency compared to rival search engines. While Altavista and Yahoo have progressively filled up their homepages with more services, links and information, Google has chosen a route that we could call 'minimalist', concentrating the homepage entirely and solely on the search engine (see Figure 11.3). This has two important advantages: the interface allows the user to fully focus on the activity he has to carry out (search for information) and it does not offer elements that can distract the user's attention from his/her activity.

Action-operation processes

Action-operation processes mean passing from conscious actions to automatic operations. An important aspect of actions is their mental planning, which Activity Theory defines as *internal plane of actions* (IPA) (Kaptelinin, 1996a). Before actually being carried out, an action is normally consciously planned by using a model. At the end of this 'orientation' phase, the more the model appears to be appropriate, the higher the likelihood that the action will be carried out properly (Kuutti, 1991; 1996). Actions, in turn, consist of operations featuring orientation and execution phases. When the model, planned in the orientation phase, is good enough and the action is carried out often and over a longer period of time, the orientation phase disappears and the action breaks down into an operation. At the same time, the process of using tools to carry out the action has been refined to the point where the action is transformed into an operation, so that in the future no further IPA's will be necessary.

ICTs, if used properly, make it possible to automate and simplify various actions, although one still has to act with the interface (be it the computer keyboard or the menu of a website) in order to produce an outcome. For example, search engines allow one to find myriads of information that would otherwise be difficult and time-consuming to find. Initially, however, one must know how a search engine works and how to act effectively on it. While this may appear banal, this is not the case when we consider all the surplus information we often get as a result of a search. There are two questions one subject has to ask to oneself: How should I act in order to carry out a search? Which words should I type in so that the search result will not be too broad and difficult to consult? Many search engines have met these needs, for example, by proposing a subdivision of websites by increasingly specific categories and sub-categories or providing the possibility of defining in greater detail the issue being searched. These options can be seen as a way to simplify the user's task but, as we said previously, it is not only important that the computer 'substitutes' human actions, but that it 'encourages' the passage from actions to operations. A subject could, for example, search for information that is not included in the search engine's predefined categories and subcategories, so the tool should allow the user to easily comprehend and learn how to search efficiently for the needed information rather than simply offering predefined categories.

For the action-operation processes principle, usability concerns those features of the electronic artifact that make it possible to shorten the orientation phase and to encourage the development of adequate IPA's.

To shorten the orientation phase the subject must be able to rely on prior knowledge and practices. The computer keyboard, for example, is a good artifact: in spite of changing the position of just a few letters, when people pass from a portable computer keyboard to normal one, they generally do not need another orientation phase. Likewise, navigation bars which are similar for various types of software help to shorten the orientation phase.

To encourage internal plans for adequate actions, the various functions and devices for clearly using an artifact show what can and cannot be done. This concept is very close to affordance, defined by Norman (1988) as the perceived and actual properties of the thing which determine just how the thing could properly be used.

These last two processes are influenced by culture and previous practices. Regarding culture, just think of the icons and graphic metaphors used in various websites and it is clear how important this factor is for rapid use. At the same time, naturally, previous practices are also an important factor: to have already experimented with an action implies not having to learn it over again and speeds up its execution when it reappears.

The simplicity of using Google certainly stems from the fact that it is based on a set-up similar to already existing search engines, so that the user does not have to learn how to use this service, nor does he have to make a mental effort to understand how it works. Google does not use graphic metaphors or special icons and typically bases its user interface on textual information. If this signifies a handicap from the aesthetic point of view, it is certainly a strong point in terms of understanding the visualized information. Metaphors and icons, in fact, are culturally defined so that users from different cultures may not be able to fully comprehend their meaning and may be forced to learn them, lengthening the orientation phase. Google, furthermore, like other international websites, automatically opens in the language of the country where the user connects up, thus not forcing the user into the difficult task of translating terms from a foreign language. Finally, concentrating solely on the searching activity and consequent limiting the number of possible actions for the user implies a very short orientation phase. On Google's homepage, in fact, the actions which the user has to automate are very limited and elementary and it is highly probable that users who have some experience on the web, on their first approach to Google, do not have to make use of any mental planning nor do they need any orientation phase.

Conclusions

Usability is an important factor influencing how final users accept web artifacts. This acceptance, from the standpoint of Activity Theory, should be understood first of all as the appropriation and insertion of technological tools in man's activities, incorporating them into functional organs or tools and human abilities which, as a whole, allow an individual to achieve a certain objective or achieve it with less effort. From this point of view, web artifacts are becoming a part of many human activities, helping people with various functions: for example, search engines allow one to easily trace back a myriad of information, and websites allow one to purchase things on-line or to download documents and certificates without having to physically move, while web platforms for on-line education allow users to continue their studies and training, going beyond the time and space limitations of school, university and work.

The evolutionary process that progressively incorporates a web artifact into a human activity extends over a shorter or longer period of time based on two additional variables: rapid automation of the tool's use and limited attention required to use it. The first variable defines the tool's 'learnability': the user has to be able to easily learn how to use it, and has to have control over the tool in the shortest possible amount of time, without having to plan the actions he has to carry out, and acting in the most automatic way possible to achieve his goal. The second variable, on the other hand, has to do with the tool's interface; the latter has to almost disappear from the scene, and should allow the user to be the author of the actions and operations he or she is carrying out without interruptions or displacements of attention caused by malfunctions or an unintelligible interface.

This re-examination of usability, based on the context in which the web user-artifact interaction is situated, defines some important principles that developers of on-line tools and services should consider in order to achieve two important goals: to increase the usability of their creations and, consequently, to increase these creations' potential of success among Internet users. If from the Activity Theory point of view this can be considered an improvement in terms of attaining certain human goals, it can also be transformed into a significant economic return from a market stand point, thanks to the public's preference of one particular web artifact over another.

References

Bannon, L.J. (1991), 'From Human Factors to Human Actors: the Role of Psychology and Human-Computer Interaction Studies in System Design', in J. Greenbaum and M. Kyng (Eds.), *Design at Work: Cooperative Design of Computer Systems*, Lawrence Erlbaum, Hillsdale, New Jersey, pp. 25–44.

Barab, S.A., Barnett, M., Yamagata-Lynch, L., Squire, K. and Keating, T. (2002), 'Using Activity Theory to Understand the Contradictions Characterizing a Technology-Rich Introductory Astronomy Course', *Mind, Culture, and Activity*, Vol. 9, No. 2, pp. 76–107.

Bødker, S. (1996), 'Applying Activity Theory to Video Analysis: How to Make Sense of Video Data in Human-Computer Interaction', in B. Nardi (Ed.), *Context & Consciousness – Activity Theory and Human-Computer Interaction,* The MIT Press, Cambridge, Massachusetts, pp. 147–174.

Carroll, J.M. (1997), 'Human-Computer Interaction: Psychology as a Science of Design', *Annual Review of Psychology,* Vol. 48, pp. 61–83.

Çakir, A. and Dzida, W. (1997), 'International Ergonomic HCI Standards', in M.G. Helander, T.K. Prabhu and P.V. Landauer (Eds.), *Handbook of Human-Computer Interaction,* North Holland, Amsterdam, pp. 407–420.

Engeström, Y. (1987), *Learning by Expanding: an Activity-Theoretical Approach to Developmental Research,* Orienta-Konsultit, Helsinki.

Engeström, Y. (1996), 'Developmental Studies of Work as a Testbench of Activity Theory: the Case of Primary Care Medical Practice', in S. Chaiklin and J. Lave (Eds.), *Understanding Practice: Perspective on Activity and Context,* Cambridge University Press, Cambridge, pp. 64–103.

Engeström, Y. (1999), 'Activity Theory and Individual and Social Transformation', in Y. Engeström, R. Miettinen, R.L. Punamäki (Eds.), *Perspectives on Activity Theory,* Cambridge University Press, Cambridge, pp. 19–38.

Faulkner, X. (2000), *Usability Engineering,* Palgrave, New York.

Hasu, M. (2001), *Critical Transition from Developers to Users. Activity-Theoretical Studies of Interaction and Learning in the Innovation Process,* Academic Dissertation, Faculty of Education at the University of Helsinki, (Retrieved on January 31, 2005, from http://ethesis.helsinki.fi/julkaisut/kas/kasva/vk/hasu/).

Hyppönen, H. (1998), 'Activity Theory as a Basis for Design for All', *3rd TIDE Congress,* 23–25 June 1998, Helsinki. (Retrieved on January 31, 2005, from http://www.stakes.fi/tidecong/213hyppo.htm).

Interbrand (2004), 'Google Gets Lucky: 2003 Readers, Choice Award Results'. (Retrieved January 31, 2005, from http://www.brandchannel.com/features_effect. asp?pf_id=195).

Jordan, P.W. (1998), *An Introduction to Usability,* Taylor & Francis Ltd, London.

Kaptelinin, V. (1996a), 'Computer-Mediated Activity: Functional Organs in Social and Developmental Contexts', in B. Nardi (Ed.), *Context & Consciousness – Activity Theory and Human-Computer Interaction,* The MIT Press, Cambridge, Massachusetts, pp. 45–68.

Kaptelinin, V. (1996b), 'Activity Theory: Implications for Human-Computer Interaction', in B. Nardi (Ed.), *Context & Consciousness, Activity Theory and Human-Computer Interaction,* The MIT Press, Cambridge, Massachusetts, pp. 103–116.

Kuutti, K. (1991), 'Activity Theory and its Applications to Information Systems Research and Development', in H.E. Nissen, H.K. Klein, R. Hirschheim (Eds.), *Information System Research, Contemporary Approaches & Emergent Traditions,* North-Holland, Amsterdam, pp. 529–549.

Kuutti, K. (1996), 'Activity Theory as a Potential Framework for Human-Computer Interaction Research', in B. Nardi (Ed.), *Context & Consciousness, Activity Theory and Human-Computer Interaction,* The MIT Press, Cambridge, Massachusetts, pp. 17–44.

Nardi, B.A. (1996), 'Activity Theory and Human-Computer Interaction'. in B. Nardi (Ed.), *Context & Consciousness, Activity Theory and Human-Computer Interaction,* The MIT Press, Cambridge, Massachusetts, pp. 7–16.

Nickerson, R.S. and Landauer, T. K. (1997), 'Human-Computer Interaction: Background and Issues', in M.G. Helander, T.K. Prabhu, P.V. Landauer (Eds.), *Handbook of Human-Computer Interaction,* North Holland, Amsterdam, pp. 3–31.

Nielsen, J. (2000), *Designing Web Usability.* New Riders Publishing, Indiana, Indianapolis.

Norman, D.A. (1986), 'Cognitive Engineering', in D.A. Norman and S.W. Draper (Eds.), *User Centered System Design: New Perspective on Human-Computer Interaction,* pp. 31–61, Lawrence Erlbaum Associates, Inc, New Jersey, Hillsdale.

Norman, D.A. (1988), *The Psychology of Everyday Things,* Basic Books, Inc., New York.

Scapin, D.L. and Bastien, J.M.C. (1997), 'Ergonomic Criteria for Evaluating the Ergonomic Quality of Interactive Systems'. *Behaviour & Information Technology,* Vol. 16, pp. 220–231.

Shneiderman, B. (1997), 'Designing Information-Abundant Websites: Issues and Recommendations'. *Journal of Human-Computer Studies,* Vol. 47, pp. 5–29.

Wixon, D. and Wilson, C. (1997), 'The Usability Engineering Framework for Product Design and Evaluation', in M.G. Helander, T.K. Prabhu, P.V. Landauer (Eds.), *Handbook of Human-Computer Interaction,* North Holland, Amsterdam, pp. 653–688.

PART III
Impact of e-Commerce
on Consumers

Chapter 12

Consumption on the Net

Laura Sartori

Beyond any doubt, the Internet is a phenomenon that influences, shapes and fills many spheres of our life. It can be thought as a new global trend that has steadily risen in popularity, growing from about 90,000 daily users in 1993 to more than 605 million in 2002 (NUA, 2004). Along with its diffusion, aspects of the Internet concerning lack of uniformity and inequalities of use have become more evident. In fact, there is a stark divide between wealthy countries and less developed regions, which have been left further behind in adopting the new technology. North America, East Asia and West Europe are the regions where Internet usage has become a daily practice for millions of people and has affected the way they work, live and consume. Indeed, many studies on the impact of the Internet are concerned with consumer behavior in order to make inferences for marketing and business strategies. Yet, the social implications of the impact of the Internet and e-commerce are not fully explored.

The chapter aims to analyze these very aspects and attempts to formulate a framework in which to explore them. What are the consequences of e-commerce over choices of consumption? Does e-commerce increase the atomism of consumer behavior or does it go along with any (old or new) forms of embeddedness in the processes of consumption? We will try to answer these questions, comparing Italy and the USA with the aid of a quantitative data set for each country.

Consequences of Consumption Through the Net: A Framework

Diffusion

To set the proper frame for analyzing the process of consumption on the web, we should examine the literature of Internet diffusion. Very few research studies have directly explored which factors influence consumption on the net. A great deal of research has focused on issues related to the *digital divide*, mainly on the inequalities and obstacles people have to tackle in the attempting to use the Internet. Gender, race, education, income and age were recognized from the beginning as important factors that divide high and low users (Ntia 1995; 1999; 2000). Research has also identified economic and infrastructural factors, such as the degree of a nation's wealth or the openness of telecommunication market, as important factors that influence online access (Guillen and Suarez, 2002).

Recently, it has been observed how the importance of socio-demographics has changed over time, at least in industrialized nations. For example, in the US, gender is now much less a source of inequality (Ntia, 2002). To better understand the source of so-called *digital inequalities*, it is necessary to examine differences in the use among those who have already access to the net and the consequences of Internet practices on its social uses (Di Maggio and Hargittai, 2001; Hargittai, 2003). We can thus imagine a richer or poorer use of the opportunities offered by the Internet given, for example, the same level of education or socio-economic status. We draw upon this in order to state a first hypothesis that needs to be further investigated. This is that the diffusion of e-commerce may be less influenced by socio-demographic and institutional factors, such as national policies of e-commerce regulation factors, but more dependent on personal experience based on familiarity with the internet, cultural guidance and habits of consumption. Grounds for our hypothesis come from longitudinal studies that reveal there is not always a linear relation between the diffusion of the Internet and an increase in the adoption of e-commerce (Lohse and Bellman, 2000). This suggests that consumption on the net cannot be explained simply by the same factors (gender, age, education and income) that were at first significant for the diffusion of the Internet.

Consumption

By looking at the consequences on consumer behavior, this hypothesis reflects the theoretical debate in economics and sociology regarding theory of action and consumption. Firstly, we need to determine whether the inclusion of the Internet in the daily practices of consumption means that the consumer is closer to the rational actor of the economic model or more similar to the actor of a social oriented action, as sociological theory suggests. Secondly, we need to explore the role of social networks in the decision making process, which now takes place in the new social space opened up by the Internet.

From this perspective, we believe that one of the main consequences of Internet use is an increased autonomy in the choices that consumers can make. This goes in parallel with new and old forms of social mediation in the process of consumption.

The first part of the hypothesis states that the Internet can be seen as an instrument through which consumers increase their autonomy both in preference formation and consumption choices. Conventional economic theory holds that the consumption preferences of rational actors, who are each oriented towards the maximization of their own personal satisfaction, are determined by constraints such as salary and the price of goods, in the absence of influence or interactions with other consumers. Sociological theory maintains, instead, that every action is formed and conducted in a context where individual autonomy is influenced by other actors (Veblen, 1899; Weber, 1922; Hirschman, 1985), by firms (Sombart, 1916; Weber, 1922; Schumpeter, 1942) and by mass media and advertising pressure (Schumpeter, 1942).

The amount of information available is one of the advantages of the Internet use (Lunt and Moor, 1998; Schlosser et al., 2000). Higher levels of information provide better opportunities to compare prices and the quality of goods and services in the market. This also offers a chance to better contain pressures exerted by firms, advertisement and the mass media. Moreover, an increased degree of autonomy offers more options for the social construction of 'active strategies' in the process of consumption. It is particularly important is to note that the Internet is a tool of primary control, offering the possibility of controlling and interacting with the outdoor environment (Schlosser et al., 2000). In this perspective, virtual consumption can be considered as an individual choice towards a new, more aware and reflexive definition, of the shopping experience.

However, it is not immediately clear whether more information, more choices and higher awareness lead towards an atomization of consumer behavior. The second part of our hypothesis maintains, instead, that the increased autonomy is still socially mediated by traditional and new forms of networks. Research has found that preferences and consumption choices are embedded in social context (Geertz, 1978; Brown and Reingen, 1987). In particular, Di Maggio and Louch (1998) pointed out how family and friends networks are crucial in purchasing processes through their suggestions and personal experiences. They term this process *search embeddedness*.

The electronic environment introduces and reinforces the uncertainty typical of economic transactions, particularly if the quality of goods is unknown and if spaces for opportunistic actions are opened to sellers (Kollock, 1994). Thus, strategies to tackle a new environment are important. On the one side, actors can use their cognitive resources to understand and handle the complexity and newness of the web. On the other side, consumers can use their social networks to ask for support and suggestions on the goods they intend to buy, in a similar way to what they do in more traditional shopping contexts (for a study on online communities, Kozinets, 2002). The interesting point here is that the Internet, spurring a new form of social network (that is, ties shaped by interaction on the web between people who do know or not each other in real life), offers new and unexplored nuances to the social mediation in consumption processes.

Consumers who decide to buy goods and services over the net have more instruments which can drive them into the decision making process. Not only do they have the traditional networks from which they get information (*search embeddedness*) for their online purchases but also they have a higher quantity of information given by opportunities found only on web. Thus, we might say there is an increase in autonomy, yet it is still socially mediated.

A Comparison Between Italy and the USA

To test our hypotheses we used two data sets,[1] one for the Italian and one for the American context. We will try to briefly describe the social profiles of Internet users

1   The Italian data set consists of a survey conducted in April 2000 by Eurisko, a research centre, on a representative sample of the Italian population (N=1008). The American

and e-consumers and the main grounds and obstacles to online shopping. Although the data in these surveys were collected before 2001, when the adoption of the Internet and broadband was less diffused, trends revealed in later and contemporary research (Istat 2001; 2002) suggest that our findings remain valid.

Social profiles of internet users and e-consumers in Italy and the USA

Looking at the demographics, it is possible to draw briefly a social profile of Internet users as well as e-consumers in Italy and the USA. Comparing the US and Italy, the main similarities are found in the role of education, years of experience with the Internet and age. Although leveling trends are reducing the gap in Internet access, education remains important.

Years of experience seems having the same effect in distinguishing e-consumers from other Internet users. In fact, the older the habit of going online, the higher is the percentage of e-consumers. Internet users and e-consumers are similar with respect to age in both countries, with more than half aged 24-44 years. However, at the same time, there are also huge differences. First of all, gender- differences are particularly marked. Two thirds of Internet users and more than 80 per cent of e-consumers in Italy are males. In comparison, gender differences in the US are not so relevant in terms of proportion of users but there are clear qualitative differences in the types of use of the Internet (Pew 2000a; 2000b). Income has a more defined role in the US. In both countries, the majority of Internet users and e-consumers have higher income levels but, in Italy, these differences are less marked than in the US Nevertheless, many indicators suggest an ongoing leveling-off of the digital divide (Norris 2001).

Grounds to online buying

Table 12.1 shows that the most common reasons stated by Italians who bought goods and services online are purchase convenience (50 per cent), ease of finding products and services (37 per cent) and the speed of this kind of shopping (35 per cent). Over time, the relative importance of price has grown as the other two factors have decreased. In general, the use of the Internet for purchases seems to be an alternative to the usual way of shopping with the advantages of convenience and greater information. Besides this, we can spot a different profile related to the exploration of this new tool: almost one third of e-consumers indicated curiosity and entertainment at the top of their list of reasons for buying online.

According to the UCLA report (Cole, 2000), the reasons for online shopping in the US (see Table 12.2) seem in line with the Italian results. The three main grounds for online shopping are convenience, saving time, and availability of information on goods and services. Also very important are issues related to ease of finding product online, possibility of comparing prices and 24 hour shopping. Another data

---

data set is a 2001 survey conducted by Pew, a research centre, on a representative sample of the American population (N=3493).

Table 12.1   Grounds for online buying in Italy (percentages)

Money saving	50.5
It is easy to find product	36.9
Time saving	35.0
Curiosity and entertainment	27.2
It is comfortable to have goods delivered home	19.4
The producer is foreigner	14.6
I find more information with clearer content compared to traditional channels	11.7
The product was unavailable on traditional markets	4.9

Source: further analysis of Eurisko data (Multiple responses on 103 cases).

Table 12.2   Grounds for online buying in the USA
(averages, 5 points scale)

General convenience	4.2
Time saving	4.0
More information available	3.9
It's easy to find products	3.8
Possibility to compare prices	3.7
Open 24/24	3.6
Money saving	3.2
More fun	2.3

Table 12.3   Reasons for online shopping

Use 1: Curiosity and entertainment	
It is fun	.80
Curiosity	.73
Use 2: Practical	
Low price	−.76
Foreigner producer	.72
Ease of fiding products	.56
Use 3: Rational	
More information	.71
It is faster	.63

Factor scores after Varimax rotation
Source: further analysis of Eurisko data, April 2000.

set (e-Marketer, 2001) confirms that online buyers appreciate the opportunity of buying during off hours (77 per cent), saving time (70 per cent), product selection (35 per cent) and shopping at stores not near their homes (59 per cent). Interestingly, attitudes towards online shopping were positively related to the number of purchases made and the amount of money spent. The more shoppers buy online, the more they appreciate the advantages of this channel (Cole, 2000).

A factor analysis on the reasons for online shopping in Italy suggests that there are three broad behavioral patterns that characterize consumers who turn to the web to buy goods and services (see Table 12.3). A first dimension can be defined as 'explorative and experimental use' where curiosity and entertainment in the use of the Internet had fairly high factor scores.

A second factor is represented by a 'practical use' as two different kinds of practical needs (price on the one side and ease of finding products and opportunity of buying foreign goods on the other side), even if negatively associated, are clustered together. This is particularly interesting because the practical use of e-commerce could be spurred by two different reasons. On the one hand, one might think of someone looking for deals (e.g. online auction and barter market) and competitive prices. On the other hand, reasons related to foreign producer and ease of finding product online point out a practical use of e-commerce separated from that of a simple convenience bounded by prices. Then, we may state that the 'practical use' of the e-commerce is supported, on the one hand, by a money saving strategy and, on the other hand, by a practical need of consumption less dependent on price.

The third factor was defined as a 'rational oriented use of the e-commerce'. This factor had high loadings on motivations related to a higher quantity of online information in addition to speed of online shopping. We can imagine this use of e-commerce being more aware, careful in gathering information and in comparing prices and quality of goods.

Table 12.4   **Barriers to online shopping in individuals with different online shopping experience, Italy and the USA**

	Italy	Italy	US[*]
	Never shop online	Already shop online	Never shop online
Prefer to see and touch goods	72.4	41.7	85.0
Worries about credit card	70.6	48.5	78.5
Prices not convenient	47.0	56.3	51.2
Not expert enough to handle the stages of online shopping	47.4	19.4	40.3
Do not findinteresting products	41.2	17.5	19.0
Needs for warranty and detailed description	19.3	15.5	–
		40.8	–

[*] In the US survey, items asked only to those who never experienced online shopping.
Source: Italy: further analysis of Eurisko data, April 2000 (N=905 never bought online; N=103 who did shop); USA: further analysis of Pew data, Nov.-Dec. 2000 (N=1034).

Taking into account all precautions concerning the data sources, it seems reasonable to conclude that the practical and the rational oriented use outlined from the Italian data set are also similar to the US context. The importance of factors such as convenience, time saving and information gathering are similar in both countries as reasons by consumers to use of e-commerce as an alternative and useful way of shopping. However, it is not possible to find similarities to the curiosity and entertainment profile found in Italy. One possible reason is that online Americans are more experienced and acquainted with the Internet and its uses, suggesting a more rational and aware use of the web after the first impact, which might have had curiosity related features. Another difference can be seen in the perception of price. Although Americans doubtlessly stress the importance of convenience, this is more related to time issues than it is for Italians.

Barriers to online shopping

According to several reports, barriers to online shopping are very similar around the world. Comparing our two first-hand data sets and other sources, it is possible to state that main barriers are pretty much similar in the two countries (see Table 12.4). The main reasons people do not want to buy are related to trust, concern over electronic instruments of payment and price.

Barriers that keep Italian Internet users from buying are traceable back to two factors. On the one hand, limited familiarity with the Internet affects the attitude to experimenting and exploring alternative online paths as compared with just navigating. On the other hand, a strong resistance is represented by a generic uncertainty and wariness, if not mistrust, towards new technology. Among those

Table 12.5   Barriers to oline shopping, Italy

Tradition in shopping behaviour	
Prefer to see and touch goods	.84
Easier and funnier in the traditional way	.79
Not sure how to protest	.64
Worries about credit card	.61
Worries about delivery time	.52
Notr enough expert to handle stages of online shopping	.49
No attraction to a new modality of shopping	
Needs for warranty and a more dtailed description	.78
Prices not convenient	.70
High delivery costs	.65
No interesting product	.65

Factor scores after Varimax rotation
Source: further analysis of Eurisko data, April 2000.

Italians who did not buy online, 72.4 per cent expressed clear needs of talking to retailers, of seeing and touching products before buying them, and more than 40 per cent do not trust home delivery arranged periods of time. Several reports agree on that the so-called 'touchy-feely' factor is one of the most common barriers across different countries (E-marketer, 2001).

More than a limited trust in e-commerce itself, we can put forward a hypothesis about a general cognitive difficulty in handling the new way of shopping, obviously compounded by a technical and practical weakness in managing the Internet. The need of supervising and of handling for oneself all the steps of the entire consumption process is still crucial.

To summarize, it is convenient to look at the results of a factor analysis run on barriers to online shopping in the Italian context (see Table 12.5). The first factor can be defined as 'Tradition on shopping experience' given that all statements clustered on this factor refer to difficulties in becoming accustomed to new boundaries (limited knowledge need to see and touch, limited confidence about payment systems, and so on). Statements on the paucity of information, difficulties in finding products online and additional delivery costs lead us to define the second factor as 'No attraction towards a new modality of shopping'.

Barriers to online shopping, shared both by Italian and US consumers, concern trust (both on the goods and on the payment technology), price, reliability about time delivery and weak customer care. In the two countries it is also observed that the more the use of the Internet, the more positive attitudes towards e-commerce are found. The more frequent consumers know how to handle the complexity of the web and the more they appreciate the opportunities offered online.

About the price barrier, it is worth noticing that online buyers, more than Internet users, believe prices on the web are not convenient, suggesting a double role for this factor. Initially, competitive prices attract new consumers but, as consumers become more experienced online, they realize that the real convenience is not on the raw price, but is spread among other issues like time saving and information. In this direction, Lohse et al. (1999) found that, in the US, consumers seem to value the time saved on the web over its cost savings.

The interesting point here is the relationship between transaction costs – specifically information costs – and price effects. We might assume that for Internet users the price difference is not worth the cost of gathering information while for e-consumers the advantages of information gathering over the Internet is far more appreciated than possible price differences. Moreover, it is possible to imagine that a detailed description of the product and associated warranties would spur consumers to keep using this new way of shopping. Once limited trust in the new technology and in different parts of the new shopping experience are overcome, consumers pay more attention to details. They appreciate and evaluate positively the information available online rather than offline.

A multivariate analysis

In previous paragraphs, different dimensions of Internet use and e-commerce were analyzed separately. Now, we turn to logistic regression, a multivariate statistical technique that provides an opportunity to evaluate at the same time the cross-effects of the different factors such as demographics, expertise and motivation to use the web. An overall evaluation of the results suggests an initial importance of demographics in adopting the use of the web. Yet, as the Internet use increases, other factors, related to cognitive and practical abilities, seem to take place in orienting and shaping attitudes towards online shopping. In both countries, education, gender and age discriminate[2] less than we might expect from the results of the bivariate analysis. Looking at the predictors of online buying, the degree of expertise and ease over the Internet emerge as the strongest variables. These two aspects are enhanced by the effects of longer experience and by the number of online activities.

Factors related both to the expertise with the new technology (years of experience, use of search engine) and cultural and individual factors (types of online activities, institutionalized habits of consumption) make a significant contribution in explaining online shopping. Our findings are confirmed by the work of Lohse et al. (1999) and Lohse and Bellman (2000) where searching for online information, years of experience and hours spent online were found as the most powerful predictors of e-commerce. Men and women with high income (more than 2,500 euro per month) and a college degree, who went online as early as 1995, who possess credit card and judge themselves as expert in the use of search engines, have the higher probability (as high as of 80 per cent) of having bought online.

Moreover, what emerged as crucial in differentiating online shopping from simply surfing the web is more related to past and present behaviors rather than demographics in both countries. This suggests that habits and individual practices have increased their importance over time, being today more important than structural (occupational status) and biological features (such as gender and age). It seems that once the Internet user has experienced virtual shopping, structural differences fade away.[3]

Summing up, a more rational decision making process seems to come with experience in online environment and an appreciation of the advantages of virtual

---

2   We run two logistic models over each country; the dependent variable was the probability that Internet users had bought online. The results are similar in the two countries. In Italy, the independent variables were: demographics (age, gender, education, and so on), having a credit card, years of experience, expertise with search engines and the two barriers 'tradition in the shopping experience' and 'no attraction for new ways of shopping' obtained from factor analysis. In the US, the independent variables were demographics and online activities (email, search for information, comparing prices and goods).

3   As we previously saw, some demographics have a role in distinguishing Internet users and e-consumers. Gender is still important in Italy as income and education are in the USA. As pointed out by Lohse and Bellman (2000), gender was an important predictor in 1997 and 1998 but not anymore in 1999.

consumption. Consumers who do decide to turn to the web to shop have more opportunities and tools to orient their preferences. The Internet is perceived as a channel of shopping alongside more traditional methods of shopping. Specifically, we know now that experience provides the spur to online purchasing.

Old and New Networks

Our results do not provide much evidence on our initial question on isolated and atomized consumers. First of all, users massively use their social networks in the first attempts and initial steps in the use of the Internet. In Italy, 58.5 per cent of Internet users asked their friends for suggestions and tips. Talking about the Internet has become more and more a topic of general conversation. For example, almost 2 persons in every 5 who never bought online know somebody who has bought online. Networks of friends remain important in the gathering and circulation of information and in introducing people to the new social space created by the Internet.

Online experience is important in mitigating uncertainty. Thus, the more consumers use the Internet the more sophisticated they become. Consider the growth in specific discussion groups, mailing lists or comparative websites. In this way, users may increase their ties to people from whom to receive suggestions and tips to use in the decision making process. It is reasonable to think that a new form of social network is under construction – the virtual network. Networks developed online might be thought of as a new field of weak social ties. Specifically at the beginning of the purchasing decision, the consumer may use these new ties to get information, enriching the process of *search embeddedness*, usually supported by the more traditional networks, such as family and friends.

Conclusions

The comparative analysis in this chapter has provided an opportunity to outline factors that influence the process of consumption on the Internet. Firstly, socio-demographics are relevant at the moment of adoption both in the diffusion process and in electronic purchases. Yet, data suggest that their relevance is going to fade as the growth of Internet access continues.

A second remark concerns the effects of cultural and institutional factors upon innovative forms of consumption. We saw similarities and differences between Italy and the USA. In both countries, familiarity and acquaintance with the virtual environment are crucial to the increased use of online purchasing. Obstacles to online shopping are very similar, albeit with some differences. What is suggested is that institutional contexts and cultural attitudes are likely to shape the actions of consumers online. Thus, it is possible that cross country differences in attitudes towards the Internet and the choice to buy online may lead to different e-commerce adoption pathways among consumers of different countries. This requires further study.

With regard to social networks, their role in mediating the process of consumption remains relevant. The increased volume of information and the autonomy of consumers do not imply the atomism of consumers. In fact, we can think that through the use of the Internet consumers become more sophisticated and more experienced, developing new forms of social (weak) ties that can be used to access more information and compare goods and services. Not only do they make use of social networks in mediating decisions of consumption (*search embeddedness*), but they can benefit from richer networks (traditional and virtual). Moreover, they can gather and use information found on the Internet by themselves or through the observations and advice of others.

Far from the isolation and atomism of consumer, we believe that in the Internet age, consumption seems to be more autonomous. However, it still needs social mediation. Thus, social actors may well re-formulate their experience of consumption through the opportunities offered by the Internet. Yet, we do not have to expect a sort of homogenization in shopping practices just because of the increasingly global diffusion of the Internet. Institutional and cultural factors intervene differently from country to country and, above all, they do not seem to be strongly related to those factors that drive Internet diffusion, though more research is needed in this important and rapidly changing area.

References

Brown, J. and Reingen, P. (1987), 'Social Ties and Word-of-Mouth Referral Behavior', *Journal of Consumer Research*, Vol. 14, pp. 350–362.

Cole, J. (2000), *The UCLA Internet Report: Surveying the Digital Future*, UCLA Center for Communication Policy (Retrieved on December 10, 2000, at www.ccp.ucla.edu/pages/Internet-report.asp).

Di Maggio, P. and Hargittai, H. (2001), *From the Digital Divide to Digital Inequality: Studying Internet Use as Penetration Increases*, Center for Arts and Cultural Policy Studies, Princeton University, Working paper.

Di Maggio, P. and Louch, H. (1998), 'Socially Embedded Consumer Transactions: For What Kinds of Purchases Do People Most often Use Networks?', *American Sociological Review*, Vol. 63, pp. 619–637.

E-marketer (2001), *Consumer Report*, March 2001 (Retrieved on May 29, 2001, restricted access at www.emarketer.com).

Geertz, C. (1978), 'The Bazaar Economy: Information and Search in Peasant Marketing', *American Economic Review*, Vol. 68, pp. 28–32.

Guillen, M. and Suarez, S.L. (2002), *Not Quite the Great Equalizer: Economic, Political and Sociological Drivers of the Global Spread of the Internet*, Wharton School, Working Paper.

Hargittai, E. (2003), 'The Digital Divide and What to Do about It', in D.C. Jones (Ed.) *New Economy Handbook*, Academic Press, San Diego, CA.

Hirschman, A. (1985), 'Against Parsimony: Three Ways of Complicating some

Categories of Economic Discourse', *Economics and Philosophy*, Vol. 1, pp. 7–21.

Kollock, P. (1994), 'The Emergence of Exchange Structures: An Experimental Study of Uncertainty, Commitment and Trust', *American Journal of Sociology*, Vol. 100, pp. 313–345.

Kozinets, V. R. (2002), 'The Field behind the Screen: Using Netnography for Marketing Research in Online Communities', *Journal of Marketing Research*, Vol. 39, pp. 61–72.

Istat (2001), *Indagine Multiscopo*, Istat, Roma.

Istat (2002), *Indagine Multiscopo*, Istat, Roma.

Lohse, G. and Bellman, S. (2000), *The Changing Online Consumer*, Wharton Forum on Electronic Commerce Working Paper, April.

Lohse, G., Bellman, S. and Johnson, E. (1999), 'Predictors of Online Behavior: Findings from the Wharton Virtual Test Market', *Communications of the ACM*, Vol. 42, pp. 32–38.

Lunt, P. and Moor, E. (1998), *The Virtual Consumer: Electronic Commerce and the Reproduction of Consumption*, European Sociological Association, working paper.

Norris, P. (2001), *Digital Divide*, Cambridge University Press, Cambridge.

Ntia (1995) *Falling through the Net: A Survey of the 'Have Nots' in Rural and Urban America* (Retrieved on April 15, 2000, at www.ntia.doc.gov/ntiahome/digitaldivide).

Ntia (1999), *Falling through the Net: Defining the Digital Divide* (Retrieved on April 15, 2000, at www.ntia.doc.gov/ntiahome/digitaldivide).

Ntia (2000), *Falling through the Net: Towards Digital Inclusion* (Retrieved on May 20, 2001, at www.ntia.doc.gov/ntiahome/digitaldivide).

Ntia (2002), *A Nation Online, How Americans Are Expanding Their Use of the Internet*, (Retrieved on May 12, 2002, at www.ntia.doc.gov/ntiahome/digitaldivide).

NUA Internet Survey (2004), *How many online* (Retrieved on March 11, 2004, at www.nua.com/surveys/how_many_online).

Pew (2000a), *Tracking Online Life: How Women Use the Internet to Cultivate Relationships with Family and Friends* (Retrieved on December 10, 2000, at www.pewinternet.org).

Pew (2000b), *The Holidays Online, e-Mails and e-Greetings Outpace e-Commerce*, December (Retrieved on January 20, 2001, at www.pewinternet.org).

USIC (2000), *State of the Internet 2000*, www.usic.org [May 2, 2001].

Schlosser, A., Novak, T.P. and Hoffman, D. (2000), *Consumer in Online Environments*, eLab, Owen Graduate School of Management, Vanderbilt University, (Retrieved on April 15, 2000, at www.2000ogsm.vanderbilt.edu/papers.html).

Schumpeter, J.A. (1942), *Capitalism, socialism and democracy*, Harper, New York.

Sombart, W. (1916), *Der Moderne Kapitalismus*, Dunker & Humblot, Berlin.

Veblen, T. (1899), *The Theory of Leisure Class*, MacMillan, New York.

Weber, M. (1922), *Wirtschaft und Gesellschaft*, Mohr, Tübingen.

Chapter 13

Affective States, Purchase Intention and Perceived Risk in Online Shopping

Elfriede Penz and Erich M. Kirchler[1]

Introduction

The Internet is perceived as a new paradigm influencing established business activities and traditionally successful strategies. The Internet is revolutionizing the business world, as shown by the emergence of pure virtual stores such as Amazon.com. It is also changing consumers' realities. Although, the Internet is on everyone's lips, no single definition exists. It is 'at once a set of common protocols, a physical collection of routers and circuits, distributed resources and even a culture of connectivity and communications' (Hoffman, Novak, and Chatterje, 1995).

Most well-known developments are occurring on the World Wide Web (WWW), the graphical part of the Internet, enabling the exchange of textual, visual, and acoustic information (Hermanns and Sauter, 1999). The WWW offers a number of important benefits both for customers and companies, such as information for consumers deciding whether to purchase or not, extended search possibilities for customers, and the possibility of comparing offers in the market. At the firm level, benefits arise from the use of the WWW as a distribution channel, a communication tool and a cost-saving information processor (Hoffman et al., 1995). As a new exchange medium, the WWW is changing the quality of relationships between companies and consumers. Consumers gain in power relative to sellers as the WWW offers access to almost unbounded information and provides a tool to exchange information and experiences (Joines, Scherer and Scheufele, 2003; Pitt, Berthon, Watson and Zinkhan, 2002; Szmigin, 2003). The Internet and WWW are used as special forms of commerce and shopping. Online shopping, in particular, refers to business-to-consumer relations of distribution and the trade of goods (Hermanns and Sauter, 1999).

From a company's perspective, a lot of effort has been put into developing websites and into deciding on strategies to successfully improve them as effective communication instruments and selling tools (Huizingh, 2002; Lee, 2004; Martin, 2002). Although the WWW offers many benefits, some critical developments

1   The authors thank Julia Arnezeder for her help in programming the simulation and collecting data.

such as cyber crimes or hacking incidents reduced the euphoria of consumers and consequently slowed down growth (Lee, 2004). Companies have learned that merely adding a website to an existing business is not enough to keep up with developments. Consequently, the need for a better understanding of consumers' perspectives and reactions to the new media has led to an increase in research on online shopping.

In this chapter, we firstly integrate research conducted in the area of online shopping into a theoretical model predicting consumers' buying intentions. Secondly, we investigate affective states and purchase intentions and their relationship to risk factors in the online-environment.

Dimensions of Online Shopping

Investigations of consumers' use of the Internet tend to focus primarily on the demand-side rather then the supply-side by studying behavioural aspects (Lee, 2004; Rosenbloom, 2003). In our research, we integrate empirical findings in a conceptual model of online shopping (see Figure 13.1) which also provides the framework for further empirical research. We assume that online shopping, or the intention to shop online, is the result of a decision process that is determined by environmental variables, such as the type of product, the specific form of shopping (online vs. offline); and psychological characteristics as well as socio-demographic profiles of potential online-shoppers. Decision processes are subdivided in stages of problem recognition, information collection, and choice of an alternative. After that, consumers purchase the product, which will be followed by evaluations of the process and satisfaction with the retailer and the product (see Figure 13.1).

Environmental dimensions

Online shopping is fundamentally different from traditional or offline-shopping, and consequently it can be assumed that consumers' shopping behaviour differs as well (Dennis, Harris, and Sandhu, 2002). Also, it should be emphasized that some goods are more suitable for online shopping (books, music, groceries and so on) than others such as personal care products, clothes, or products that require sellers' assistance like the car (Chiang and Dholakia, 2003; Kwak, Fox and Zinkhan, 2002; Monsuwe, Dellaert and Ruyter, 2004). Goods can be classified into search goods, which are usually standardized products (e.g., books or CDs) that require only limited direct examination (Shim, Eastlick, Lotz and Warrington, 2001) and experience goods, which usually have to be experienced personally (Chiang and Dholakia, 2003). The more goods can be presented in a tangible way, the more suitable they are for online shopping. Koernig (2003) demonstrated that services can be presented in a tangible way by using appropriate cues such as facts and figures. This leads to more positive attitudes towards the good and increases the probability of online-purchases. Besides the design of the offered goods, the design of the webpage, in general, presents an important environmental dimension determining the atmosphere experienced by consumers (McCarthy and Aronson, 2000; Wang and Tang, 2003). The experienced atmosphere of an online store leads to positive emotions and, consequently, to favourable attitudes towards online shopping, the presented goods, and higher satisfaction with a purchase (Eroglu, Machleit and Davis, 2003). The design of a webpage contributes also to sensations of 'flow' (e.g. Novak, Hoffman and Duhachek, 2003). Flow can be experienced during the navigation if high challenges on the one hand are matched with high skills and efficacy on the consumer side (Novak et al., 2003; Novak, Hoffman and Yung, 2000). Moreover, the online environment itself boosts interactivity and consequently may lead to flow experiences.

Psychological aspects

Motivational and values research shows that the perceived risk of online shopping and trust in retailers are important determinants of online shopping. Consumers usually perceive risk when they are not sure about the outcome of their behaviour. In the online environment, perceived risk is defined as 'subjectively determined expectation of loss by an Internet shopper in contemplating a particular online purchase' (Forsythe and Shi, 2003, p. 869). Perceived risk was found to have a negative impact on the evaluation of online-purchases and thus can inhibit online shopping (Forsythe and Shi, 2003; Teo and Yeong, 2003). Finally, risk-reducing strategies such as using reference group appeal, marketer's reputation or the brand image are proposed (Tan, 1999).

Trust is a multidimensional construct and can be defined as a psychological state that is expressed by beliefs, confidence or positive expressions about situations or persons. Trust results either from fair cooperation or from the evaluation of risky choice situations (e.g., learning about online product offers or payment procedures)

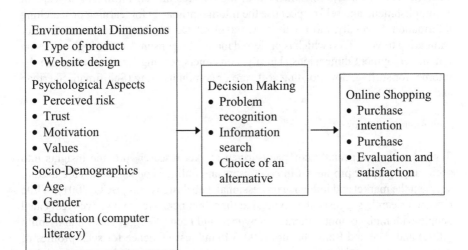

Figure 13.1   Dimensions of online shopping

(Chen and Dhillon, 2003). Interdependence and cooperation between consumers and retailers is mediated by the reputation of a retailer and the information provided on a website (Grabner-Kraeuter, 2002). Fear of insecure transactions is the strongest inhibitor to online shopping as are requirements to disclose private information (Joines et al., 2003). Guaranteea of confidentiality of private information and security features increase consumers' trust (Belanger, Hiller, and Smith, 2002) along with the functioning of the hardware and software to ensure online transactions (Grabner-Kraeuter, 2002). The trustworthiness of unfamiliar retailers was studied by Murphy and Blessinger (2003) by using mock web pages. Strategies that improve the consumers' trust include legal and regulatory compliance, confirmation of common expectations, testimonials or business alliances.

Consumers' motivation to shop online presents another psychological dimension (e.g. Joines et al., 2003; Korgaonkar and Wolin, 1999; Wolfinbarger and Gilly, 2001). It is argued that consumers' motivation to shop online differs from those held in the offline retail environment for identical products. Hedonic rather than utilitarian motives are suggested as a key influence on the adoption rates of interactive media. Enjoyment in using the unique features of the Internet is a consistent and strong predictor of positive attitudes towards interactive shopping and may be one of the most important motives for online shopping (Childers, Carr, Peck and Carson, 2001). In contrast, Parsons (Parsons, 2002) found, that Tauber's personal and social motives (Tauber, 1972) also influence online shoppers.

Values in general have long been studied with regard to consumers' attitudes and behaviour. Values refer to 'an enduring belief that a specific mode of conduct or end-state of existence is personally and socially preferable to alternative modes of conduct or end-states of existence' (Rokeach, 1973; Schiffman, Sherman, and Long, 2003). With regard to Internet activities, three specific value profiles were found in a recent survey. Firstly, consumers with high scores on self-fulfilment, a sense of accomplishment, and self-respect use the Internet primarily for learning or searching information. Secondly, most activity is travel related (e.g., making reservations or comparing travel offers) which is preferred mainly by consumers with high values on fun and enjoyment dimensions. Thirdly, consumers seeking for excitement use the Internet for surfing, downloading software or communicating (Schiffman, Sherman and Long, 2003).

Socio-demographics

Several studies, especially company-driven market research, provide insights into socio-demographic profiles of Internet users and online-shoppers which are used to segment the market and influence professional web designs (e.g., BCG, 2001). While market research suggests that typical online-shoppers are young, well educated people with high computer literacy, Koyuncu and Lien (2003), Swinyard and Smith (2003) and Wee and Ramachandra (2000) found less evidence for such profiles of online-shoppers. Online-shoppers usually spend more time on their computer and on the Internet and find online shopping easy and entertaining. They are also less fearful regarding financial loss when online shopping than others. However, since more and more consumers are acquainted with computers and use the Internet, typical socio-demographic characteristics are fading. Online-shoppers are becoming similar to traditional consumers because they *are* traditional consumers (Gutzman, 2000).

Consumer decision-making

Traditional purchase decision processes are frequently conceptualised as moving from problem recognition, information search, to evaluation of different alternatives, ending in making a choice (Solomon, 2002). With regard to online shopping, a bulk of studies was conducted on the process of information search (e.g., Peterson and Merino, 2003). Since the Internet empowers consumers by making price, company, product, and competitors' information available, it is expected that information search is a crucial stage in the shopping process which differs from the traditional brick-and-mortar shopping situations. The decision to visit an online store was studied by Moe and Fader (2001) who analysed visitor traffic and consequently developed a taxonomy of shopping strategies. This study revealed that consumers who intent to purchase products online view only a few categories and review product information repeatedly. Hedonic browsing is substantially different, with no planned purchase intent, resulting sometimes in spontaneous purchases. Usually the time spent per page is short and product information is not considered much (Moe and Fader, 2001). Burke (2002) asked consumers about traditional and online shopping features which they consider in the decision making process, and found that durable goods are expected to be described with full information. Moreover, these goods should be offered jointly with the necessary services that make the act of buying quick and convenient.

After buying, consumers are expected to evaluate the process and the product. If experiences are satisfying, consumers may increase their online shopping frequency and become loyal customers (Anderson and Srinivasan, 2003). Companies dedicate much attention to keeping shoppers as loyal customers. Satisfaction and loyalty depend mainly on the price of a product (Reibstein, 2002) but also substantially on the match of expectations and experiences.

Perceived Risk as Determinant of Experiences and Online Shopping

This review of the literature suggests that the type of product, as well as familiarity with the retailer, are highly relevant determinants of online shopping. We assume that trust increases if search goods are bought from well-known retailers. The perceived risk of buying a product which does not fulfil the consumer's own wishes or of being cheated by the retailer should be low. In the case of buying experience goods from unknown retailers, consumers are likely to judge the risk they run as high. We define the perceived risk to buying a good as resulting from the combination of acquaintance with the web-site retailer, and the type of good at stake. Online shopping experiences and behaviour were investigated in a shopping situation. Participants had a possibility of buying a product. They were requested to provide information about various affective experiences. We expected:

1. that the consumers' willingness to purchase online increases with decreasing perceived risk. In other words, consumers are more likely to buy online if they are already acquainted with at website or retailer and if the product at stake is a search good rather than an experience good;

2. depending on perceived risk, satisfaction with a website varies and should depend on different informational aspects of the website. In other words, consumers perceiving a situation as risky are likely to be sensitive to other information than consumers perceiving low risk;

3. during the shopping process, consumers consider different aspects of a webpage. These aspects lead them to experience of positive feelings, well-being, satisfaction, and trust in the retailer.

Pre-Test: determining risk of online shops

A sample of 73 students, 21 to 35 years old (M = 24.04, SD = 2.4), was recruited; 44 per cent were male, 56 per cent female. The majority studied Economics and Business Studies (76 per cent), 15 per cent were enrolled in Psychology. On average, participants purchased products online on four separate occasions (range: 1 to 25).

Perceived risk with respect to different websites was investigated using questionnaires that asked students to indicate which webpages they knew and to differentiate between bookstores and music stores (search goods) and sellers of clothing (experience goods). Respondents were presented with a list of 18 websites of different stores and asked whether they perceived buying an item as risky or not. Overall, almost all participants had already bought books or CDs online (98.7 per cent); only 11.7 per cent perceived that as risky transaction. The most familiar website to the respondents was www.amazon.de (92.37 per cent), whereas www.austrobuch.at was known by nobody. With regard to clothes, only 1.3 per cent had already bought online and 63.1 per cent perceived buying clothes online as risky. The website www.otto.com was known by 15.4 per cent of respondents, and www.ipuri.com was known by nobody. Based on these results, we consider buying books or CDs at www.amazon.de as low risk purchases; buying books or clothes by www.austrobuch.at or www.otto.com as medium risk purchases, and buying clothes at www.ipuri.com as risky.

Empirical study: online shopping and risk

Method To test the influence of risk of an online-shop on consumers' experiences and intention to buy, we invited participants to surf through the webpages of one of the four selected stores, representing low, medium or high risk. They were endowed with a virtual sum of money (€ 72). While surfing, they were asked to indicate how convenient a page was designed, what features on a page they perceived as facilitating interaction, whether they searched for additional information about an item or services (such as paying for packaging, delivery), and how they judged the design of the page in general. Additionally, questions were asked on whether convenience, interaction facilitation, information about the product, additional services, and design were related to experiences of positive feelings, well-being, satisfaction, and trust. The experiment ended when respondents quit surfing or when they were ready to buy an item. On average, respondents considered a purchase 7.8 times (SD = 4.7), relevant aspects of the website (ranging between one and 26) and indicated the influence on their affective state at that time. At the end, they were asked to indicate whether the web-site had fulfilled their overall satisfaction with the webpage, and whether they had intended to buy an item or not. Moreover, they were asked to indicate how they judged various aspects of the webpages in relation to online shopping (e.g., design of the home-page, navigation, information about the company, after sales service, payment procedure; all answers on seven point scales ranging from 1 = very good to 7 = very bad). Figure 13.2 presents the experiment as a path diagram and shows an example of a webpage used in this study.

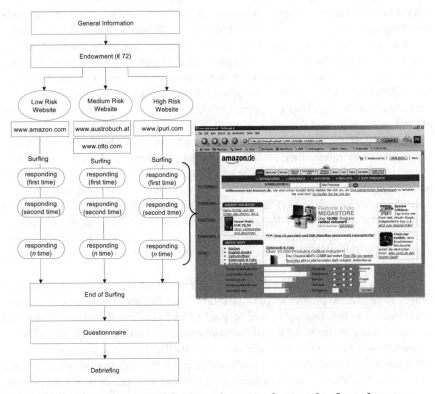

Figure 13.2   Path diagram of the experiment and example of a webpage
Source: Amazon.de welcome page reprinted with permission.

In the selection of respondents, we considered the following characteristics: age and education, computer literacy, amount of time spent on the computer and on the Internet, and enjoyment of online shopping. Based on the socio-demographic profiles of typical online-shoppers (Swinyard and Smith, 2003) students fitted the criteria of frequent internet surfers and online-shoppers very well. Overall, 293 students from Universities in the Eastern part of Austria participated in October 2001. On average, they were 23.9 years old (SD = 3.56); 48 per cent were male, 52 per cent female. The majority of participants studied Economics and Business Studies (83 per cent); 17 per cent studied Psychology. Regarding online shopping experiences, 44 per cent had never purchased items online. Those experienced in online shopping had, on average, purchased online 1 to 20 times within the past year (median = 1).

The experimental design is one-factorial with three risk levels. At each testing session, 30 respondents participated. Every participant sat in front of a PC on which the webpage of one of the four randomly chosen stores was open. After a general instruction, participants were endowed with a virtual credit-card and invited to start the shopping process, limited to one hour.

Results and discussion The assumption that perceived risk of an online-store determines purchasing intentions was tested by analysing frequencies of participants intending to buy under low, medium or high risk conditions. In the low risk condition (www.amazon.de), 78 per cent of participants intended to buy. In the medium risk conditions (www.austrobuch.at; www.otto.com), 51 per cent intended to buy, and in the high risk condition (www.ipuri.com), only 40 per cent were ready to buy (Chi-square(2)= 25.7; p < .001). As predicted, the willingness to buy online varies significantly with perceived risk, operationalized as knowledge of a store and type of product.

The assumption that satisfaction with a webpage depends on risk and, under varying risk conditions, different aspects of a page become relevant was tested first by analysing average satisfaction. The analysis of variance revealed that satisfaction with the website differed significantly between the three risk conditions (low, medium, high risk websites) (F(2)=15.40; p<.001). In addition Scheffé post-hoc test showed that satisfaction with the low risk website (mean = 2.29, s.d. = .86) differed significantly from the medium (mean = 2.99, s.d. = 1.20) and the high risk condition (mean = 3.16, s.d. = 1.20). It can be concluded, that the higher the risk of the website, the lower the satisfaction with the website.

Secondly, aspects considered relevant during surfing were factor analysed, and factors were used as predictors of satisfaction. Four factors explained 62.7 per cent of variance. The first factor, 'design', explained 16.7 per cent of variance. It referred to visual features of the website and the representation of products. The second factor explained 16.5 per cent of variance and was labelled 'personal contact', meaning the opportunity to complain, give feedback on products or communicate with other consumers. The third factor 'information' explained 15.8 per cent of variance and referred to information about payment, security, and product availability. Finally, the fourth factor, explaining 13.7 per cent of variance, concerns the opportunity to download 'trials and samples' (see Table 13.1).

In general, features on low risk websites were evaluated as good to moderate. In contrast, features on high risk websites were evaluated rather negatively (means

Table 13.1   Factor analysis of the aspects of websites

	Design	Personal contact	Information	Trial and sample
Design of homepage	.79	.11	.05	.05
Design of e-shop	.76	.17	.11	.02
Catalogue design	.71	.08	.18	.12
Representation of products	.64	.04	.04	.41
Navigation	.62	.04	.22	-.04
Option for complaints	.11	.85	.25	-.02
Option for feedback	.15	.82	.16	.07
Option for discussion groups	.11	.75	-.01	.40
After Sales Service	.13	.68	.13	.26
Information on payment	.12	.03	.87	.05
Information on security	.11	.22	.74	.07
Payment procedure	.29	.01	.72	.07
Company information	.15	.17	.56	-.17
Download of literature sample	.04	.17	.02	.87
Download of acoustic sample	.06	.24	-.04	.87
Product information	.36	.13	.29	.51
Cronbach's alpha	.79	.84	.77	.76
Eigenvalue	5.27	2.24	1.86	1.28

Note: Principal component analysis; Varimax with Kaiser normalization rotation.

Table 13.2   Means and standard deviations of revealed factors of websites

	Low risk n = 92		Medium risk n = 134		High risk n = 66	
	Mean	SD	Mean	SD	Mean	SD
Factor Design	2.7	.9	3.2	1.2	3.0	1.1
Factor Personal Contact	3.8	1.2	4.6	1.4	5.0	1.3
Factor Information	3.4	1.2	3.5	1.3	3.9	1.2
Factor Trial and sample	3.3	1.5	4.2	1.4	5.1	1.3

Note: 1 = very good ... 7 = very bad.

Table 13.3   Predictors for satisfaction in three risk conditions (low, medium, high risk website)

	Low risk website β	Medium risk website β	High risk website β
Factor 'Design'	.52**	.61**	.60**
Factor 'Personal Contact'	.18*	-.00 ns	.25*
Factor 'Information'	.12 ns	.24**	−.02 ns
Factor 'Trial and sample'	.05 ns	.10 ns	.14 ns
R2	.46	.59	.58
Adjusted R2	.44	.58	.55

Note: Method: Backward, * p < .05; ** p < .01.

ranging between 3.0 and 5.1). The characteristics of personal contact and trial and sample were evaluated very negatively with high risk websites. Table 13.2 describes the revealed factors in terms of means and standard deviations.

In a next step, the extracted factors were used as predictors of satisfaction with the website in three risk conditions (low, medium, high risk website). In the low and the high risk conditions, design and personal contact significantly predicted satisfaction with the website. In the medium risk condition, design and information are predictors for satisfaction. Trial and sample did not predict satisfaction in any condition (see Table 13.3).

It was further assumed that consumers consider different features of a webpage during the shopping process. We divided the surfing process into four stages and counted what features were indicated by participants as relevant. Due to data limitations, only a small sub-sample could be used. A sequence of 31 respondents who answered the questions four times during their online session will be analysed. As shown in Figure 13.2 (left side), design was mentioned as relevant by 47.2 per cent of respondents, followed by information (41.7 per cent) and convenience (33.3 per cent). Chronologically, however, design attracted the most attention only in the beginning. During surfing, convenience and information became more relevant. Interaction and additional services were not considered much during the entire online shopping process.

Finally, the features of a website were assumed to lead to positive feelings, well-being, satisfaction, and trust in the retailer. For each website-feature that was considered important, respondents indicated how that particular feature influenced their affective state at that time (−1 = negative influence, 0 = neutral/no influence, +1 = positive influence). Therefore, the average impact of each website-aspect on affective states was calculated. The respective means and standard deviations are displayed in Figure 13.3 (right side).

		Positive Feel.		Well-Being		Satisfaction		Trust	
	N	Mean	SD	Mean	SD	Mean	SD	Mean	SD
	7	.57	.54	.57	.54	.86	.38	.57	.79
	9	.71	.49	.57	.54	.86	.38	.56	.53
	8	.33	.82	.14	.90	.14	.90	.38	.92
	12	.17	.72	.18	.75	.42	.90	.27	.78
	2	.00	.00	.00	.00	.50	.71	1.00	.00
	4	.00	.82	.25	.96	.50	1.00	.25	.96
	1	-1.00	--	.00	--	-1.00	--	.00	--
	2	.00	1.40	.00	--	.50	.71	.50	.71
	7	.17	.98	.43	.54	.00	.89	.00	.63
	9	.43	.78	.13	.64	.38	.92	.25	.71
	13	.08	.67	.17	.58	.00	.85	.15	.80
	15	.17	.83	.08	.86	.15	.90	.31	.75
	3	.00	1.40	.00	1.00	.00	1.40	.00	1.40
	4	.33	.60	.33	.60	.25	.96	.67	.60
	4	1.00	.00	.00	.00	.75	.50	.33	.60
	3	.67	.60	.33	1.10	.00	1.00	.00	1.00
	17	.00	.84	.18	.73	.27	.60	.31	.70
	11	.45	.69	.27	.65	.27	.90	.10	.54
	10	.00	.47	-.10	.57	-.20	.79	.00	.70
	5	-.20	.84	-.25	.50	-.75	.50	.00	.00

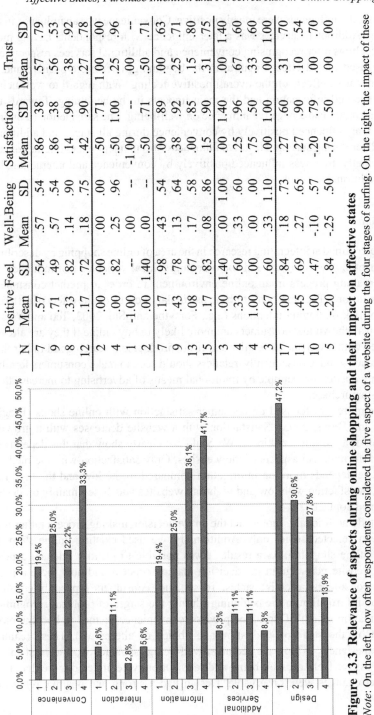

Figure 13.3 Relevance of aspects during online shopping and their impact on affective states

Note: On the left, how often respondents considered the five aspect of a website during the four stages of surfing. On the right, the impact of these aspects on respondents' affective states; (-1 = negative impact, 0 = neutral/no impact, 1 = positive impact).

Overall, the influences were mostly positive. Convenience was an influence in the beginning. Additional services was a later influence with respondents having more positive feelings after recognising convenience and additional services respectively. Design caused mixed effects: neutral in the beginning, later more positive and, at the end, negative effects on the overall positive feeling. With regard to well-being, convenience and information had the main impacts in the beginning. Towards the end, design again had a negative influence on well-being. The satisfaction of online-shoppers was influenced positively by convenience during all stages and additional services later during surfing. Negative influences on satisfaction had interaction and design. Finally, trust was influenced positively by convenience and interaction, but also by additional services.

Conclusion

This chapter aimed at integrating research in the area of online shopping by describing environmental, psychological and socio-demographical variables that influence the decision making process in an online environment in order to predict consumers' buying intentions. The empirical study, in particular, focused on the effect of different degrees of risk on buying intentions (e.g., Forsythe and Shi, 2003; Teo and Yeong, 2003). It was shown that consumers are more likely to buy online if they are already acquainted with a website or retailer and if the product is a search good rather than an experience good. Consequently, retailers should seek to make consumers familiar with their website, for example by traditional means of advertising to increase their intention to purchase.

Furthermore, we focused on consumer satisfaction with online shops (Eroglu, Machleit and Davis, 2003). Satisfaction with a website decreases with a growing perception of a website's riskiness. We could not clearly show that this depends on different informational aspects of the websites. Only satisfaction with the medium risk website depends more on information compared to the low and the high risk websites. Satisfaction with low and high risk websites was based mainly on design and personal contact.

The study additionally monitored the entire decision making process rather than focusing on selected stages only. Additionally, we used existing online shops to simulate online shopping. As a result, it was possible to identify relevant aspects of a real website per stage in the decision making process and how these aspects influence consumers' affective states. To sum up, consumers especially consider design and information in the beginning (during the stages of problem recognition and information search). During the process, convenience seemed to become more important (in the stage of evaluation and choice of alternative). These features lead to experiences of positive feelings, well-being, satisfaction, and trust in the retailer. Positive feelings, well-being and satisfaction were affected more than trust and higher changes were observable. Design had a strong and positive relevance for online-shoppers in the beginning, but became less significant and even led to negative affective states.

Consequently, the design of online shops and their appearance on the WWW have to be developed with care. Design can serve as orientation at the entrance to the online context, but should not be overestimated in the further process of shopping. Consumers are becoming more interested in additionally provided services or require information because they simply are in another stage of their decision.

References

Anderson, R.E. and Srinivasan, S. S. (2003), 'e-Satisfaction and e-Loyalty: A Contingency Framework', *Psychology and Marketing,* Vol. 20, pp. 123–138.

BCG (2001), *Winning the Online Consumer*, Boston Consulting Group.

Belanger, F., Hiller, J.S. and Smith, W.J. (2002), 'Trustworthiness in Electronic Commerce: The Role of Privacy, Security, and Site Attributes', *Journal of Strategic Information Systems,* Vol. 11, pp. 245–270.

Burke, R.R. (2002), 'Technology and the Customer Interface: What Consumers Want in the Physical and Virtual Store', *Journal of the Academy of Marketing Science*, Vol. 30, pp. 411–432.

Chen, S.C. and Dhillon, G.S. (2003), 'Interpreting Dimensions of Consumer Trust in e-Commerce', *Information Technology and Management,* Vol. 4, pp. 303–318.

Chiang, K.-P. and Dholakia, R.R. (2003), 'Factors Driving Consumer Intention to Shop Online', *Journal of Consumer Psychology,* Vol. 13, pp. 177–183.

Childers, T.L., Carr, C.L., Peck, J. and Carson, S. (2001), 'Hedonic and Utilitarian Motivations for Online Retail Shopping Behavior', *Journal of Retailing*, Vol. 77, pp. 511–535.

Dennis, C., Harris, L. and Sandhu, B. (2002), 'From Bricks to Clicks: Understanding the e-Consumer', *Qualitative Market Research*, Vol. 5, p. 281.

Eroglu, S.A., Machleit, K.A. and Davis, L.M. (2003), 'Empirical Testing of a Model of Online Store Atmospherics and Shopper Responses', *Psychology and Marketing*, Vol. 20, pp. 139–150.

Forsythe, S.M. and Shi, B. (2003), 'Consumer Patronage and Risk Perceptions in Internet Shopping', *Journal of Business Research*, Vol. 56, pp. 867–875.

Grabner-Kraeuter, S. (2002), 'The Role of Consumers' Trust in Online shopping', *Journal of Business Ethics*, Vol. 39, pp. 43–50.

Gutzman, A.D. (2000), *Technologies that Capture Motivated Shoppers,* Insights – EC Tech Advisor, http://ecommerce.internet.com/news/insights/ (November, 8, 2003).

Hermanns, A. and Sauter, M. (1999), *Management Handbuch Electronic Commerce*, Vahlen, München.

Hoffman, D.L., Novak, T.P. and Chatterje, P. (1995), Commercial Scenarios for the Web: Opportunities and Challenges', *Journal of Computer-Mediated Communication,* Vol. 1 (December).

Huizingh, E.K. (2002), 'Towards Successful e-Business Strategies: A Hierarchy of Three Management Models', *Journal of Marketing Management*, Vol. 18, pp. 721–747.

Joines, J.L., Scherer, C.W. and Scheufele, D.A. (2003), 'Exploring Motivations for Consumer Web Use and their Implications for e-Commerce', *The Journal of Consumer Marketing*, Vol. 20(2/3), p. 90.

Koernig, S.K. (2003), 'e-Scapes: The Electronic Physical Environment and Service Tangibility', *Psychology and Marketing*, Vol. 20, pp. 151–167.

Korgaonkar, P.K. and Wolin, L.D. (1999), 'A Multivariate Analysis of Web Usage', *Journal of Advertising Research*, Vol. 39, pp. 53–68.

Koyuncu, C. and Lien, D. (2003), 'e-Commerce and Consumer's Purchasing Behavior', *Applied Economics*, Vol. 35, pp. 721–726.

Kwak, H., Fox, R.J. and Zinkhan, G.M. (2002), 'What Products Can Be Successfully Promoted and Sold Via the Internet', *Journal of Advertising Research, January/ February*, pp. 23–38.

Lee, P.-M. (2004), 'Behavioral Model of Online Purchasers in e-Commerce Enviroment', *Electronic Commerce Research*, Vol. 4, pp. 75–85.

Martin, N.M. (2002), 'Task-Technology Fit: Brick and Mortar Beware?', *Journal of American Academy of Business*, Vol. 1, pp. 278–281.

McCarthy, R.V. and Aronson, J.E. (2000), 'Activating Consumer Response: A Model for Web Site Design Strategy', *Journal of Computer Information Systems*, Vol. 41, pp. 2–8.

Moe, W.W. and Fader, P.S. (2001), 'Uncovering Patterns In Cybershopping', *California Management Review*, Vol. 43, p. 106.

Monsuwe, T.P., Dellaert, B.G.C. and Ruyter, K.D. (2004), 'What Drives Consumers to Shop Online? A Literature Review', *International Journal of Service Industry Management,* Vol. 15, pp. 102–121.

Murphy, G.B. and Blessinger, A.A. (2003), 'Perceptions of No-Name Recognition Business to Consumer e-Commerce Trustworthiness: The Effectiveness of Potential Influence Tactics', *The Journal of High Technology Management Research*, Vol. 14, pp. 71–92.

Novak, T.P., Hoffman, D.L. and Duhachek, A. (2003), 'The Influence of Goal-Directed and Experiental Activities on Online Flow Experiences', *Journal of Consumer Psychology*, Vol. 13, pp. 3–16.

Novak, T.P., Hoffman, D.L. and Yung, Y.-F. (2000), 'Measuring the Customer Experience in Online Environments', *Marketing Science*, Vol. 19, pp. 22–42.

Parsons, A.G. (2002), Non-Functional Motives for Shoppers: Why We Click', *The Journal of Consumer Marketing*, Vol. 19, pp. 380–392.

Peterson, R.A. and Merino, M.C. (2003), 'Consumer Information Search Behavior and the Internet', *Psychology and Marketing*, Vol. 20, pp. 99–121.

Pitt, L.F., Berthon, P.R., Watson, R.T. and Zinkhan, G.M. (2002), 'The Internet and the Birth of Real Consumer Power', *Business Horizons*, Vol. 45, pp. 7–14.

Reibstein, D.J. (2002), 'What Attracts Customers to Online Stores, and What Keeps Them Coming Back?', *Journal of the Academy of Marketing Science*, Vol. 30, pp. 465–473.

Rokeach, M.J. (1973), *The Nature of Human Values*, Free Press, New York.

Rosenbloom, B. (2003), 'Behavioral Dimensions of e-Commerce: Augmenting Technology and Economics', *Psychology and Marketing*, Vol. 20, pp. 93–98.

Schiffman, L., Sherman, E. and Long, M. (2003), 'Toward a Better Understanding of the Interplay of Personal Values and the Internet', *Psychology and Marketing*, Vol. 20, p. 169.

Shim, S., Eastlick, M.A., Lotz, S.L. and Warrington, P. (2001), 'An Online Prepurchase Intentions Model: The Role of Intention to Search', *Journal of Retailing*, Vol. 77, pp. 397–416.

Solomon, M.R. (2002), *Consumer Behavior*, Prentice Hall, Upper Saddle River.

Swinyard, W.R. and Smith, S.M. (2003), 'Why People (Don't) Shop Online: A Lifestyle Study of the Internet Consumer', *Psychology and Marketing*, Vol. 20, pp. 567–597.

Szmigin, I. (2003), *Understanding the Consumer*, Sage, London.

Tan, S.J. (1999), 'Strategies for Reducing Consumers' Risk Aversion in Internet Shopping', *The Journal of Consumer Marketing*, Vol. 16, p. 163.

Tauber, E.M. (1972), 'Why Do People Shop', *Journal of Marketing*, Vol. 36, pp. 46–59.

Teo, T.S.H. and Yeong, Y.D. (2003), 'Assessing the Customer Decision Process in the Digital Marketplace', *Omega*, Vol. 31, pp. 349–363.

Wang, Y.-S. and Tang, T.-I. (2003), 'Assessing Customer Perceptions of Website Service Quality in Digital Marketing Environments', *Journal of End User Computing*, Vol. 15, pp. 14–31.

Wee, K.N.L. and Ramachandra, R. (2000), 'Cyberbuying in China, Hong Kong and Singapore: Tracking the Who, Where, Why and What of Online Buying', *International Journal of Retail and Distribution Management*, Vol. 28, pp. 307–316.

Wolfinbarger, M. and Gilly, M.C. (2001), 'Shopping Online for Freedom, Control and Fun', *California Management Review*, Vol. 43, pp. 34–55.

Chapter 14

Risk Perception in Online Shopping

Marco G. Mariani and Salvatore Zappalà

Introduction

Human beings have developed the ability to escape or change dangerous or potentially dangerous situations that threaten their psycho-physical wellbeing. The perception of risk plays an important role in this process of adaptation to the environment. But in this day and age a growing number of people are working in environments different from what a few decades ago would have been called 'natural'. Internet is one of those environments and its peculiarity consists of the prevalence of virtual as opposed to physical relationships with other persons acting in the same environment. In these environments, activities that are perceived in daily life as ordinary and not dangerous can be perceived as risky. For example, as we will discuss in this chapter, a typical adult human being activity such as consumer behaviors can take on special risky implications when it is carried out in the Internet environment.

The Internet's World Wide Web is an essentially new environment for consumers. It appears as a complex context due to the quantity and quality of information and the competencies required: a consumer needs to login into one out of dozens of commercial websites, search and find a specific product, read about its features and payment details and eventually make a purchase; subsequently, s/he receives the merchandise directly at home. This has clear advantages for the customer; among others the high number of goods or services to choose from, the possibility to purchase at any time and at low cost. But what are the perceived risks when purchasing online? Which factors influence the underlying psychological processes? What are the consequences of such processes for individuals' behavior?

This chapter answers these questions by reviewing some of the studies on risk perception in the use of technology and consumer behavior and by reporting the results of two studies we conducted on risk perception in e-commerce. Finally, in the conclusion some considerations on how to reduce risk perceptions of online consumers are presented.

Risk Perception

Several definitions of risk refer to concepts such as probability and loss (Vlek and Stallen, 1981). Risk perception can be considered both a function of the probability that an undesired event may occur as well as a function of the extent of the negative consequences associated with the undesired event (Murray, 1991). An 'objective' evaluation of risk, based on statistical estimates, is contrasted with a 'subjective' perception of risk, characterized by judgements inspired by personal experience or individual reasoning.

The subjective aspects of risk perception have stimulated great interest in the marketing sector because it is an intuitive process, easily understood, and allows marketing people to assume customers' points of view (Mitchell, 1999). Risk perception also proves to be a versatile concept and it has been used to investigate many different fields of human experience, such as public and individual health, industrial and household use of technology, financial and economic behaviors, and so on.

The concept of risk was used for the first time in scientific research in the 1920s in studies on economic and financial decision-making (Knight, 1921). But it was in the 1960s that risk perception started to be increasingly used in two important contexts: shopping and use of technology.

Bauer (1960) pointed out that consumer evaluate shopping behavior as a risky one when consumption choices have uncertain consequences as to possible gains/ losses. Afterwards Cox and Rich (1964) revealed that risk perception influences the decision to purchase or not at a distance, by telephone, as well as the decision on which product to purchase. In the same period Cunningham (1967) asserted that risk derives from the probability and consequences of negative events.

In 1969 Chauncey Starr published a seminal article, 'Social benefit versus technological risk', which drew the attention of the scientific community to the topic of risk in using technology, initiating a school of thought that still now is rich in contributions. Starr stated that using technology means accepting risks and that 'people are more willing to accept voluntary risks (e.g. smoking) ..... than involuntary risks (e.g. electric power)' (Starr, 1969, p. 1237). The concepts of benefit and voluntariness as expressed by Starr were further used in the 1970s to investigate risk perception in many social and individual contexts.

With respect to shopping behavior, Jacoby and Kaplan (1972) identified five components of risk:

1. *economic* – possible loss of money in case that what has been bought does not function adequately and/or could be bought at a lower price;
2. *performance* – possibility of the product not functioning as expected;
3. *physical* – probability of the product damaging one's health;
4. *psychological* – possibility that the product does not meet the purchaser's expectations;
5. *social* – possibility that the purchase conveys a negative image of the purchaser.

In addition to these components of risk, Roselius (1971) added another component, *temporal* risk, defined as the possibility of wasting time during the purchasing process. In the same period Bettman (1973) distinguished between *inherent risk*, or risk associated with a specific product category (i.e., washing machines), and *handled risk*, or risk related to the specific product one intends to purchase (i.e., the washing machine A as opposed to B).

In regard to risk associated with technology use, at the end of the 1970s Fischhoff et al. (1978) published an article that brought about the well-known psychometric paradigm and showed that risk perception and its components can be measured. At almost the same time at University College of London, the anthropologist Mary Douglas, along with other colleagues, developed the Cultural Theory. This theory emphasizes the role that culture and collective worldviews play in explaining individuals' reactions to risk (Douglas and Wildavsky, 1982).

In the 1980s communication of risk, the information flow on risk issues that is established between experts and the public, became of wide interest (for example, Kasperson et al., 1988). In this field the theoretical research focused on the role played by the media in spreading and changing the perception of risk, while the practical research focused on understanding how and what to communicate in particular situations of risk.

In the 1990s the concepts of trust and credibility were used to explain the failure of certain risk communication procedures, by studying not only the effect of the contents but also the role of the source of the message (Slovic, 1993). Within the context of purchasing, research showed that risk perception is influenced by emotions related to the consumption experience (Chaudhuri, 1997) and increases the level of search activities (Dowling and Staelin, 1994).

Risk perception in e-commerce

Despite the apparent benefits of online purchases, many consumers are still reluctant to use e-commerce, probably because the risks they perceive associated with online shopping are greater than the possible benefits. Forsythe and Shi (2003) define risk perception in online shopping as 'the subjectively determined expectation of loss by an internet shopper in contemplating a particular online purchase' (p. 869).

Bhatnagar, Misra and Rao (2000) used factor analysis to investigate advantages and risks of online shopping. Two dimensions were observed: the first, called convenience, concerns the advantages of online shopping and includes items such as 'web vendors provide better customer service and after sales support', 'web vendors are more reliable' or 'web vendors deliver orders in a more timely manner'. The second dimension regards the financial risks related to the use of the credit card, and includes items such as 'Providing credit card information on the web ... is riskier than providing it over the phone to an off-line vendor, ... is riskier than providing it to some unknown store when travelling, ... is the single most important reason I don't buy through the web'. They further observed that subjects evaluated electronic household products priced at over 50 dollars, legal services, hardware and software products that cost over 50 dollars and sunglasses as the riskiest product to purchase on the web. Products considered least risky to purchase on the web were records and music CD's, books and travel. Bhatnagar, Misra and Rao (2000) argue that when consumers purchase a book or a music CD they know exactly what they are buying, while complex electronic products or goods related to one's personal image, such as sunglasses, introduce greater uncertainty and are thus perceived as riskier.

Finally, internet shoppers are older and less risk averse than Internet non-shoppers (Donthu and Garcia, 1999). Other socio-demographic variables related to risk perception are gender (males perceive as less risky those products with which they have more experience, such as electronic ones, while perceive shopping for food or clothing as riskier) and the experience of using the Internet (whoever has spent more time using the Internet considers it less risky to buy electronic products) (Bhatnagar, Misra and Rao, 2000).

Types and sources of perceived risk in e-commerce

Studies on risk perception have identified the six components of perceived risk described above. Research has also described the four most prevalent components among internet shoppers: financial risk, product performance risk, psychological risk and the risk of loss of time/convenience (Forsythe and Shi, 2003).

Financial risk derives from consumers' sense of insecurity when using credit cards. Consumers' unwillingness to provide credit card information is one of the main obstacles to online shopping (Maignan and Lukas, 1997) and many consumers believe that their credit card numbers can be easily stolen online (Caswell, 2000). The risk inherent in product performance derives from the possibility of choosing down-market goods, and from consumers' inability to accurately judge the quality of online products. Regarding psychological risk, the Internet is often perceived by consumers as an environment in which violations of privacy can occur. This is a very relevant problem for customers (Benassi, 1999) that are inhibited by the perception of lack of control over their own personal information while navigating online (Hoffman et al., 1999; Jacobs, 1997). The last type of risk, the loss of time, refers to the difficulty of finding appropriate websites or delays in receiving a product.

Forsythe and Shi (2003) also investigated the relationship between these types of risk and three customers' online behaviors: 1) frequency of searching with the intent to buy, 2) frequency of online shopping and 3) amount of money spent on the web. Financial risk was the best predictor of the three behaviors and it was negatively correlated to all of them; the product performance risk was negatively related only to the frequency of online shopping and the psychological risk did not influence any of the purchasing behaviors examined.

For Lim (2003), the four main sources of risk in e-commerce according to consumers are: technology, sellers, other consumers and the product.

Technological risks include, for instance, download delays, limitations in the interface, search problems or lack of internet standards. The second source of risk is related to the seller that may be perceived as 'impersonal and distant'; this anonymity may lead to potential risks as, for example, that the company does not deliver the product. The third source of risk in online shopping derives from the social pressure exerted by consumers' friends and family through unfavourable opinions and comments. Finally, products sold on the Internet can also increase risk perception when too little product information is given to consumers.

The Concept of Trust

Risk perception is often associated with trust, a dimension that is in some aspects the opposite of risk. In all fields of social interaction, people give significant importance to the credibility of their interlocutor and, thus, to trust (Slovic, 1993). In the business environment, for example, trust and credibility take on a primary role in capital investment, sales and marketing, transcultural communication, negotiations, and more generally in developing any sort of project (Gambetta, 1988). Thus, trust is an important condition as it helps to reduce the perception of risk (Mitchell, 1999).

Although the importance of trust is widely recognized in many disciplines, and in spite of the extensive literature on the subject, a unique definition shared by all has not been achieved (Blomqvist, 1997). Following the definition proposed by Blomqvist (1997), trust implies that individuals find themselves in a potentially vulnerable position vis-à-vis another person who is considered to have both more specific knowledge as well as the will to behave correctly. Trust is an actor's expectations towards his counterpart's competence and goodwill.

Two different theoretical perspectives have tried to explain why someone trusts someone else. The first is based on personality traits and the second on social processes. Personal dispositions in the process of attributing trust are emphasized by Rotter (1967) who considers trust as an individual's generalized expectation that s/he can rely on words and promises of another individual. The social perspective, on the other hand, sees trust as a culturally determined process (Fisman and Khanna, 1999) influenced by the actors' values, the context in which the relationship is going on, the order in which events occur (Cvetkovich, 1999) and the perception that the trustee is competent (Sjöberg, 1999).

A more recent approach to the study of trust, the cognitive one, considers trust a complex structure based on observations, reasoning and social stereotypes, which processes and integrates information on the trustee's values, morality and goodwill (Castelfranchi and Falcone, 2000). When it is difficult to make a decision, due to lack of information or specific competencies, individuals may make their choice on the base of the trust they place in certain actors. Thus, trusting someone allows to reduce the complexity of uncertain situations (Grabner-Kraeuter, 2002).

In the past, economic analysis did not pay much attention to trust in business negotiations since it was thought that the market could bring to light every instance of 'deceit'. Recently scholars have begun to consider the market as not perfectly competitive (due to differences in knowledge between actors) and this has led to attributing a significant role to trust in implicit negotiations and developing expectations regarding future behaviors/actions (Blomqvist, 1997).

In sum, the meaning of trust is not easy to define, both because of the many points of view on it, and because it is seen as a situation-specific variable which varies according to context. Literature reports associations between trust and perception of risk, even though the levels of such associations, albeit significant, explain only about 10 per cent of the variance between the two variables and correlation is at approximately 0.30 (Sjöberg, 1999).

Trust in online shopping

In online shopping consumers are rather vulnerable and trust becomes a very important aspect to take into account (Wang and Emurian, 2005). Trust is a process; like window-shopping, it begins to develop (or not) from the first contact, that is, from browsing the website itself. Having enough trust to purchase online means that the buyer has to believe that the seller is professionally competent, wants to profit legitimately and fairly and will honour promises (Gefen, 2002).

Jarvenpaa, Tractinsky and Vitale (2000) hypothesized that trust is influenced both by the store size, as perceived from viewing the website, and by perceived reputation; in turn, reputation influences risk perception and together they determine the intention to purchase at an internet store. The model, tested with Australian and Israeli subjects, is valid in the two national contexts, while strength of association between the variables changes. Furthermore, results show that the antecedents of trust play different roles depending on the amount of money spent.

In summary, research on risk perception, conducted in various fields (e.g. economics, health and technology), has made clear that risk is a general construct but that consumers perceive risks related to single characteristics of the product or service being purchased (i.e., the economic, performance or social risk). Risks arise also when shopping online; they may concern the product, the seller, but also the financial and security issues. Trust is an important dimension of shopping behavior; it is negatively related to risk perception. It starts being developed quite early in the transaction, since the first contact with the seller. Research has shown that trust influences risk perception also in online shopping.

Empirical Research on Risk Perception in e-Commerce

We conducted two studies to investigate risk perception and online consumers' behavior. The first study was focused on the relationship between trust, risk perception and the intention to purchase online, and the second one examined the influence of trust and internet self-efficacy on risk perception.

Study 1: Trust, risk and intention to purchase online

This study tested the hypotheses that site usability and trust influence risk perception, and that these three variables determine purchasing intentions (see Figure 14.1). More detailed discussion on usability and site usability for international business are in the chapters by Mazzoni (Chapter 11) and Fulford (Chapter 10) in this book.

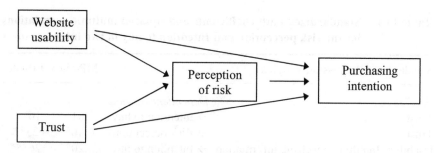

Figure 14.1   Model on risk perception in shopping online used in first study

Subjects of the research were 83 Italian internet users. Males were 59 per cent of the sample, the average age was 28.4 years old, and high school graduates were 48 per cent. Subjects were contacted through mailing lists, chat lines and directly by e-mail. On average respondents use personal computers for 26.5 and the Internet for 9.6 hours each week; 47 per cent of them had bought online at least once, and they use the computer to send/receive e-mail (96 per cent), search for information on the Internet (81 per cent), listen/play music (48 per cent), and download software from the Internet (46 per cent).

Subjects who agreed to participate were directed to a website, created for the study, where they found instructions about the two other Internet websites to navigate, the product to buy and the online questionnaires to compile. In each website they had to search for a specific music CD and then proceed with the purchasing process, interrupting it only when it was time to provide the credit card number. Five different subjects, frequent Internet users, had previously rated the two websites that we used in the survey, among ten websites, as the most preferred (MP-site) and the least preferred (LP-site) website in which to buy music CDs.

Half of the subjects initially simulated the purchase on the MP-website, while the other half started the purchase simulation on the LP-website. Once each simulation was completed, subjects answered an online questionnaire concerning, among others, the following aspects of the just visited website:

- usability, measured by the two subscales 'ease of use' and 'intelligibility of information';
- trust towards the website;
- risk perception of shopping at the website;
- intention to purchase from the website.

The model was tested in the two websites and coefficients reveal a good fit to the data (Byrne, 2001) (see Table 14.1). In both websites the intention to buy is predicted by 'usability-intelligible website information' and 'risk perception'. Moreover, risk perception is negatively predicted by trust, and trust does not influence the intention to buy.

Table 14.1   Standardized path coefficients and squared multiple correlations for the risk perception and Intention to buy in two internet stores

Standardized Regression Weights		MP-site	LP-site
Predictors	*Dependent variable*		
Trust	→ Intention to buy	.01	.16
Trust	→ Risk perception	−.46***	−.23**
Usability–Intelligible website information	→ Intention to buy	.20**	.26***
Usability–Intelligible website information	→ Risk perception	−.19**	−.04
Usability–Ease of use of the website	→ Intention to buy	.07	.18*
Usability–Ease of use of the website	→ Risk perception	−.23**	−.15
Risk – Risk perception of shopping online	→ Intention to buy	−.35***	−.24**
Squared Multiple Correlations			
Risk perception of shopping in the Internet store		.30	.10
Intention to buy from the Internet store		.20	.28

* p<.10; ** p<.05;*** p<.01
fit indexes: MP-site: Chi square/df = 0.36; AGFI = 0.97; CFI=1.00; RMSEA = .00
          LP-site: Chi square /df = 0.67; AGFI = 0.95; CFI=1.00; RMSEA = .00

Differences between the two websites show the usability subscales negatively related to risk perception on the most preferred website. In other words, this website is characterized by a higher perception of usability and, thus, by a lower perception of risk. Such association does not appear in the least preferred website. On the least preferred website, instead, the intention to buy is predicted by the perception of 'ease of use of the website'.

More concretely, results suggest that the intention to buy at an Internet store is not influenced by trust but by the perception of risk. Moreover, an easy to use website, with textual contents and graphics easy to understand, immediate and exhaustive, facilitates the development of the consumer's intention to buy (usability → intention to buy). Furthermore, a website is not considered a potentially risky situation when, navigating in it, the seriousness and competence of the seller is made evident; honest and transparent instructions also reduce the perception of risk (trust → risk perception).

These results agree with the conclusion of Roy et al. (2001) that usability is an important aspect of the online shopping process. In our model, usability-intelligible web site information influences the intention to buy at an Internet store. Future research should study specific aspects of trust, usability and perception of risk when shopping in different types of internet sites.

The model has shown acceptable goodness-of-fit statistics; the relationships between the variables are consistent for the two websites and are similar to results observed by Jarvenpaa and Tractinsky (1999). Nonetheless, the relationships are rather low and the model explains a small portion of the intention to buy variance. A wider comprehension of the online shopping process may be reached by adding other explanatory variables, such as emotions, motivations, and shopping orientations (on this issue, see chapter 15, by Scarpi, in this book).

Study 2: Components of risk perception

Given the relevance of risk perception in online shopping, we investigated the role of two of its important components: severity of perceived consequences and probability of perceived losses. The study is based on a model (see Figure 14.2) that is similar in some aspects to the one presented above. Following Cunningham (1967), we hypothesized that risk perception in online shopping is influenced by the severity of perceived consequences and the probability of perceived losses (in both cases a positive correlation is expected), and that the perception of probability and the perception of consequences are reciprocally associated (Bettman, 1973).

Additionally, we hypothesized that the perception of probability is influenced by Internet self-efficacy. Self-efficacy is defined as a set of beliefs about one's own skills and the expectations of being more or less able to manage different kinds of tasks (including online navigation, search and purchasing tasks) (Bandura, 1997).

Self-efficacy, used to explain the intention and effective behavior of subjects in different tasks, has been measured in relation to computing (computer self-efficacy), internet use (internet self-efficacy) or e-mailing (e-mail self-efficacy) (Decker, 1999). Internet self-efficacy, for example, is defined as the belief of an individual of being able to accomplish online tasks (Eastin and LaRose, 2000).

Besides, we hypothesized that the perception of probability is also influenced by trust. Finally, in accordance with the literature, we measured three kinds of risk perception in online shopping, that is risk related to: a) consumer incompetence (CI), b) seller mistakes (SM) and c) fraudulent behaviors (FB).

Internet users were contacted by mailing lists, chat lines and directly by e-mail. Subjects accepting to participate in the survey (N = 104), received a questionnaire by e-mail. They were on average aged 32 years old, about two thirds were males and

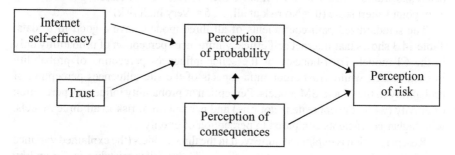

Figure 14.2   Model on risk perception in shopping online used in the second study

Table 14.2 Items of the 'Online Risk Perception Scale'

For you, in online shopping, how much risk is there about:

Negative events caused by consumer incompetence (CI)
Incorrect evaluation of items
Making a mistake in the procedures for online shopping
Not being able to find specific information and instructions on items use

Negative events caused by seller mistakes (SM)
Insufficient post sale assistance
Delivered goods are not the ordered ones
Delivered goods are damaged
Crash (abort) of the online shopping procedures

Negative events caused by fraudulent behaviors (FB)
Getting incorrect online information about items
Dishonest use of personal data which you sent the seller
Somebody read your personal data on your PC
Fraudulent use of credit card code

A confirmatory factor analysis on these items tested a three correlated factors model
(Chisquare (36) =48.4; p= 0.08; cmin/df= 1.3; GFI=.93; AGFI=.87; CFI=.98; RMSEA=.05).

52 per cent were high school graduates. Subjects mainly used the computer to search for information on the Internet (99 per cent), send/receive e-mail (98 per cent), work on files (92 per cent), browse (84 per cent) and use chat/mailing lists (72 per cent). On average they used PCs for 34 hours and Internet for 18 hours a week. Fifty-three per cent of them have bought online at least once.

Structural Equation Model was used three times to test the model. Firstly, in relation to negative events caused by consumer incompetence; secondly, on negative events caused by seller mistakes; and thirdly, on negative events caused by fraudulent behaviors. Table 14.2 shows the items we used to measure the three types of risk, on a six point Likert scale (0 = No risk at all, ... 5 = Very high risk).

The standardized path coefficients of all three models have a good fit to data. Table 14.3 shows that Internet self efficacy influences perception of probability only in the CI model. Trust-honesty of the seller influences perception of probability in each model, while Trust-ergonomic aspects of the site influences perception of probability in the CI and SM models. Perception of probability influences perception of gravity (while the opposite is not true) and perception of risk in all three models, with higher coefficients compared to perception of gravity.

Risk perception is explained quite well in the three models (the explained variance of risk caused by consumer incompetence is .79, by seller mistakes is .76 and by fraudulent behaviors is .67), while, in contrast, the amount of explained variance of perception of probability and of gravity are both low, ranging from .13 to .25 in the three models.

Results show that the basic structure of the model is valid for the three kinds of risk (CI, SM and FB), but that the impact of predictors is different in the three types of risk. Findings also suggest that there is a relationship between perception of probability and perception of gravity. In other words, from a psychological point of view, when an online consumer perceives one of these two components (for example, the probability of a negative event) s/he will also tend to consider the second component (in this case, the consequences of that event). It has to be noted that the perception of probability that a negative event will happen is more important in determining the perception of risk. These results are similar to those observed exploring lethal risks (Sjöberg, 1994) and non-lethal risks (Bettman, 1973).

The perception of honesty of the seller is important in reducing the idea of risk in the three conditions; on the contrary, the perception of professionalism of the seller does not influence the perception of risk. As argued by Luhman (1979), trust allows future anticipation, in that people experiencing trust behave as if they expect positive future events. Our results show that trust influences perception of probability by reducing the anticipation of negative events, or by imagining that these, if they occur, could be satisfactorily resolved by interacting with a honest seller.

Trust-ergonomic aspects of the site influence the perception of probability of risks related to consumer incompetence and seller mistakes. In other words, the easier the

Table 14.3   Standardized path coefficients of the three models

		Risk of negative events caused by:		
		Consumer Incompe- tence (CI)	Seller Mis- takes (SM)	Fraudulent Behaviors (FB)
Internet self-efficacy	→ Percept. of Probability	0.16*	−0.07	0.03
Trust–honesty of sellers	→ Percept. of Probability	−0.21*	−0.32**	−0.35**
Trust–professional. sellers	→ Percept. of Probability	0.14	−0.09	0.12
Trust–ergonomic aspects	→ Percept. of Probability	−0.39**	−0.21*	−0.15
Perception of probability	→ Percept. of Gravity	0.50**	0.39**	0.46**
Perception of probability	→ Percept. of Risk	0.78**	0.83**	0.76**
Perception of gravity	→ Percept. of Risk	0.18**	0.13**	0.12*

* $p<.05$; ** = $p<.01$. Fit indices of the model on:

Consumer Incompetence: Chi square /df = 1.14; AGFI = 0.90; CFI=0.99; RMSEA=.04
Seller Mistakes: Chi square /df = 1.17; AGFI = 0.90; CFI=0.99; RMSEA=.04
Fraudulent Behaviors: Chi square /df = 1.30; AGFI = 0.89; CFI=0.98; RMSEA=.05.

website is to use, less probable purchasers will consider their own mistakes in the buying procedure or sellers' mistakes when delivering goods.

Internet self-efficacy is important only regarding the probability of risks caused by consumer incompetence. Those who feel they can operate efficiently on the Internet also consider negative events caused by their own errors as less likely. This finding confirms Bandura's hypothesis (1997) that high self-efficacy is associated with low risk perception. Internet self-efficacy has no effect on probability of risks caused by sellers' mistakes and fraudulent behaviors.

Conclusion

Our two studies are consistent with previous studies reporting that risk perception decreases the intention to shop online. They also confirm that the perception of risk of a negative event is influenced by the perception of probability more than the perception of gravity. Besides, the two studies add important considerations about the determinants of the intention to buy online and the online risk perception. Each actor and each step of the online shopping process is related to some source of risk: the (more/less competent) consumer, the (dis/honest) seller, the (un/easy) website, the (un/knowable) product, and so on. Our results show that different variables mitigate risks related to different sources: internet self efficacy reduces risks related to consumer incompetence; honesty of seller is useful to mitigate consumer incompetence and seller mistakes but, for instance, has nothing to do with fraudulent behaviors; professionalism of the seller is not related to risk perceptions, at least when buying music CD. This suggests that the intention to buy online is a complex process resulting from the interaction of consumer, seller and the website as a medium, without overlooking type of product and its price.

If risk perception is so important when shopping online, how do consumers and firms deal with it to increase consumers' security? A very high level of risk perception in online shopping can indeed make consumers so cautious as to prevent them pursuing the commercial advantages offered by the net. Methods frequently used by consumers to reduce risks concern the search for information from formal and informal sources, such as trade journals reporting reviews on reliability and convenience of websites stores, or the participation in internet consumers forums. Penz and Kirchler's study (see Chapter 12), highlights the importance of reputation when shopping online by well or less known companies. Reputation and image can thus guide consumers towards potential low risk situations (Akaah and Korgaonkar, 1988; Tan, 1999).

To reduce consumers' risk perception companies have used marketing strategies entailing promises to reimburse money, guarantees and product testing (Schiffman and Kanuk, 1994). A study by Akaah and Korgaonkar (1988) showed that money-back guarantees are considered the most important factor in reducing risk, followed by the producer's name, the cost of the product, the distributor's reputation, delivery of free samples, the approval of a trusted person and brand experience. Consumers have also shown interest in sellers' references (for example the company's history and its most important customers) considering this as an important factor in reducing risk (Tan, 1999). Experts' judgements and opinions regarding different products have likewise proven to be useful (Tan, 1999).

More recent strategies to reduce risk include the adoption of website certification by government bodies and merchant and consumer associations. The Euro-label project (www.euro-label.com), for example, supported by the European Commission, is based on the acceptance by sellers of the European Code of Conduct based on European Union legislation on e-commerce and selling at a distance. The Code prescribes, for example, using secure payment systems, a clear procedure for treatment of complaints and respect for consumers' privacy.

It is in any case advisable that companies adequately map out the risks that consumers may perceive when purchasing in their websites, keeping in mind, as pointed out above, that different risks require different prevention strategies.

References

Akaah, I.P. and Korgaonkar, P. (1988), 'A Conjoint Investigation of the Importance of Risk Relievers in Direct Marketing', *Journal of Advertising Research*, Vol. 28, pp. 38–44.

Bandura, A. (1997), *Self-efficacy: The Exercise of Control,* Freeman, New York.

Bauer, R. (1960), 'Consumer Behaviour as Risk Taking', in R.S. Hanchock (Ed.), *Dynamic Marketing for a Changing World,* American Marketing Association, Chicago.

Benassi, P. (1999), 'Trust: an Online Privacy Seal Program', *Communication of ACM*, Vol. 42, pp. 56–59.

Bettman, J.R. (1973), 'Perceived Risk and its Components: a Model and Empirical Test', *Journal of Marketing Research*, Vol. 10, pp. 184–190.

Bhatnagar, A., Misra, S. and Rao, H.R. (2000), 'On Risk, Convenience, and Internet Shopping Behaviour', *Comunications of ACM*, Vol. 42, pp. 98–105.

Blomqvist, K. (1997), 'The Many Faces of Trust', *Scandinavian Journal of Management*, Vol. 13, pp. 271–286.

Byrne, B.M. (2001), *Structural Equation Modelling with AMOS*, LEA, London.

Castelfranchi, C. and Falcone, R. (2000), 'Social Trust: a Cognitive Approach', in C. Castelfranchi and Y. Tan (Eds.), *Deception, Fraud and Trust in Virtual Society,* Kluwer Academy, London, pp. 55–90.

Caswell, S. (2000), 'Women Enjoy e-Shopping Less than Men', www.ecommerce. com, January, p. 11.

Chaudhuri, A. (1997), 'Consumption Emotion and Perceived Risk: A Macro-analytic Approach', *Journal of Business Research*, Vol. 39, pp. 81–92.

Cox, D.F. and Rich, S.T. (1964), 'Perceived Risk and Consumer Decision-making: The Case of Telephone Shopping', *Journal of Marketing Research,* Vol. 4, pp. 32–39.

Cunningham, S. (1967), 'The Major Dimensions of Perceived Risk', in D. Cox (Ed.), *Risk Taking and Information Handling in Consumer Behavior,* Harvard Business School, Boston, pp. 82–108.

Cvetkovich, G. (1999), 'The Attribution of Social Trust', in G. Cvetkovich and R. Löfstedt (Eds.), *Social Trust and the Management of Risk,* Earthscan Publications Ltd., London, pp. 53–61.

Decker, C.A. (1999), 'Technical Education Transfer: Perceptions of Employee Computer Technology Self-Efficacy', *Computers in Human Behavior,* Vol. 15, pp. 161–172.

Donthu, N. and Garcia, A. (1999), 'The Internet Shopper', *Journal of Advertising Research,* Vol. 39, pp. 52–58.

Douglas, M. and Wildavsky, A. (1982), *Risk and Culture,* University of California Press, Berkley.

Dowlin, G.R. and Staelin, R. (1994), 'A Model of Perceived Research and Intended Risk-handling Activity', *Journal of Consumer Research,* Vol. 21, pp. 119–134.

Eastin, M.S. and LaRose R. (1996), 'Internet Self-efficacy and the Psychology of the Digital Divide' *Journal of Computer-Mediated Communication,* Vol. 6, http://www.ascusc.org/jcmc/vol6/issue1/eastin.html.

Fischhoff, B., Slovich, P., Lichtenstein, S., Read, S. and Combs, B. (1978), 'How Safe is Safe Enough? A Psychometric Study of Attitudes towards Technological Risks and Benefits', *Policy Sciences,* Vol. 9, pp. 127–152.

Fisman, R. and Khanna, T. (1999), 'Is Trust a Historical Residue? Information Flows and Trust Levels', *Journal of Economic Behavioral Organization,* Vol. 38, pp. 79–92.

Forsythe, S.M. and Shi, B. (2003), 'Consumer Patronage and Risk Perceptions in Internet Shopping', *Journal of Business Research,* 56, pp. 867–875.

Gambetta, D. (1988), *Trust, Making and Breaking Cooperative Relations,* Basil Blackwell, New York.

Gefen, D. (2002), 'Reflections on the Dimensions of Trust and Trustworthiness among Online Consumers', *ACM SIGMIS Database,* Vol. 33, pp. 38–53.

Grabner-Kraeuter, S. (2002), 'The Role of Consumer Trust in Online Shopping', *Journal of Business Ethics,* Vol. 39, pp. 43–50.

Hoffman, D., Novak, T. and Peralta, M. (1999), 'Building Consumer Trust Online', *Communication of the ACM,* Vol. 42, pp. 80–85.

Jacobs, P. (1997), 'Privacy: What You Need to Know', *Infoworld,* Vol. 19, pp. 111–112.

Jacoby, J. and Kaplan, L.B. (1972), 'The Components of Perceived Risk', *Proceedings of the Third Annual Conference of the Association for Consumer Research,* Vol. 3, pp. 382–393.

Jarvenpaa, S.L. and Tractinsky, N. (1999), 'Consumer Trust in an Internet Store: a Cross-Cultural Validation', *Journal of Computer-Mediated Communication,* Vol. 5, http://www.ascusc.org/ jcmc/vol5/issue2.

Jarvenpaa, S. L., Tractinsky, N. and Vitale, M. (2000), 'Consumer Trust in an Internet Store', *Information Technology and Management,* Vol. 1, pp. 45–71.

Kasperson, R.E., Renn, O., Slovich, P., Brown, H.S., Emel, J., Goble, R., Kasperson, J.X. and Ratick, S. (1988), 'The Social Amplification of Risk: A Conceptual Framework', *Risk Analysis*, Vol. 16, pp. 473–486.

Knight, F. (1921), *Risk, Uncertainty and Profit*, Harper & Row, New York.

Lim, N. (2003), 'Consumers' Perceived Risk: Sources versus Consequences', *Electronic Commerce Research and Application*, Vol. 2, pp. 216–228.

Luhman, N., (1979), *Trust and Power*, Wiley, Chichester.

Maignan, I. and Lukas, B.A. (1997), 'The Nature and Social Uses of the Internet: a Qualitative Investigation, *Journal of Consumer Affair*, Vol. 31, pp. 346–371.

Mitchell, V.W. (1999), 'Consumer Perceived Risk: Conceptualisations and Models', *European Journal of Marketing*, Vol. 33, pp. 163–195.

Murray, K.B. (1991), 'A Test of Services Marketing Theory: Consumer Information Acquisition Activities', *Journal of Marketing*, Vol. 55, pp. 10–25.

Roselius, T. (1971), 'Consumer Rankings of Risk Deduction Methods', *Journal of Marketing,* Vol. 35, pp. 56–61.

Rotter, J.B. (1967), 'A New Scale for the Measurement of Trust', *Journal of Personality*, Vol. 35, pp. 651–665.

Roy, M.C, Dewit, O. and Benoit, A.A. (2001), 'The Impact of Interface Usability on Trust in Web Retailers', *Internet Research: Electronic Networking Applications and Policy,* Vol. 11, pp. 388–398.

Schiffman, L.G. and Kanuk, L.L. (1994), *Consumer Behavior*, Prentice-Hall, Englewood Cliffs.

Sjöberg, L. (1994), 'Perceived Risk vs. Demand for Risk Reduction', *Rhizikon: Risk Research Reports,* Vol. 18, pp. 1–45.

Sjöberg, L. (1999), 'Perceived Competence and Motivation in Industry and Government as Factor in Risk Perception', in G. Cvetkovich and R. Löfstedt (Eds.), *Social Trust and the Management of Risk,* Earthscan Publications Ltd., London, pp. 89–100.

Slovic, P. (1993), 'Perceived Risk, Trust and Democracy', *Risk Analysis*, Vol. 13, pp. 675–82.

Starr, C. (1969), 'Social Benefit versus Technological Risk', *Science*, Vol. 165, pp. 1232–38.

Tan, S.J. (1999), 'Strategies for Reducing Consumers' Risk Eversione in Internet Shopping', *Journal of Consumer Marketing*, Vol. 16, pp. 163–180.

Vlek, C. and Stallen, P. (1981), 'Judging Risks and Benefits in the Small and in the Large', *Organizational Behavior and Human Decision Processes*, Vol. 28, pp. 235–271.

Wang, Y.D. and Emurian, H.H (2005), 'Trust in e-Commerce Interface: Consideration of Interface Design', *Journal of e-Commerce in Organizations*, Vol. 3, pp. 42–60.

Chapter 15

The Fun Side of the Internet

Daniele Scarpi

Internet Today

In the early 1990s, the Internet was regarded as an exciting invention well suited primarily for communications within academia, and only a few companies were trying to exploit the business opportunities of this invention (Thomas and Wyatt, 1999). But the Internet developed quickly, including a commercial infrastructure, and since the mid-1990s an increasing number of firms are resorting to Information Technology and to e-Commerce as major facilitators of business activities, making the Internet a global commercial resource (European Commission, 2003).

Today, e-commerce is a rapidly growing phenomenon around the entire planet, and in more than a few countries it grows at a *tremendous* rate. For instance, expenditures in some European countries (e.g. the UK) have experienced a 10-fold or even 12-fold increase since 2000, while recent statistics report that at least 12 million British consumers do shop online, 60 per cent of them at least once a month (European Commission, 2004; Hall, 2003).

However, although the UK is among the countries where online shopping is more widespread, online expenditures amount to about a disappointing 6 per cent of total retail spend (Hall, 2003), and the use of the Internet as a distribution channel is still limited (Forsythe and Shi, 2003). For instance, whilst 45 per cent of the adult population goes online in the UK, only 58 per cent of these Internet users buy online. Thus, about one half of today's British Internet users never purchase on the web. Figures for other European countries are even lower, sometimes dramatically (e.g. in Italy only 3 per cent of adult population buys online).

This evidence highlight that still today many people are suspicious or discouraged in using such technology, although the number of online buyers is rising. To increase the diffusion of e-commerce it is thus necessary to take into account not only firms' adoption process, but also *consumers'* attitudes towards the Internet. The objective of this chapter is to provide an empirical analysis of online shopping structured around two factors that appear to influence consumer purchase behaviour: the shopping orientation of consumers and product characteristics.

Although the literature considers these two factors from various different perspectives, there is shared agreement about their importance for understanding and directing consumers' behaviour online. We therefore believe an analysis of these factors could not only provide useful hints for academics, but could also offer practical suggestions to managers for improving their online marketing strategies.

Hedonism and Utilitarism Online

Consumers' buying behaviour has been traditionally portrayed as rational and goal oriented (Howard and Sheth, 1969). However, in more recent years the literature has focused upon the role of emotions and pleasure in consumer behaviour, and typically discusses shopping orientation in terms of 'economic' versus 'recreational' orientation (e.g. Bellenger and Korgaonkar, 1980) or 'hedonic' versus 'utilitarian' orientation (e.g. Hirschman and Holbrook, 1982; Griffin et al., 2000). It is by now widely held that consumers' buying behaviour is not purely rational goal-directed or goal-seeking, and research has definitively shown that buying processes are constructive and context-dependent, impulse buying is rather widespread, shopping and buying processes often follow a wide and diverse range of motives, emotions play a significant role in the process, experiential aspects of the buying process itself are at times very important, and utilitarian motives and strategies are often complemented by more hedonic ones (Bagozzi and Gopinath, 1999; Hirschman and Holbrook, 1982; Hoffman and Novak, 1996; Oliver et al., 1997). In fact, consumers may enjoy looking around and fantasizing, perceiving shopping as a moment of evasion, an adventure, reflecting shopping's potential entertainment. Thus, enjoyment could result from the fun and play arising from the shopping experience *per se*, and not just because some pre-specified end-goal has been achieved. As Babin et al. (1994) suggest, 'shopping consists of both rational and emotional motives'.

But whilst a large stream of recent literature has focused on the role of emotions, fun and joy in buying behaviour (e.g. Bagozzi and Gopinath, 1999; Oliver et al., 1997), little consideration has been given to the role of consumers' shopping orientation in the adoption of web retailing by Internet users, apart from recent studies by O'Cass and Fenech (2003; Fenech and O'Cass 2001). As remarked by O'Cass and Fenech (2003), research is needed on how consumers feel when shopping in the traditional brick-and-mortar environment versus the Internet 'virtual' environment. Indeed, the literature is still very far from a systematic and sound examination of online shopping.

A deeper understanding of the role of the Internet as a distribution channel could be provided re-interpreting the special features of the Internet in light of the hedonic-utilitarian research paradigm. On one hand, the literature has already highlighted the typical advantages the Internet can offer as a distribution channel: for instance that purchases can be easily done from home or from the office, without any need of moving, thus saving time and effort. On the other hand, when put into the hedonic-utilitarian research framework, these characteristics gain greater strength and provide new considerations and insights. For instance, consumers behaving in a utilitarian way perceive the act of shopping as a necessary task, from which they get neither joy nor pleasure and whose time they try to minimise, and could therefore derive from the Internet an added value unseen and unheard of in the physical world. On the other hand, consumers who enjoy the act of shopping *per se* and thus exhibit a hedonic approach, could also derive an added value from the Internet, even though of a different nature. For instance, they could enjoy buying online because of the novelty of this form of shopping, the fun of a new way of making purchases, the feelings of curiosity, adventure and exploration.

However, the features of the online distribution medium need to be considered in conjunction with the characteristics of the product if we want to gain a deeper understanding of how consumers behave online, and to derive relevant implications for increasing the diffusion of e-commerce. There is no doubt some products seem to be more suited than others to online shopping, and goods like software, books and CDs still accounts for the majority of online purchases (Lee and Johnson, 2002). In fact, by facilitating the acquisition of information, the Internet might suits certain product categories: as Peterson et al. (1997) note, when the value proposition is intangible or informational, the electronic channel has key advantages. Burke (1997) suggests that the Internet is an unsuitable distribution channel for heavy, bulky, and fragile items, low-margin items, product requiring in-store demonstration, and products that are needed urgently. In contrast, when the delivery cost accounts for a small proportion of the cost of the good, because the product is expensive and infrequently purchased, Internet selling becomes possible (Peterson et al., 1997). Indeed, some expensive and infrequently purchased products are successfully sold online (e.g. personal computers).

In the 1980s, Bloch and scholars (Bloch et al., 1986) started categorizing products, considering their 'emotional-aesthetic' content, and their 'functionality'. On this basis, they identified a number of 'hedonic' and 'utilitarian' products. Hedonic products are aesthetic goods providing pleasure or fun, like for instance perfumes, chocolate, clothes, jewels, and the like. In contrast, utilitarian products are functional goods which are bought to perform a specific rational task, for instance screws, desk computers, furniture for the offices, machinery, and the like (Youn et al., 2000). About ten years later, specifically focusing on the potential of interactive media such as the Internet, Klein (1998) proposed a categorization of products on the basis of the balance between 'search' and 'experience' attributes they posses. Full information on the most important attributes can be obtained prior to purchase for search-products (for instance, personal computers). In contrast, for experience-products, full information on the most important attributes cannot be obtained without direct experience, or is more costly than direct experience (for instance, an ice-cream).

These different product types, and the related characteristics, may effect consumers' online purchase intentions and behaviour, and also strategic e-retail decisions, including website design and assortment planning (Alba et al., 1997).

An Empirical Example of Hedonism and Utilitarism Online

Aims

In this section we provide an analysis of online shopping structured around the two main factors that appear to influence consumer purchase behaviour on the Internet, namely: product characteristics, and the shopping orientation of consumers. Our purpose is threefold:

1. verify if and how far the utilitarian and hedonic approaches exist and combine on the Internet;
2. examine consumers' orientation towards online shopping;
3. identify consumers' preferred buying modality on the Internet.

Considerations guiding the analysis

According to the literature on hedonism, it is now accepted that shopping can be a source of pleasure other than the product that is bought (Hirschman and Holbrook, 1982; Griffin et al. 2000). Moreover, the way consumers approach the web may influence their online behaviour. Thus, differences in the shopping orientation of consumers may affect the choice of the distribution channel, favouring (or hindering) e-commerce rather than more traditional ways of making purchases. For instance, consumers behaving hedonically might prefer traditional retail channels, since they enjoy the entertainment value of shopping *per se*, with or without purchase. On the other hand, consumers behaving in a more utilitarian way value getting the job done efficiently, and may appreciate the savings in time and effort that the Internet can offer.

We argue that the higher the perceived hedonic value of a traditional shopping trip, the less is the readiness to forgo it for browsing the web. However, some customers may attribute a hedonic value to the process of browsing and purchasing on the web: such customers, who are probably curious about computers and new technologies, might appreciate electronic purchasing as an experience providing pleasure and hedonic feelings. Similarly, other customers, utilitarian towards the web, might consider it as a mean to save both the time and the trouble of embarking in a shop expedition. Thus, we have empirically tested the relation between approach to the distribution channel and probability of buying online, expecting that a hedonic approach to the traditional distribution channel correlates negatively with the probability of buying online. On the other hand, we expect that a more utilitarian approach to the traditional distribution channel correlates positively with the probability of buying online.

However, a buying experience on the Internet could be happen completely online (e.g. the consumer sees and buys the product straight from the Internet), or could have some connections with the traditional physical buying context (e.g. the consumer could decide to buy online after having seen the product in a shop offline). Visiting a brick-and-mortar shop could have a functional meaning, like product trial and the building up of a reference point for the price, but it could also have a social meaning, like the interaction with the shop assistants and with other customers. Moreover, offline stores are still the distribution channel that is best known and more familiar to consumers. Thus, one could argue consumers prefer to purchase a product on the Internet after having been to an offline store. We have tested such proposition, expecting to find empirical evidence supporting it.

Finally, we want to draw attention on the fact that a consumer buying online cannot touch, feel, and try the good, and may also have insufficient information on quality attributes relevant to him/her (Forsythe and Shi, 2003). The perceived risk may thus be extremely high. Moreover, some products such as clothes, whose quality attributes (fit or quality of material) can be assessed before purchase in a traditional brick-and-mortar store, shift towards becoming 'experience' products when sold online. In fact, when shopping for clothes on the Internet, consumers have to rely on other attributes, such as the reputation of the brand. Alternatively, they may rely on offline experience, like from visiting a physical retail outlet.

Simply put, we provide an empirically-grounded answer to the following question: which is the preferred modality of making purchases on the Internet?

We therefore consider different buying scenarios: a know brand against an unknown brand, a purchase straight from the Internet against a purchase after visiting a shop offline. We also consider different product categories, namely clothes and personal computers.

According to the product categorization theory of Bloch and scholars (Bloch et al. 1986), clothes are hedonic products, while computers are utilitarian products. Following Bloch et al. (1986), we considered 'everyday clothes', not luxury 'boutique clothes', and desk-computers, not laptops. According to Klein (1998), clothes are experience goods, while computers are search goods. Clothes and computers are among the most frequently quoted products in the hedonic-utilitarian research framework, and are considered sort of archetypical for their categories.

Methodology

Data were collected through a questionnaire adapted from Babin et al.'s (1994) five-point Likert scale for the measurement of utilitarism and hedonism. Because of the features of the Internet, some concepts where reshaped when measuring constructs in the electronic environment. For instance, we translated 'shop' with 'web site', and 'shopping' with 'browsing'[1]. By means of this questionnaire we recorded data for four factors: hedonism in the traditional channel (Hedoshop), utilitarism in the traditional channel (Utishop), hedonism in the web (Hedoweb), and utilitarism in the web (Utiweb). We also asked respondents how many times they had connected to the

---

1 As neither shopping nor browsing imply buying; e.g. original item of Babin et al. (1994) 'I continued to shop, not because I had to, but because I wanted to', was adapted for the Internet: 'I continued to browse, not because I had to, but because I wanted to'.

Internet in the last week, how long their latest connection lasted, and whether they had bought online in the last semester.

The questionnaire was administered to 250 students enrolled in management and statistics courses at a leading British business school. The age of respondents was between 19 and 27 years (mean: 22.3; median: 23.5); 65 per cent were females. We believe the use of students was justified, as they are shoppers of the products we considered in the study and are likely to access to the Internet either from home or from the University.

Results

Hedonism and utilitarism online

All scales displayed acceptable reliability (Cronbach's alpha ranges between .74 and .87). This confirms previous scales on traditional hedonic and utilitarian approach toward shopping (Babin et al., 1994; Griffin et al., 2000), and highlights the presence of internally consistent constructs for such concepts on the Internet.

First we verified if hedonism and utilitarism exist also on the Internet, and how they are compared to their offline counterparts. Results are presented in Table 15.1.

These results are in line with previous research regarding the offline context (Babin et al., 1994), as hedonism and utilitarism are not fully independent constructs nor are they perfectly correlated. They are different, but not two opposite poles.

Table 15.1 also illustrates that hedonism and utilitarism exist also on the Internet, and they exhibit a correlation similar to their offline counterparts. Moreover, it is looking at the relation between the constructs that differences emerge between the two distribution channels. In fact, no significant correlation emerges between *any* behaviour in the traditional channel and *any* behaviour in the web: the two channels are very independent, and *fully* capable on their own to evoke any kind of behaviour.

Table 15.1 Hedonism and utilitarism in the two distribution channels

	Hedoshop	Utishop	Hedoweb
Hedoshop	–		
Utishop	.27*	–	
Hedoweb	ns	ns	–
Utiweb	ns	ns	.33*

* correlation significant at the 0.01 level

Offline approach and buying online

We ran a t-test to verify if consumers perceiving a high value from shopping in the traditional channel are less prone to switch to the Internet. The data show that the degree of hedonism is significantly different among consumers who purchased on the electronic channel and those who did not. Results are summarised in Table 15.2. The column 'mean' reports the mean score for hedonism and utilitarism of those who bought online and those who did not.

Electronic channel customers show a significantly less hedonic orientation toward the traditional brick-and-mortar shop; consumers who have never purchased through the web are those perceiving a high degree of hedonism in the traditional shopping environment. On the contrary, we did not find any significant difference as far as utilitarism is concerned: the degree of utilitarism is about the same for Internet buyers and non-Internet buyers. These results highlight that a hedonic approach to the traditional distribution channel *does* negatively correlate with the probability of buying online, but a utilitarian approach to the traditional distribution channel *does not* correlate with the probability of buying online.

Table 15.2   Offline approach and buying online

	BuyOnline	Mean	Significance
Hedoshop	Yes	2.8	0.01
	No	3.1	
Utishop	Yes	2.8	ns.
	No	2.8	

Approach to the internet and its use

We analysed the relationship between Internet orientation and number and frequency of connections. Table 15.3 summarises the relation among hedonism and utilitarism toward the web, number and length of connections.

The data show there is a significant correlation between hedonism on the web and both the length of connection and their number. Not only are these the only significant correlations, they are also by far the highest (the other, non significant correlations

Table 15.3   Approach to the internet and its use (correlation)

	Number of connections	Length of connections
Hedoweb	.29*	.33*
Utiweb	ns	ns

* significant at the 0.01 level.

Table 15.4   Preferred online buying modality

	Straight on the Internet	Try in the shop
Cloth of a known brand	3.8	2.2
Cloth of an unknown brand	4.3	2.9
Computers of a known brand	3.6	2.4
Computers of an unknown brand	4.2	3.5

Note: 1= would certainly buy, … 5= would certainly NOT buy.

do not exceed 0.03). Thus, consumers behaving hedonically surf more frequently and longer. This is consistent with the idea of hedonic consumers being experiential, curious, trying to exploit the hedonic potential of their shopping environment, and enjoying the Internet in itself (Hoffman and Novak, 1996).

Preferred modality of making purchases on the internet

Finally, we investigate which is the preferred modality of buying online. As aforementioned, we have considered different scenarios basing on different brands (known vs. unknown), different products (clothes and computers), and different buying modalities (buying straight from the Internet vs. buying online after seeing the product in a brick-and-mortar shop). Results are summarised in Table 15.4 (the higher the value, the higher the reluctance towards buying).

Reading Table 15.4 vertically (columns) one can see that, all else equal, consumers prefer to buy a known brand over an unknown brand (3.8 and 4.3 for clothes, and 2.2 vs. 2.9 for computers). This is to be expected because of the very meaning of branding, and because of the capability of a known brand to reassure consumers about the quality of the product. Reading Table 15.4 horizontally (rows) one can see that consumers prefer to buy online less then buying at a physical shop (e.g., 3.8 vs. 2.2, and 3.6 vs. 2.4 for goods of a known brand).

These patterns of preference are all statistically significant and do not change due to the different product category. In fact, Holbrook and Hirschman (1982) remark that hedonism and utilitarianism are the outcome of the *interaction* of many elements. Among these elements there are the characteristics of the product but also other important factors like shopping environment and consumer personality.

Conclusions

Result show that also the Internet has a fun side, and is capable of evoking feelings of joy, fun and curiosity. More specifically, consumer-related factors interact with product-related factors in determining the online purchase process and the use of the Internet. As product and consumer factors act both as constraints and as determinants of e-purchases, managers can play an important role. For instance, a manager should try easing the difficulties arising from product characteristics, reducing risk perceptions and providing a shopping environment which facilitates purchase and also delivers enjoyment and value. In this perspective, we discuss the main implications and provide some actionable suggestions for e-marketing operators.

Hedonism and utilitarism exist also on the web: they display correlation patterns similar to those already known in the traditional brick-and-mortar world, but they are independent from it. In fact, they are not transposed from the offline world to the Internet, but they originate specifically for the web, that is fully capable on its own of evoking both orientations. This should be carefully kept in mind, and should guide both the choice of the distribution channel, and the design of the web site. This chapter provides empirical evidence that considerations and relations appropriated for the physical world need to be reshaped when transposed to the electronic environment, and not merely 'copied and attached'. A first managerial implication is that hedonism has a systematic impact on the probability of buying online. Moreover, there are hedonic experiences emerging specifically for the web, and they can originate in strongly hedonic consumers as well as in strongly utilitarian consumers. Shoppers may for instance derive pleasure from 'hunting for bargains' on the Internet.

A 'pleasurable' online shopping experience should satisfy the requirements of the consumers who have a more hedonic orientation to shopping, stimulating exploration, curiosity and entertainment. Basing on the empirical evidence collected from this analysis, we suggest that, similarly to the role of atmospheric in offline retailing, the use of colours, music and other sensory features of the website should be carefully studied and selected, not to interfere with, but to *enhance* the shopping experience. Users' gratification from using the website is in fact suggested as an important driver of repeated use of the site (Szymansky and Hise, 2000). The basic rationale is that if the electronic shopping environment evokes positive affect, consumers will perceive greater value, which in turn might serve as a reward encouraging further patronage. In fact, we found hedonism correlates with connecting to the Internet for longer times and with higher frequency: the way consumers behave online and the way they approach the web are related. Accordingly, inadequate exploration of the site is a commonly quoted mistake, alongside with insufficient variety of brand selection (Cowles et al., 2002). This chapter provides empirical data supporting these considerations.

Traditional channel managers should therefore reinforce hedonic and pleasant experiences in shopping expeditions through the use of product display, shop layout, and events for customers. On the other hand, managers operating online should focus on providing a shopping interface conforming to the different requirements of consumer-buying situations, rather than concentrating on issues strictly related to the product-category. In fact, the specific product does not seem to play a substantial role in influencing the preferred buying modality on the Internet, as the characteristics features of the Internet still prevail over product-category related differences. Consumers feel uncomfortable with the lack of physical inputs and prefer to purchase online something they are familiar with, let it be because they know the brand, or because they were reassured by touching/feeling the product in an offline store. The interactive features of the web should therefore be exploited to the full, and should be used with the rationale of playing a fundamental role in providing customers with tangible cues that can overcome the need of touching the product. For instance video streaming could be used to show the product in operation, illustrating its functions, characteristics and use. Additionally, video streams can also enhance the perceived hedonic value of the site.

References

Alba, J., Lynch, J., Weitz, B., Janiszewski, C., Lutz, R., Sawyer, A. and Wood, S. (1997), 'Interactive Home Shopping: Consumer, Retailer and Manufacturer Incentives to Participate in Electronic Marketplaces', *Journal of Marketing*, Vol. 61, pp. 38–53.

Babin, B.J., Darden, W.R. and Griffin, M. (1994), 'Work and/or Fun: Measuring Hedonic and Utilitarian Shopping Value', *Journal of Consumer Research*, Vol. 20, pp. 644–656.

Bagozzi, R.P. and Gopinath, M. (1999), 'The Role of Emotions in Marketing', *Academy of Marketing Science*, Vol. 27, pp. 184–206.

Bellenger, D.N. and Korgaonkar, P.K. (1980), 'Profiling the Recreational Shopper', *Journal of Retailing*, Vol. 56, pp. 77–92.

Bloch, P.H., Sherrell, D.L. and Ridgway, N. (1986), 'Consumer Search: An Extended Framework', *Journal of Consumer Research*, Vol. 13, pp. 119–126.

Burke, R.R. (1997), 'Do You See What I See? The Future of Virtual Shopping', *Journal of the Academy of Marketing Science*, Vol. 25, pp. 352–360.

Cowles, D.L., Kiecker, P. and Little, M.W. (2002), 'Using Key Informant Insights as a Foundation for e-Retailing Theory Development', *Journal of Business Research*, Vol. 55, pp. 629–636.

European Commission (2003), *e-Europe 2003 Action Plan*, Brussels (www.europa. eu.int/information_society/eeurope/plus).

European Commission (2004), *The European e-Business Report*, 3rd Synthesys Report of the e-Business W@atch, EC Enterprise Directorate, Brussels.

Fenech, T. and O'Cass, A. (2001), 'Internet Users' Adoption of Web Retailing: User and Product Dimensions', *Journal of Product and Brand Management*, Vol. 10, pp. 361–381.

Forsythe, S.M. and Shi, B. (2003), 'Consumer Patronage and Risk Perceptions in Internet Shopping', *Journal of Business Research*, Vol. 56, pp. 867–875.

Griffin, M., Babin, B.J. and Modianos, D. (2000), 'Shopping Values of Russian Consumers', *Journal of Retailing*, Vol. 76, pp. 33–53.

Hall, M. (2003), 'Online Living: Still a Few Clicks Away from Becoming a Reality', *Sunday Times*, September 21st 2003.

Hirschman, E.C. and Holbrook, M.B. (1982), 'Hedonic Consumption: Emerging Concepts, Methods And Propositions', *Journal of Marketing*, Vol. 46, pp. 92–101.

Hoffman D.L. and Novak, T.P. (1996), 'Marketing in Hypermedia Computer-Mediated Environments: Conceptual Foundations', *Journal of Marketing*, Vol. 60, pp. 50–68.

Holbrook, M.B. and Hirschman, E.C. (1982), 'The Experiential Aspects of Consumption: Consumer Fantasies, Feelings and Fun', *Journal of Consumer Research*, Vol. 9, pp. 206–211.

Howard, J.A. and Sheth, J.N. (1969), *A Theory of Buyers Behavior*, Wiley, New York.

Klein, L.R. (1998), 'Evaluating the Potential of Interactive Media through a New Lens: Search versus Experience Goods', *Journal of Business Research*, Vol. 41, pp. 195–203.

Lee, M.Y. and Johnson, K.K.P. (2002), 'Exploring Differences between Internet Apparel Purchasers, Browsers and Non-Purchasers', *Journal of Fashion Marketing and Management*, Vol. 6, pp. 146–157.

O'Cass, A. and Fenech, T. (2003), 'Web Retailing Adoption: Exploring the Nature of Internet Users Web Retailing Behavior', *Journal of Retailing and Consumer Services*, Vol. 10, pp. 81–94.

Oliver, R.L., Rust R.T. and Varki, S. (1997), 'Customer Delight: Foundations, Findings, and Managerial Insight', *Journal of Retailing*, Vol. 73, pp. 311–336.

Peterson, R.A., Balasubramanian S. and Bronnenberg, B.J. (1997), 'Exploring the Implications of the Internet for Consumer Marketing', *Journal of the Academy of Marketing Science*, Vol. 25, pp. 329–346.

Szymanski, D.M. and Hise, R.T. (2000), 'E-Satisfaction: An Initial Examination', *Journal of Retailing*, Vol. 76, pp. 309–322.

Thomas, G. and Wyatt, S. (1999), 'Shaping Cyberspace-Interpreting and Transforming the Internet', *Research Policy*, Vol. 28, pp. 681–698.

Youn, S., Sun, T. and Wells, W.D. (2001), 'Commercial Liking and Memory: Moderating Effects of Product Categories', *Journal of Advertising Research*, Vol. 41, pp. 7–13.

Chapter 16

Risk Perception as a Motivational Barrier for Online Purchasing

Annamaria Silvana de Rosa, Elena Bocci and Sara Saurini

Risk Perception and the Social Representations Theory

Alone among the other means of modern mass communication, the Internet offers 'images', 'conceptions' and 'representations' of reality that can influence the processes by which each user constructs his/her own understanding of the world. *Social Psychology*, therefore, is a crucial reference point for a more general theory of knowledge about this phenomenon. Applied to the study of mass communications, it can contribute by defining the public's interactive relationship with mass and personal media and the circularity of the relationship between social and individual contexts. However, the rapid expansion of technology has increased public attention to the risks inherent in the new technologies. As stated by Luhmann (1996): 'Even the relationship between benefits and possible costs seems to have become unfavorable. The rejection of new technologies now arises because of the risks that must be run when introducing new technology' (p. 99). Mass communication have a determining role in forming public opinion about the risks related to specific events. The average person's first contact with a potential social crisis is often via the new media or is obtained from other people who relay what they heard on the news. The new media, aiming to retain their audience's interest, do not merely repeat the technical information provided by experts, but simplify complex issues as well as introduce exciting views (Joffe, 1999).

The aim of this chapter is to identify, in the light of the Social Representations Theory, key criteria for risk perception in e-commerce in the tourism sector.

The Social Representation Theory (SRT), introduced in 1961 by the social psychologist Serge Moscovici and subsequently revised and developed by Moscovici himself (Moscovici, 1981, 1986, 2000a, 2000b, 2001) along with many other researchers including Abric (1994, 2003), Bonardi and Roussiau (1999), de Rosa (1987, 1994, 2001), Deaux and Philogene (2001), Doise (1985, 1993, and Clémence and Lorenzi-Cioldi, 1993), Farr and Moscovici (1984), Jodelet (1989), Markova (2003) and Moliner (2001). It has become a world wide, multi-lingual cultural venture that has moved beyond the boundaries of social psychology towards social sciences as cultural anthropology, educational psychology or media studies.

Replacing and updating Durkheim's notion of 'collective representation', Moscovici defines social representations as cognitive 'systems having a special logic and language, a structure of implications related both to values and concepts', (Moscovici, 1969, p.6). Furthermore, he points out that a social representation is:

> a system of values, ideas and practices with a twofold function: first to establish an order which will enable individuals to orient themselves in their material and social world and to master it; and secondly, to enable communication to take place among the members of a community by providing them with a code for social exchange and a code for unambiguously naming and classifying the various aspects of their world and their individual and group history (Moscovici, 1976, p. 13).

The SRT maintains that social practices reflect and create circular-dialogue type dynamics and that there are culturally shared codes for interpretation and attribution of meaning. The theory is also concerned with social action. In his 1961 work on the social representations of psychoanalysis, Moscovici studied communicative actions like propaganda and propagation, and later Jodelet (1989) described social representation of insanity as thoughts and also as social practices resulting from representations. Citing Pitkin, Moscovici (2001) wrote: 'to a certain extent, a representation that 'stands for' can also '*act for*' or 'act on behalf of' or 'instead of' those it represents' (p. 21). The link between social representations, practices, actions and behavior is so strong that it can be identified in a 'behavioral style': 'behavioral styles came from the study of social representations; underlying that we have social representations of intention, of behavior, of rules of behavior, etc.' (Moscovici, 2000a, pp. 265–66).

A social representation is, therefore, a shared reality, a result and condition of communication and social interactions. According to the 'structural approach' developed by the Aix-en-Provence school (including, among others, scholars such as Abric, Flament, Guimelli, and Verges), the basically stable *central nucleus* of a representation is made up of information and values associated with the object of the representation that are more widely shared and socially more significant. A *peripheral system* develops around the 'central nucleus', and is made up of information and values that are shared by a limited number of subjects belonging to specific social and cultural framework (Abric, 2003).

Two processes generate social representations: anchoring and objectifying. These processes make the 'unfamiliar familiar', as they transfer and anchor new information, new event, and any kind of social changes to information already available to individuals so that they can compare and give a meaning to the new social objects. New information are objectified by reproducing it among the things we can see, touch and thus control (Moscovici, 2000b).

In the SRT the 'content' of representations is an element that plays a lively role in representational dynamics. A social representation is always a representation of something (the object) and of somebody (the subject) whose respective features impact on representation. Therefore, the development of a social representation involves an active role on the part of the subject in many communication and social interactions. In fact, each subject selects, interprets, evaluates, and classifies information from the surrounding world, hence, also from the media, and tries to reconstruct them in the universe that is familiar to him/her (Losito, 1994).

The media are one of the most significant components of the context in which objectification and anchoring processes take place. The media provide new information and reproduce information already available on social objects. Placing social objects in order of importance, media propose them to the public in the same order. Media give this information a meaning which is organized on the basis of an explicit and/or implicit reference to values, thus, as a consequence they do not only affect opinions and attitudes but also contribute to development, structuring and possible change of social representations.

Joffe (1999) has proposed applying SRT to a set of risk concepts. Individuals use historical, cultural and societal ideas in shaping their social representations of risk. Since our response to risk is essentially a response to menace or threat, emotional factors play a major role in how we react. Identity is the earliest expression of an emotional tie we have with another person. To form particular representations, a core motivation is identity protection, that is to say, the protection of the in-group and self-identity. Unfamiliar events evoke unease. People's representations serve to create feelings of comfort and security, defending individuals from a sense of personal vulnerability to threat. However, this defensive process is not an individualistic one. Different groups ascribe to different representations in accordance with the identities requiring protection (Joffe, 1999).

Social Representations 'Mediated By' the Internet

Main objectives and hypotheses

We conducted a study in the field of new media to explore the representations 'of' the Internet and 'mediated by' the Internet in users with different levels of Internet expertise. The main goals were to:

1. identify the content, structure and polarity of the representation of the Internet and of activities conducted through internet. We used a free association task by proposing subjects to associate words to the stimulus phrases: 'Looking for tour packages via traditional channels means ...', 'Looking for tour packages via Internet means ...' and the simple stimulus word 'Internet'. Given the character of the subject population, (tourists/'surfers') we assumed that the social representations concerning the stimulus phrases would be positively polarized. We also assumed that the representation of the Internet would play a mediating role within the representations evoked by the two other more specific and action oriented stimulus phrases and operate as a resistance or an acceptance factor in approaching the new media and its related social practices;

2. establish the function of the Internet as a potentially useful tool for travel planning and its influence on the user's decisional process and buying behavior;
3. delineate the decision-making processes preceding the purchase of a tour package and the use of different media (the Internet and the traditional agency).

Data collection tools

The study was conducted from January to July 2001 using a multi-method approach (de Rosa, 1990). Due to the fast changing scenario in the diffusion of Internet practices it is important to temporally and culturally contextualize our results. Data was collected using a questionnaire consisting of open and closed questions and the 'Associative Network', a projective tool based on the free associations technique developed by de Rosa (1995, 2003). The questionnaire allowed for the collection of information on:

- subjects' travel habits;
- frequency of Internet use and the self-rating of Internet expertise;
- most frequently used Internet tools;
- 'surfing' to find tour packages;
- socio-demographic variables (sex, age, education, profession).

The associative network required subjects to associate words to three stimuli: 'Internet', 'Looking for tour packages via Internet means ...' and 'Looking for tour packages via traditional channels means ...'. This technique reveals the structure and content of representations evoked by stimulus phrases as well as the evaluative component implicit in the representations. This component is measured in a polarity index which derives from the subjects' positive, negative or neutral evaluation of each evoked word. Thus, the associative network provides an evaluation that is less influenced by social desirability.

Results

Subjects' socio-demographic characteristics and internet practices

Subjects that took part at the study were 120 Italians (tourists/surfers) with different levels of expertise on the Internet. In addition, all of them had travelled in the two years prior to the study and a majority had used the web to search tour packages (69 per cent). Subjects were divided into 12 groups resulting from the combination of three independent variables: sex; age (up to 30, 31 to 40, over 41) and education (high school or less; university). Other variables, such as users' perceived level of expertise and the Internet use profiles derived from subjects' answers, were used as independent variables. The sample was balanced in relation to sex (50 per cent male and 50 per cent female) and age (33.3 per cent in each age category). About education, 50 per cent of the subjects had an university degree, 40 per cent a secondary school diploma, and only 10 per cent had less than a secondary school education. The subjects were predominantly white-collar workers (32 per cent) but there were 24 per cent of professionals and 20 per cent of students. Only 6 per cent had a blue-collar job.

We observed that younger subjects (up to 30 years) were the most frequent users of the Internet to look for tourist information (43 per cent), compared with subjects from 31 to 40 years (28 per cent) and those over 40 (29 per cent). They also more frequently asked advice from friends and acquaintances when planning their vacations (45 per cent). Only 26 per cent of subjects from 31 to 40 y.o. and 29 per cent of those over 40 used this information source. Besides, 93 per cent of subjects experts on the Internet were men, while women were more frequent among subjects with an average or little expertise (56 vs. 44 per cent of males).

When asked 'did you ever find interesting tourist packages via Internet?' a higher percentage of subjects with secondary school education replied positively (53 per cent) compared to subjects with university degree (38 per cent) and with middle school education (9 per cent). Surfers with more Internet experience (65 per cent of subjects using internet from more than two years) consult the Web when planning vacations. The level of expertise in the use of the Internet clearly differentiate between subjects that choose Internet as a tourist information tools, remember the names of tourist sites visited and intend to purchase tour packages via Internet in the near future, and subjects that did no one of these activities.

The questionnaire also investigated to what degree touristic offers on the Web were considered as interesting and, consequently, if surfers purchased them or, at least, had the intention to make an online purchase in the near future. Fourty four per cent of the subjects had found interesting packages via the Internet; 61 per cent of them had found two interesting offers and 39 per cent more than two. Only the 11 per cent of the sample actually had made an online purchase of a tour package and only 8 per cent expressed high satisfaction with the purchase. These subjects were satisfied because of the speed/ease of service (50 per cent), the perceived trustworthiness/ seriousness of the seller (20 per cent), the good opportunities (20 per cent) and, finally, the capacity to meet purchaser's needs (10 per cent).

The reasons subjects gave for not purchasing online are linked to lack of trust (27 per cent) and security (20 per cent), the belief that Internet is only an information tool (20 per cent) and, to a lesser degree, that offers were unsatisfactory (13 per cent) or unable to meet personal needs (7 per cent).

The percentage of subjects who say that they intend to purchase tour packages via Internet in the near future is decidedly higher. The percentage of those that already had a purchasing experience and those that intend to try in the near future leaps from 11 to 51 per cent. The fundamental motivation expressed by subjects to purchase tour packages online in the near future is an economic one (27 per cent).

Among subjects who have no intention to purchase tour packages in the near future, lack of trust and security (respectively 41 and 32 per cent) are once again the most important themes. The lack of interpersonal relations and of opportunities for comparison (respectively, 12 and 3 per cent) are other two additional barriers.

'Looking for tour packages via traditional channels means...'

The words associated to the stimulus 'Looking for tour packages via traditional channels means ...' were submitted to factor analysis through the Spad-T program. The first factor includes words describing traditional channels as something that require a *reciprocal commitment on the part of the agent and the client*. On one hand, when purchasing tour packages, travel agencies are able to offer greater guarantees concerning information provided and payment security. On the other, travel agencies require a substantial personal commitment, i.e. time wasted by physically going to the agency and browsing through catalogs to obtain information. Words located along the positive semi-axis of the factor include, for example, 'security', 'help', 'guarantee'. On the negative semi-axis are found terms like 'mobilize', 'browse'.

The second factor has the twin tracks of *help obtained* and *effort required from the user*. On the positive semi-axis traditional channels offer 'competent' and 'expert' employees. The opposite semi-axis contains words underscoring the efforts of clients to use traditional tools ('slowness', 'buy', 'look for').

The third factor contains words that on the positive semi-axis offer a *description* of traditional channels as having less information and offerings and requiring both economic and time efforts ('waste of time', 'smaller offering', 'higher costs'). On the negative semi axis, however, using these channels there is an increased possibility of contact with other people and of personal relationship ('experience', 'traditional', 'trust', 'human contact').

The list of words obtained from subjects was then analysed using the Evoc program. This software identifies the structural elements of the representational field (the central nucleus and the peripheral elements) by producing a *Rank x Frequency* table in which the frequency of words and the average order of appearance are cross tabulated. Such a table has four quadrants. The upper left quadrant contains words that were mentioned by many subjects (high frequency) and were mentioned among the first positions (a low rank order) and they are the 'candidates' for the central nucleus of the representation. The words of the peripheral elements are found in the other three quadrants (as they include words mentioned from few subjects and/or mentioned by subjects among the last words).

The Evoc results confirm that the candidates for the representation's central nucleus describe traditional travel agencies as safe ('reliability', 'experience') and making an interpersonal relationship possible ('human relationship'; 'human contact', 'advice'). Human relations and professionalism are, therefore, fundamental elements in the choice to use a travel agency.

We then turned to the DiscAn program to examine the *conversational dynamics* used by subjects when producing associations. DiscAn provides information on

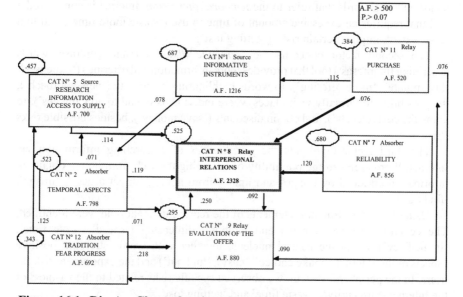

Figure 16.1 DiscAn Chart showing the categories and their functional role in the discourse dynamic of words (stimulus *'Looking for tour packages via traditional channels means ...'*)

the role of words in the discourse and their relationships expressed in terms of probability. The software compiles lists of lexical units (words, syntagma, etc.) from the body of texts and calculates the probability of transition from one category to the immediately preceding or subsequent ones (first level Markov chains). Categories with greater input than output are defined *absorbers*; those with greater output than input are *sources. Relays* are categories that have a simple connective function that neither reduces nor extends the discourse dynamics.

Figure 16.1 presents the categories with the highest activity factors (higher than 500) and all links with a probability higher than 0.07. It shows that seeking information has a *source* role (*Research information/Access to supply*). *Evaluation of the offer* have an intermediate *relay* position, mutually and exclusively linked to *Interpersonal Relations*. In the discourse dynamic, *Reliability,* but also other aspects of traditional channels (*Tradition and Fear of Progress*, as well as *Temporal aspects*) have an *absorber* role (to make the figure more readable, most of the input links to these categories are not displayed).

'Looking for tour packages via internet means ... '

The same data processing procedures were used for the list of words associated to the stimulus 'Looking for tour packages via Internet means'. The Spad-T analysis identified three factors, describing multiple perspectives on the Internet. The first factor includes words that refer to the *temporal dimension*. Internet is considered a tool that requires an excessive amount of time to use ('waste more time') and to a lesser extent, implies certain risks ('getting lost').

The second factor concerns the *economic dimension* and contrasts words describing Internet as a tool that provides more information and offerings ('expenses', 'last minute', 'more offering'), to words highlighting its novelty ('new approach'), the possibility to virtually visit places where individuals intend to go ('images'), to know the costs ('costs'), and obtain discounts ('save money'), besides possible risks ('risk').

The third factor highlights the *peculiarities* of researching information via Internet. Words refer to the possibility of accessing the web from home, obtaining information enriched by images and links ('from home', 'direct access', 'image', 'find out').

Using Evoc the structural elements of the representational field were identified. The economic ('save money') and temporal dimension ('speed', 'save time', 'immediacy') are in the central nucleus, together with words stressing positive aspects of the Internet ('make choice', 'easy', 'find out') and the exposure to risk for users. In the peripheral system, we observed specific risks related to the vastness of the Internet: 'insecurity', 'waste time' and 'getting lost'.

To facilitate the DiscAn analysis, 11 categories were created. They were grouped into five macro areas: Internet as an information source; the information search

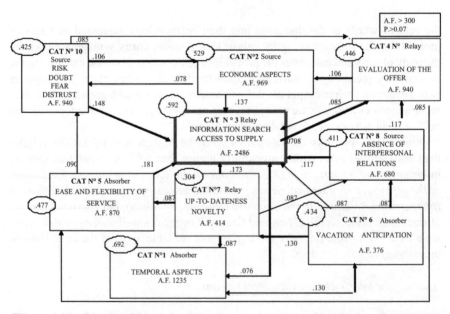

Figure 16.2 DiscAn Chart showing the categories and their functional roles in the discourse dynamic of words (stimulus *'Looking for tour packages via internet means...'*)

phase; the evaluation of the offer; the economic and emotional aspects related to departure; and finally a macro area including three sub-categories (temporal aspects; risk, doubt, fear, distrust; up-to-dateness).

The results obtained from DiscAn are reported in Figure 16.2. The central category is *Information search /Access to supply* which has the highest activity factor. The most important discourse *sources* are *Economic aspects* and *Risk, doubt, fear, distrust*. Risks are related to the *Information search* phase, the *Evaluation of the offer* and, reciprocally, with the category *Economic aspects*. The third *source* is the category *Absence of interpersonal relations* which is equally linked to relays *Information search* and *Evaluation of the offer*.

Since many of the terms that refer to the three *sources* on the chart have negative connotations we believe that users started to associate words by describing limits and negative aspects of Internet; then, via the connecting elements, the *relays*, such as *Access to supply* and *Evaluation of the offer*, considered the advantages of the Internet over traditional channels. Then they went on closing the associative discourse with words referring to specific positive characteristics of the Internet, *Ease and flexibility of service* and *Vacation anticipation*.

It has to be noted that both the categories *Ease and flexibility in service* and *Vacation anticipation* have links with two sources. The former is connected to the category *Risk, doubt, fear, distrust* and the latter is connected with the source *Absence of interpersonal relations*. The category *Information search/Access to supply* therefore forms a crossroad in the associative dynamic which passes from the disadvantages to the advantages of looking for tour packages via Internet and vice versa. Therefore, data show that Internet is prevalently used in the information gathering stage, and this activity has a positive connotation. But, on the other hand, negative aspects are evident at the beginning of the discourse and, also, when concluding the online transactions. In fact, once again, these final steps are connected with the risks, doubts, fear and distrust seen in our subjects' responses.

'Internet'

The factors extracted by Spad-T for the last stimulus, *Internet,* draw a descriptive-evaluative representation of the Internet. The representation of the Internet by subjects with 'low expertise' and that one of subjects with an 'average' or 'excellent' level of expertise in Internet use are very different. Users with low expertise shared a more stereotyped and reductive representation of the Internet and mainly highlighted its negative aspects. Average and experienced users were more analytical and noted the Internet's complexity and multiple dimensions.

In particular, the first factor is characterized, on the positive semi axis, by terms concerning the Internet's possibilities for communication and purchasing, such as 'chat', 'money'. The Internet's perceived difficulties are reported with words located on the negative semi axis ('chaos', 'difficult', 'confusion', 'speed', 'slowness'). The subjects on the positive semi axis are men, up to 30 years old, high school graduates and students, average and expert users. They log on several times a week, consult websites, visit chat rooms, and use the Internet to look for information for both work/study and free time activities, such as tourist information. The subjects on the negative semi axis are women, subjects with less experience with internet, university graduates, and people from 31–40 years old. They mainly use the Internet to obtain information for work/study purposes.

A subsequent Evoc analysis on the same data showed that the terms that are most frequently and early cited refer to the Internet as a 'useful' tool for collecting 'information' and for 'communication'. Words in the peripheral system include, in the upper right quadrant, kinds of search that can be conducted via Internet as well as motivations for Internet use, such as work, travels, music, study, knowledge, curiosity, entertainment. Other words refer to the Internet's innovativeness ('novelty', 'progress', 'technology'). The lower right quadrant, containing words with the lowest frequency and that were elicited last, introduces words related to the temporal dimension such as 'time', 'free time', and even contradictory terms as 'slowness' and 'speed'.

As we did with the previous stimulus, words associated to the stimulus *Internet* were grouped in 14 categories and analysed using DiscAn. Categories that were elicited at the beginning of the task, the *sources*, describe the Internet's characteristics and environments. Figure 16.3 shows the categories with the highest frequencies (activity factors higher than 600) and links with a probability higher than 0.05. Five sources were identified, the most important being *Usefulness*. There was only one

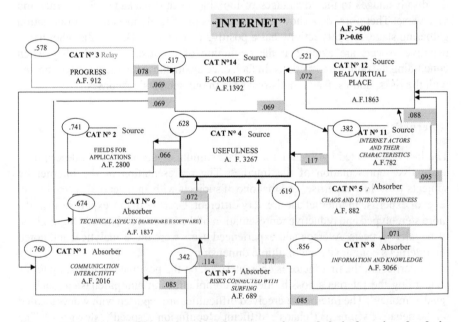

Figure 16.3 DiscAn Chart showing the categories and their functional role in the discourse dynamic of words *(stimulus* 'Internet')

relay, *Progress* and five absorbers, including, in descending order of activity factors, *Information and knowledge, Communication interactivity, Technical aspects, Chaos and untrustworthiness, Risks connected with surfing.*

The DiscAn analysis shed further light on the aspects identified using the associative network technique. *e-Commerce* transactions is not directly related to *Risks related to surfing*. These two categories are mediated by the category *Communication and interactivity*. It is as if interpersonal relationships have a fundamental importance for the subjects and, instead of the fear of being swindled after an online payment, the risk of alienation takes center stage. This may be due to the fact that this type of transaction is still not widely diffused among our subjects, that stated that they use the Internet mainly to gather information.

Conclusions

The results we obtained show that subjects with higher level of expertise with the Internet choose Internet to search tourist information, remember the names of tourist sites they visited and intend to purchase tour packages via Internet in the near future. Having high online skills encourages a positive attitude towards the Internet and a more developed representation focalized on communication and ways to use the Internet. Improved skills would encourage the representation's evolution, increasing the percentage of subjects willing to make purchases online and facilitating purchasing by surfers who already demonstrated an inclination to purchase online (51 per cent of the subjects answering positively to the question: 'Do you intend to purchase tour packages via Internet in the near future?'). Strategies designed to modify the perceptions of subjects more resistant to change their ideas about online purchases, (the 49 per cent of the subjects who answered negatively to question posed above) are needed.

The results obtained from the questionnaire items and the associative network confirm that subjects ascribe a more positive connotation to looking for tour packages 'via Internet' than to looking for tour packages 'via traditional channels'.

Considering the Spad-T and Evoc results provides information on the key criteria, that is the basic dimensions that differentiate the two representations (Table 16.1). Traditional channels are characterized by the presence of *interpersonal relations, source reliability, purchase* as well as *higher costs*. The Internet is characterized by *possibility of choice, save money* but also *risks*.

The temporal dimension is another relevant key criterion. It was expressed in terms of two poles: *save time* and *waste of time*. The representation of traditional channels includes only *waste of time*. In the structure of the representation evoked by the stimulus 'Looking for tour packages via Internet', *save time* is in the central nucleus with *speed* and *immediacy* (mentioned quite early by many subjects) while waste of time is in the peripheral system, mentioned by few subjects.

The DiscAn results confirm that people using traditional channels have a fear of progress and prefer the reliability provided by personal contact with a travel agent to

Table 16.1   Presence(+)/ absence(-) of key criteria in Spad-T and Evoc results to the words evoked via the associative networks

| Key Criteria | Looking for tour packages via | | | |
| | Traditional channels | | Internet | |
	Spad-T	Evoc	Spad-T	Evoc
Interpersonal relations	+	+	-	-
Source reliability	+	+	-	-
Purchase	+	+	-	-
Higher costs	+	+	-	-
Risks	-	-	+	+
Possibility of choice	-	-	+	+
Save money	-	-	+	+

the advantages offered by the web (e.g. 'save money', 'greater choice'). On the other hand, people who use the Internet take into account risks related to economic issues and to search and evaluation of the offer.

For the subjects in this study, therefore, the dimension of risk is a central element of the representation of searching tour packages on the Internet. This risk is mainly tied to possible difficulties encountered by users during the actual economic transaction. This perception is considerably amplified in subjects with lower levels of expertise in Internet use.

After considering the complex social representations held by our subjects, we conclude that, on the whole, they do not appear to fully exploit the potential offered by Internet to act as *pro-sumer* (Toffler, 1980). This is because the Internet is still prevalently used in the information gathering phase, rather than in evaluation and purchase phases. Results show that at least during 2001, when we collected these data, risk perception was still playing a central role as a motivational resistance factor for online purchasing, as probably plays such a role in the adoption of most innovations.

The challenge, therefore, is to find a way to use re-intermediation to re-establish trust between businesses and customers who are coming to terms with e-commerce. On the basis of the results of this study, the following recommendations may be suggested:

- reconstruct a dialog between producer and online consumer (key criterion: interpersonal relationship);
- use strategies designed to transmit the reliability of the brand's image: i.e. who we are, corporate history, links, etc.;
- use strategies geared to increase to users' trust in the information source (key

criterion: source reliability);
• adopt all possible technical solutions to provide increased economic security for online transactions (key criterion: eliminate risk).

These measures would encourage the representation to evolve, increasing the number of subjects willing to make purchases online and facilitating other subjects' already demonstrated inclination to purchase.

References

Abric, J.C. (1994), *Pratiques sociale et représentation,* P.U.F., Paris.
Abric, J.C. (2003), *Méthodes d'étude des représentations sociales*, Eres, Ramonville Saint-Agne.
Bonardi, C. and Roussiau, N. (1999), *Les Représentations Sociales,* Dunod, Paris.
de Rosa, A.S. (1987), 'The Social Representations of Mental Illness in Children and Adults', in W. Doise and S. Moscovici (eds.), *Current Issues in European Social Psychology,* Cambridge University Press, Cambridge.
de Rosa, A.S. (1990), 'Per un Approccio Multi-Metodo allo Studio delle Rappresentazioni Sociali', *Rassegna di Psicologia*, Vol. 8, pp. 101–152.
de Rosa, A.S. (1994), 'From Theory to Meta-Theory in S.R.: The Lines of Argument of a Theoretical-Methodological Debate', *Social Science Information,* Vol. 33, pp. 273–304.
de Rosa, A.S. (1995), 'Le 'Reseau d'Associations' Comme Methode d'Etude dans la Recherche sur les Representations Sociales: Structure, Contenus et Polarite du Champ Semantique', *Le Cahiers Internationaux de Psychologie Sociale*, Vol. 28, pp. 96–122.
de Rosa, A.S. (2001), 'The King is Naked. Critical Advertisement and Fashion: The Benetton Phenomenon', in K. Deaux and G. Philogene (eds.) *Representations of the Social*, Blackwell, Oxford.
de Rosa, A.S. (2003), 'Le Reseau d'Associations': Une Technique pour Detecter la Structure, les Contenus, les Indices de Polarite, de Neutralite et de Stereotypie du Champ Semantique lies aux Representations Sociales', in J.C. Abric (ed.), *Méthodologie d'Etude des Representations Sociales,* Eres, Ramonville Saint-Agne.
Deaux, K. and Philogène, G. (2001), *Representations of the Social.* Blackwell, Oxford.
Doise, W. (1985), 'Les Représentations Socials: Definition d'un Concept', *Connexions,* Vol. 45, pp. 243–253.
Doise, W. (1993), 'Debating Social Representations', in G.M. Breakwell and D.V. Canter (eds.), *Empirical Approaches to Social Representations,* Clarendon Press, Oxford.
Doise, W., Clémence, A. and Lorenzi-Cioldi, F. (1993), *The Quantitative Analysis of Social Representations',* Harvester Wheatsheaf, London.
Farr, R.M. and Moscovici, S. (1984), *Social Representations,* Cambridge University

Press, Cambridge.

Jodelet, D. (1989), *Les Représentations Sociales,* P.U.F, Paris.

Joffe, H. (1999), *Risk and 'the Other'*, Cambridge University Press, Cambridge.

Losito, G. (1994), *Il Potere dei Media,* NIS-Carocci Editore, Roma.

Luhmann, N. (1996), *Sociologia del Rischio,* Bruno Mondadori, Milano.

Markova, I. (2003), *Dialogicality and Social Representations. The Dynamics of Mind.* University Press, Cambridge.

Moliner, P. (2001), *La Dynamique des Représentations Sociales,* PUG, Grenoble.

Moscovici, S. (1969), 'Préface', in C. Herzlich (ed.), *Santé et Maladie.* Mouton, Paris.

Moscovici, S. (1976), *Social Influence and Social Change,* Academic Press, London.

Moscovici, S. (1981), 'On Social Representations', in J.P. Forgas (ed.), *Social Cognition. Perspectives on Everyday Understanding,* Academic Press, London.

Moscovici, S. (1984), 'The Phenomenon of Social Representations', in R.M. Farr and S. Moscovici (eds.) *Social Representations,* Cambridge University Press, Cambridge.

Moscovici, S. (1986), 'L'ére des Représentations Sociales', in W. Doise, and A. Palmonari (eds.), *L'étude des Représentations Sociales,* Delachaux et Nestlé, Neuchatel.

Moscovici, S. (2000a), 'What is in a Name?', in M. Chaib and B. Orfali (eds.), *Social Representations and Communicative Processes,* Jonkoping University Press, Jonkoping.

Moscovici, S. (2000b), *Social Representations. Explorations in Social Psychology,* Polity Press, Cambridge.

Moscovici, S. (2001), 'Why a Theory of Social Representations', in K. Deaux and G. Philogene (eds.), *Representation of the Social,* Blackwell, Oxford.

Toffler, A. (1980), *The Third Wave.* Morrow, New York.

Chapter 17

Conclusions: Common Themes and Future Perspectives

Salvatore Zappalà and Colin Gray

Although the chapters in this book were grouped in three different sections that reflected clear differences in research emphasis, a number of interesting common themes emerged. It is also clear that, with most of the chapters based on research conducted between 2002 and 2003 (albeit updated by reference to more recent developments), the discussion and findings are focused on the earlier processes and stages of adoption and use of e-commerce in particular, and of e-business applications more broadly. However, with the pace of technological innovations, plus associated organizational and social innovations, still increasing and still impacting on firms, consumers and work behaviors, it is important to understand the early stages of the processes of adoption and use, as well as the changing social and economic contexts in which they take place.

The aim of this final chapter is to identify and pull together the key issues and lessons that have emerged from the findings presented in the book. These common themes, linking the three sections and the chapters within them, include social influence processes, staged learning and adoption, and risk. The chapter will then conclude in a brief review of current ICT trends affecting consumers and organizations plus some speculative reflections on future developments.

Social Influence Processes

One of the common themes of this book is the impact of ICT on social processes. Individuals get involved in social processes to understand, evaluate, decide whether to adopt or not, or how to improve ICT and e-business. Rogers' social network theory of diffusion of innovation is one of the most influential works referred to in the first section. Different forms of social processes, involving different actors, have been discussed in the book.

The owners of small and large firms in the same district, cluster or forums influence each other. Discussion and evaluation of costs, advantages and difficulties experienced by early adopters within the cluster, or by competitors, stimulate small firm owners to think about adoption, and/or to imitate successful early adopters revealing the advantages of e-business.

Small firm owners are also influenced by business support agencies. These agencies, among the other things, stimulate SMEs to become more aware of ICT, to pursue national or regional subsidies or to develop support networks. Another relevant source that may influence entrepreneurs to adopt ICT are the firm's employees, especially the more technologically skilled or in contact with consumers' needs. Once adopted, entrepreneurs and technologically skilled employees will show social intra-organizational influence processes, trying to make the new technology widely accepted, used and competently managed by the other, more reluctant, employees. Thus, each business is involved in a rich net of formal and informal relationships which bring up pros and cons of the e-business innovation adoption that need to be take into account.

As mentioned at several places in the book, national and European policies currently aim to raise ICT awareness, promote support networks and to encourage technology transfer (Gray, 2003; Technopolis Group, 2005a). Increasingly, this is taking the form of encouraging the development of clusters of firms either as physical and spatial entities (similar to previous policies aimed at developing industrial districts) or as virtual, ICT-linked groupings of different firms, sometimes also known as 'digital business ecosystems' (Power and Jersian, 2001). The need to better understand the group dynamics and social relations between firms grows stronger as these developments proliferate. Thus, as current policies are evaluated, it becomes clear that e-business is having different kinds of impacts on small and medium firms. An increasing relevant issue, not a focus of this book, is that one of metrics, or how to measure business performance of firms' presence on the internet and firms' selling online (Straub *et al.*, 2002).

The decision to adopt or not, is based also on many objective, financial and technical considerations on ICT, such as revenue and costs, security issues, software and hardware compatibility, and so on (e-Business W@tch, 2004; Kraemer *et al.* 2004). But also Governments are considering the costs to increase ICT awareness and adoption. In her chapter Jane Tebbutt asks whether continue to 'assist "weaker" firms to embrace the advantages of ICT ... or helping stronger firms become even better'. Good practices and new policies recently examined in the 'European Conference on Innovation and e-Business', held in May 2005, suggest, for instance, the 'need to understand the firms' and also 'to talk to business in their own terms' (Technopolis Group, 2005b). Thus, to pursue these strategies there is a continuing need to investigate everyday social processes and influences exerted within the social context of businesses. This appears a useful way to understand processes that can make current and future ICT adoption a collective and group adoption.

To increase their practical relevance, however, social processes have to be considered within specific industrial contexts. This is the approach adopted by the European e-Business W@tch project and, in this book, also by Jane Tebbutt. Additionally, managerial processes and technology implementation were described in the ICT industry and the aviation repair industry (chapters 4 and 7). These two 'case studies' show that strategic and competitive environments, labour processes, employees' ICT competencies, and so on, are very different in the two industries.

It is clear that adoption choices need to be more consistently mapped within distinct industries.

An additional impact of ICT on small firms concerns a theoretical and practical, issue that we have not specifically addressed in this book. This is the relationship between technology adoption, organizational change and innovation. Such relationships have been debated from long time in relation to various types of technology (see Majchrzak and Borys, 1998, for a review). It has been argued that the mere implementation of technology does not determine how organizations are structured and how work is accomplished and that complex relationships exist between ICT and new ways of working in network organizations (Sonnentag, 2000; Symon, 2000). An OECD project (E-Commerce Business Impacts Projects – EBIP) provides evidence that ICT contributes to improving firm performance when complementary investments in skills or organizational change are present. In this book, the chapter by Wendt and colleagues describes the detailed restructuring of work processes required by the implementation of electronic communication and business between craft enterprises and Airbus. The European Conference on Innovation and e-Business confirms that e-business is not just about buying technology, nor does it always have any direct effect on the economic performance of the firm. It is an important driver for innovation, just like education, finance or skills, requiring a redefinition of business processes and doing things differently (Technopolis Group, 2005b).

SMEs need to understand that ICT adoption raises new tasks and that these new tasks may alter the pre-existing socio-technical system (Hollnagel and Cacciabue, 1999). Thus, to avoid negative impacts of ICT adoption good implementation practices needs to be developed and shared in advance among small firms, even to overcome the well-known lack of managerial competencies within most of the small firms.

Staged Adoption Processes

Across the volume, steps and stages concerning ICT and e-marketing adoption, structure and contents of websites were described. Stages in consumers' decision making and, particularly, in moves towards online purchasing have also been described. This stage process helps consumers and small firms to manage problems and to become more self-acquainted with the technology. Many case studies show this process. For instance, Internet forum, as described by Mochrie, Galloway and Deakins (chapter 6), suggests that firms may 'taste the water' of ICT gradually.

This process is probably led by the evolution of technology but also by the learning processes which characterize customers but also employees and firms. Imitation of a model, as may be the case of a successful early ICT adopter, is a powerful learning instrument. Action learning, experiential learning and learning by 'trial and errors' are other well-established approaches (Lewin, 1948; Kolb, 1984), well known to children and teachers and used a lot in the design of management development programmes. However, learning styles differ and, with the advent of the 'knowledge economy', the focus now is on the outcomes of learning and the role that formal and informal learning has on patterns of use and adoption of ICT.

The key role played by ICT in the management of knowledge in small firms was specifically addressed by Corso and colleagues (2003) who state that ICT applications can 'play a key role in this process. By providing quick and easy access to external sources of knowledge and new and more intense communication channels with partner organizations, ICT can erase traditional constraints on SMEs innovation ability, while leveraging their flexibility and responsiveness'. Increasingly, the Internet helps SMEs to participate in useful networks or to pursue commercial and industrial linkages without a strong need for spatial proximity.

The development of the key prior motivation to adopt and the development of a firm's internal capacity to manage the adoption of technology and the progres to more advanced applications, sometimes called its 'absorptive capacity', remain key areas for research. In fact, only larger firms can allow to invest large amount of money and to start e-business activities at higher sophisticated level. The six Italian case studies conducted by Butera and partners (Butera, 2001) showed that only a large bank was able to start with e-business activities, while the other five small and medium firms progressed across the typical stage process, from the brochure web, to e-commerce, to e-business. Thus, for many small firms the demand for more capital and capabilities, including psychological readiness, means that they take a more evolutionary approach that may improve efficiencies and reduce risks to market without transforming their business model in any revolutionary way.

Consumers' and Firms' Risk Perception

The spreading of ICT in modern social life is requiring not only businesses but also consumers to cope with the new communication instruments. Probably the first customers' reaction, or opinion, to e-commerce is considering it as a risky activity. Most of the chapters of the third section deal with this issue. There are obvious differences among consumers, especially concerning internet related skills. A recent survey by AC Nielsens (2005) reports an increase in the number of people buying online; more exactly, it is reported that 600 million people, one tenth of the world population, has bought on line at least once in their life. It has to be noted that the survey was conducted online among Internet users. These findings confirm that the best predictor of online shopping is 'being an Internet user' and having already bought online in the past.

Firms need to reduce the perception of online shopping as risky behavior for, at least, another 10 per cent of the world population. This book has described several strategies to pursue this relevant objective and, among others, the ergonomic and content aspects of the websites, sellers' presentation and type of communication can be used to lower the perception of risk. It is also maintained that when buying online some customers appreciate more the website contents and features than the products' description, while someone else considers the possibility of a personal relationship with the seller as the most important difference between traditional travel agencies and online agencies. Thus, as also suggested by Internet marketing experts, discussing and interacting with consumers to better understand their requests and needs may improve loyalty.

But e-commerce is not a risky activity only for consumers. Also small firms are reluctant to adopt e-commerce because of, for instance, perceived financial risks associated with the lack of commercial benefits or legal concerns associated to domestic and cross border transaction (European Commission, 2002). There is also a reluctance on the part of small firm owners to move away from established and familiar business routines that have worked well in the past for an uncertain future of trading electronically. Indeed, the most common reasons given by two-thirds of small firm owners in Britain in 2003 for not adopting e-commerce was simply that it was not seen as suitable for their business (SERTeam, 2003).

Thus, again, consumers and firms share the same basic processes, but a better comprehension of consumers' fears may help firms to offer more secure services.

Recent Developments

The technical side of the argument in support for adopting e-commerce has rested on an assumption that broadband adoption rates and connectivity speeds will continue to grow. Having set a policy target in 1999 to become the 'best place in the world to do e-business', the UK government proudly announced that, by May 2005, more than half of British households had broadband and that broadband diffusion activities were increasing (Cabinet Office, 2005). However, social network theories of innovation adoption (discussed in chapter 1 and 2), also indicate that adoption rates slacken as adoption nears saturation point and as new technological applications attract the intention of the ever-curious early adopters (Rogers, 1983). The dramatic rise in adoption of the ubiquitous mobile phone and new wireless applications show that the need for closer connectivity and faster (and more accessible) communication are still powerful drivers of consumer adoption. There are, however, still wide differences in the adoption of relatively familiar technologies like broadband and newer wireless applications between the EU and other industrialized economies and even wider differences between EU Member States (e-Business W@tch, 2005). Moreover, there are also signs that quality issues are beginning to emerge as businesses and consumers are becoming more familiar to the wonders of instant communication and more instrumental in its use. The crude adoption rates do not reveal the qualitative effects as businesses and consumers become more discerning as they upgrade to more advanced and sophisticated models and new applications. Nor do the crude rates reveal much about the churn as new adopters enter while some earlier adopters discard applications that are no longer 'state of the art' or have failed to meet their expectations.

Public policy at all levels – regional, national and multi-national (EU, OECD, World Bank, etc.) – continues to link economic development and competitiveness to increases in the effective application of ICT to improvements in communication and productivity. With the growing importance of China and India as global poles of manufacturing and technology development, these policies have taken on a new urgency. In the EC's recent review of its *eEurope2005* strategy, there is more than a hint of anxiety over the lack of progress and the absence of expected benefits (European Commission, 2004). However, the review did not herald a change in policy but rather a renewed call to get back on track. At national level, the UK government, for instance, was much more upbeat about progress and reaffirmed its belief in the underlying model of encouraging universal broadband access (and near universal adoption) to encourage more open communication in society and continuous developments of applications to foster innovation, knowledge based businesses and new working practices, including e-commerce. In the recent review of its digital strategy, the UK government is very clear:

> the effective use of broadband is the key to improved productivity and economic competitiveness. This is well understood by our competitors and our inward investors. A survey by the Institute of Directors (2004) found that 84 per cent of respondents using broadband saw a quantifiable increase in productivity and 61 per cent said broadband had delivered cost savings (Cabinet Office, 2005, p.16).

This is reassuring for those sharing the belief that increased diffusion of broadband will lead to more creative use of the Internet and a proliferation of new, and previously unimagined, e-business opportunities. However, in the US, which is on a par with the EU average but has lower broadband adoption rates than several Asian and Scandinavian economies, there are signs that adoption rates may be slowing down. Trends in ICT adoption and use by consumers and firms are regularly monitored by the Pew Internet & American Life Project and reveal that, between 2002 and 2005, the intensity of online consumer activities is largely determined by having home access to broadband. The decision to get broadband at home is driven by intensity of online use, with cost and price playing a very secondary role. Intensity of online use by consumers is driven by years of online experience and connection speed. More recently, home use and speed of connections has been a much stronger determining factor than years of experience.

In a presentation to the 33rd Telecommunications Policy and Research Conference in September 2005, the Pew Director of Research John Horrigan provided clear evidence that broadband and the Internet adoption curves in the US have either hit a plateau or, in some cases, are actually declining. However, there was also evidence of different patterns of early adopter and late-adopter patterns for various ICT applications, reflecting uncertainties over costs and benefits. After very rapid early adoption, high-speed broadband connections in households appear to have stabilized at around one-third of the adult population of the US (considerably below comparable broadband adoption in Britain). On one hand, this adds to the evidence already provided in this book in support of the social network approach to the adoption of innovations but, on the other, it points to a need for a better understanding of technology aversion. It also strongly suggests that the various digital divides that have been observed within Europe and between industrialized and less developed countries will not steadily drift away and may be subject to influences such as age, incomes and levels of education. Comparing 2005 survey findings with 2002 (Horrigan, 2005), key trends in US consumer Internet use are:

- the largest group is comprised of moderately experienced dial-up internet users who have been online for more than a year but less than six years. This fell from 34 per cent of adult internet users in October 2002 to 23 per cent in May 2005;
- the number of experienced (online for six or more years) dial-up internet users, those most likely to participate in e-commerce, has fallen by one-third since October 2002, from 19 million to 13 million in May 2005;
- new internet users (online for a year or less) made up 4 per cent of the internet population in May 2005, compared with 6 per cent in October 2002 (and the conversion rate from dial-up connections to broadband was very low);
- currently 32 per cent of the US adult population does not use the internet, a number that has held steady in the first six months of 2005. Few new users seem to be coming online and data show that only 23 per cent of internet users who have adopted in the past year have done so with high-speed connections.

This suggests a long term, if not permanent, digital divide with two thirds of US consumers using the Internet – though split evenly between those using high-speed broadband connections and those using slower dial-up connections that are unsuitable for e-commerce – and one-third either self-excluded or excluded by external factors such as income, education or lack of stable habitation (Horrigan, 2005). The latest Pew study also revealed that the moderately experienced Internet users who still rely on dial-up connections are significantly older, poorer and educated to lower levels than the more advanced broadband adopters. In its optimistic report on Britain's progress as an e-economy, the UK review of digital policy also acknowledged an endemic internal digital divide that has to be addressed. There is a strong correlation between household income and Internet access, with higher socio-economic classes three times more likely to have home access than lower socio-economic classes. Indeed, increases in Internet adoption by households has been entirely among the wealthier groups. The rate of connection among the lower groupings has remained around 20 per cent since 2001.

These trends among consumers are similar to the patterns of Internet connection and website adoption among small firms. In UK the adoption of computers by small firms has hit a plateau, albeit a high plateau of 92 per cent of all small firms in Britain (SERTeam, 2005). The adoption rates of websites, networked computers and Internet e-mail is slowing down. The survey also confirmed that e-commerce, in the form of the capacity for accepting and processing online payments has yet to take off (in four years it has only grown from 7 per cent of small firms to 11 per cent). However, the survey also confirmed the dramatic increase in the adoption of broadband connections among small firms that nearly doubled from 35 per cent in 2003 to 67 per cent in 2005. Small firms with broadband connections were significantly more likely to conduct purchasing transactions, searching purchase information (such as prices, product specification, availability, delivery, and so on), seeking other market and regulatory information and even ordering goods, components and services online. However, there were clear size effects with microfirms (less than 10 employees) and the self-employed less likely to be conducting these online transactions, a pattern also observed elsewhere in Europe (e-Business W@tch, 2005; UNCTAD, 2005).

Future Trends

Socio-economic, educational and size effects also maintain a digital divide between industrialized and developing countries. The latest report on e-commerce, the information economy and development by the United Nations Conference on Trade and Development (UNCTAD, 2005), reveals tremendous growth in the adoption of computers, the Internet and broadband connections in many small firms in developing countries. There are now around one billion Internet users in the world, with more in Asia, followed by Europe, than in North America. Given the tailing off in US adoption curves, it is perhaps not surprising that 2003–2004 adoption rates in developing countries (30 per cent) grew at twice the rate of those in industrialized countries (16 per cent). Although from a low base, the 67 per cent growth in Internet adoption in Africa is quite spectacular. However, the poorer countries in sub-Saharan Africa remain in a state of digital deprivation, with Egypt, Morocco and South Africa accounting for half of Africa's 21 million Internet users. The gaps in adoption of other ICT applications necessary for e-commerce, such as broadband and computers, are also crucial. In its 2004 report, UNCTAD stated clearly that 'the digital divide in terms of broadband in many less developed countries could have serious implications for their enterprises' and that computers 'are indispensable for the development of the information economy and in particular for the application of ICT in e-business processes'. Broadband subscription rates are currently high in Africa but it will be many years before the levels of subscribers approach those of developed countries. The 2004 computer adoption rates in Africa (2 per cent) were miniscule compared with North America (74 per cent) or Europe (31 per cent).

However, this book does not have its focus on digital divides *per se* but rather on their implications on future developments of e-commerce as they will affect consumers and small firms. There are at least two interesting areas to which a focus on this type of digital divide leads us. They can be termed *e-credit* and *e-tourism*. The first refers to the fact that a great deal of poverty and underdevelopment in developing countries stems from wide and increasing inequalities in conditions and terms of trade. In a recommendation, which would also be relevant to small firms in industrialized economies that suffer from information asymmetries with respect to large firms, UNCTAD (2005) argues that 'an important avenue for improving developing countries' access to trade related finance and e-finance, ... , is the extensive use of opportunities provided by the Internet to overcome information asymmetry between creditors and borrowers'. The report suggests that this could be achieved by 'moving away from the informal economy by creating transparent conditions for collecting credit information on developing countries' enterprises, and by moving rapidly towards e-credit information infrastructures and e-credit scoring and e-rating techniques'. This has clear relevance to the problems faced by many small firms not only in developing countries but in Europe as well.

The second area for e-commerce application and future development is already happening. Indeed, de Rosa and colleagues in chapter 16 discuss how consumers' perceptions of the Internet and of online tourist booking services impact on each other. The UNCTAD focus on e-tourism partly reflects the fact that many tourist destinations are located in developing countries. However, the online tourism industry is already quite mature with a great deal of concentration (mergers, takeovers, dominant firms and so on) and consolidation already taking place in that industry. However, there is scope for niche firms of specialists to appeal to particular segments of consumers. Most of these e-tourism services are based in developed countries and UNCTAD (2005) sees a need for the development of a parallel 'ICT diffusion and use among tourism providers, and in particular within small and medium-sized tourism enterprises, are crucial for the effective development of e-tourism in developing countries'.

Finally, the advent of mobile and wireless technologies is already having an impact on consumers and firms of all sizes. Indeed, with the advent of palmtops, Bluetooth and new generation mobile phones, the nature of Internet connections and the work-life balance is already changing in certain industries. For instance, the 2005 SERTeam survey in Britain suggests that m-commerce may be poised to edge out or substantially alter e-commerce. While broadband connections rose significantly in 2003–2005, there was a more than doubling in the use of wireless applications, from 14 per cent in 2003 to 29 per cent in 2005. In the context of the digital divide discussed above, UNCTAD (2005) states unequivocally that 'mobile telephony is the ICT that has the most significant impact on development, particularly in developing and least developed countries. In these countries, mobile phones are used for more than simple communication, often as a business tool by means of which producers and buyers can shop around for prices and vendors can be paid'. The number of mobile phone subscribers in Africa increased from 15 million in 2000 to over 80 million in 2004. However, mobile telephony is an area that Europe dominates with an average adoption rate of 75 per cent of all inhabitants compared with 60 per cent for the US and just 9 per cent for Africa.

These are just a few of the more obvious changes and issues related to e-commerce that are beginning to impact on consumers and businesses. Despite the meteoric rates of adoption of the Internet, memories of old analogue, dial-up 56kps modems have faded in most firms and in many households. In most parts of the world, the adoption of broadband connections is largely determined by infrastructural access. However, as wireless and satellite technologies improve, and as the costs of subscriptions fall, high-speed connections to the Internet will become the norm. The issue remains, as the contributors to this book have discussed, one of addressing and adapting to change. The overall Internet and broadband adoption rates may have stabilized in the US and may stabilize in Europe but the aggregate adoption curves only mask many underlying adoption curves which move at varying rates as applications are developed and new features added. For example, the proportion of small firms in Britain that have their own websites have stabilized but many are static. From an e-commerce perspective it is much more interesting to look at the adoption rates of those that use new markup languages to be more appealing to consumers. It is also more interesting to see how consumer behaviors relate to, say, blogs, online telephony and smart tags change, how websites are used and how consumers expect them to be used. And there are still plenty of non-technological changes that will affect the development of e-commerce, such as reports that large firms are tuning their backs on outsourcing and dropping their e-commerce links with smaller firms in favour of controlling operations in house. Whether or not true, changes like that can alter consumers and small firms behavior which, ultimately, alter the types of innovation that attract early adopters. However, the central message of this book is that what determines whether a consumer or a small business owner embraces the change or flinches from it is still to be found in understanding the processes of social interaction, learning and risk perception.

References

AC Nielsens (2005), Global Consumer Attitudes towards Online Shopping (Retrieved on November 10, 2005, at www.acnielsen.com/news).

Butera, F. (2001), *Il Campanile e la Rete, e-Business e le Piccole e Medie Imprese in Italia*, Sole 24 Ore, Milano.

Cabinet Office (2005), *Connecting the UK: The Digital Strategy*, Prime Minister Strategy Unit, March, London.

Corso, M., Martini, A., Pellegrini, L. and Paolucci, E. (2003), 'Technological and Organizational Tools for Knowledge Management: In Search of Configurations', *Small Business Economics*, Vol. 21, pp. 397–408.

e-Business W@tch (2004), *The European e-Business Report, 3rd Synthesis Report*, European Commission: Enterprise Directorate, Brussels.

e-Business W@tch (2005), *The European E-Business Report 2005*, European Commission: Enterprise and Industry Directorate, Brussels.

European Commission (2002), *Benchmarking National and Regional e-Business Policies*, Synthesis Report, Enterprise Directorate, Brussels.

European Commission (2004), *Challenges for the European Information Society beyond 2005*. COM(2004) 757 final. November, 2004. Brussels.

Gray, C. (2003), 'Managing the Impact of Broadband on Microfirms and Their Networks', *The European Journal of Teleworking*, Vol. 9, pp. 4–16.

Hollnagel, E. and Cacciabue, P.C. (1999), 'Cognition, Technology and Work: An Introduction', *Cognition, Technology and Work*, Vol. 1, pp. 1–6.

Horrigan, J. (2005), 'Broadband Adoption at Home in the United States: Growing but Slowing', Paper presented to the 33rd Annual Telecommunications Policy Research Conference, September 24, USA.

Institute of Directors (2004), *Broadband: Its Impact on British Business*, I.o.D., London.

Kolb, D.A. (1984), *Experiential Learning*, Prentice Hall, Englewood Cliffs, NJ.

Kraemer, K., Zhu, K., Xu, S., Korte, W. and Gareis, K. (2004), 'What Drives e-Business Diffusion among Firms? Evidence from European Companies', in e-Business W@tch (2004), *The European e-Business Report, 3rd Synthesis Report,* EC Enterprise Directorate, Brussels, pp. 195–203.

Lewin, K. (1948), *Resolving Social Conflicts; Selected Papers on Group Dynamics*, Gertrude W. Lewin (ed.), Harper & Row, New York.

Majchrzak, A. and Borys, B. (1998), 'Computer-Aided Technology and Work: Moving the Field Forward', in C. Cooper and I. Robertson (eds.), *International Review of Industrial and Organizational Psychology*, Vol. 13, pp. 305–354.

Power, T. and Jersian, G. (2001), *Ecosystem: Living the 12 Principles of Networked Business*, Financial Times, Prentice Hall, London.

Rogers, E. (1983), *The Diffusion of Innovations*, Free Press, New York.

Small Enterprise Research Team (SERTeam) (2003), *NatWest/SERTeam Quarterly Survey of Small Business in Britain*, Vol. 19, No. 4.

Small Enterprise Research Team (SERTeam) (2005), *NatWest/SERTeam Quarterly Survey of Small Business in Britain*, Vol. 21, No. 3.

Sonnentag, S. (2000), 'Working in a Network Context – What are we talking about? Comment on Symon', *Journal of Occupational and Organizational Psychology*, Vol. 73, pp. 415–418.

Straub, D., Hoffman, D., Weber, B. and Steinfield, C. (2002), 'Measuring e-Commerce in Net-Enabled Organizations: An Introduction to the Special Issue', *Information Systems Research*, Vol. 13, pp. 115–124.

Symon, G. (2000), 'Information and Communication Technologies and the Network Organization: A Critical Analysis', *Journal of Occupational and Organizational Psychology*, Vol. 73, pp. 389–414.

Technopolis Group (2005a), *European Conference on Innovation and e-Business, Preparatory Paper*, 26–27 May, Brussels.

Technopolis Group (2005b), *European Conference on Innovation and e-Business, Output Paper*, 26–27 May, Brussels.

UNCTAD (2005), *Information Economy Report 2005*, United Nations Conference on Trade and Development, Geneva.

Index